True Sisterhood

SUNY Series in American Social History
Charles Stephenson and Elizabeth Pleck, Editors

True Sisterhood

Michigan Women and Their Kin
1820-1920

Marilyn Ferris Motz
Bowling Green State University

State University of New York Press
Albany

Published by
State University of New York Press, Albany

©1983 State University of New York

Printed in the United States of America

For information, address State University of New York Press, State University Plaza,
Albany, N.Y., 12246

Library of Congress Cataloging in Publication Data
Motz, Marilyn Ferris, 1951–
True sisterhood.
(SUNY series in American social history)
Bibliography: p.
Includes index.
1. Women—Michigan—History—19th century. 2. Married women—Michigan—His-
tory—19th century. 3. Sisters—Michigan—History—19th century. 4. Mothers and
daughters—Michigan—History—19th century. 5. Family—Michigan—History—19th
century. I. Title. II. Series.
HQ1438.M5M67 1983   305.4'09774   82-19198
ISBN 0-87395-715-6
ISBN 0-87395-716-4 (pbk.)

To my parents, C. Robert Ferris and Maro Martin Ferris

Contents

Tables

Illustrations

Photograph Credits

All photographs are in the Michigan Historical Collections, Bentley Historical Library, University of Michigan, Ann Arbor, Michigan.

1. Wives and relatives of University of Michigan Faculty, James B. Angell Photograph Collection.
2. Family portrait in Charles and Elsie Cooley's home in Ann Arbor, Charles Horton Cooley Photograph Collection.
3. Josiah Littlefield, Hazel Littlefield Smith Photograph Collection.
4. Picnic at North Lake, Charles Horton Cooley Photograph Collection.
5. Four generations of the Cooley/Angell Family, Cooley Family Photograph Collection.
6. Frances Pomeroy, Raab Family Collection.
7. Hannah Bingham, Hannah Bingham Photograph Collection.
8. Elizabeth Margaret Chandler, frontispiece, *The Poetical Works of Elizabeth Margaret Chandler: With a Memoir of her Life and Character* by Benjamin Lundy (New York: Baker, Crane & Day, 1845).
9. Cooley brothers, Cooley Family Photograph Collection.
10. Four generations of Horton/Cooley/Angell Women, Cooley Family Photograph Collection.
11. Lucy Ann Wyman Smith (sketch), Margaret Knowles Collection.
12. Eli Regal (ambrotype), Eli Regal Photograph Collection.
13. Elsie Cooley's kitchen, Charles Horton Cooley Photograph Collection.
14. Regal children (ambrotype) Raymond Davis Photograph Collection.
15. Frances Pomeroy, Raab Family Collection.
16. Florence Pomeroy holding Margaret Pomeroy, Raab Family Collection.
17. Kate Taylor Cooley and children, Cooley Family Photograph Collection.
18. Mary Hall Littlefield, Hazel Littlefield Smith Photograph Collection.
19. Florence Pomeroy and boarders on steps of Frances Pomeroy's Ann Arbor boarding house, Raab Family Collection.

Acknowledgments

THIS work was completed with assistance from a Ford Foundation Research Grant administered by the Center for Continuing Education of Women at The University of Michigan and a Predoctoral Fellowship from Rackham Graduate School, The University of Michigan. I would like to thank particularly the co-chairs of my doctoral dissertation committee. Elizabeth Pleck was instrumental in introducing me to the field of women's history and establishing the direction of my research. John King was extremely helpful in guiding me through several revisions of the manuscript. Their criticism as well as encouragement is greatly appreciated. Robert Berkhofer, Marion Marzolf, and Louise Tilly, members of my dissertation committee, were all generous with their assistance and helpful in their suggestions. The responsibility for any errors is of course my own.

My fellow graduate students in the Program in American Culture at The University of Michigan and my colleagues in the Department of Popular Culture at Bowling Green State University have provided an exchange of ideas which has helped shape my interpretations. Many of the concepts represented here grew out of discussions with fellow students Rosemary Kowalski, Helen Levy, Mary Sies, and Barbara Winkler. I greatly appreciate both their intellectual contributions and their personal support.

I would also like to thank Jo Mahoney and Joyce Swope for their excellent typing of the manuscript. The staff at the Bentley Historical Library at The University of Michigan were uniformly helpful. Mary Jo Pugh, reference archivist, uncovered the numerous collections of women's letters which made this study possible. I would also like to thank those who donated their family papers for the purposes of historical research. I have attempted to respect the dignity and privacy of the correspondents while still presenting their stories honestly and fully. They are, of course, the real authors of this book.

I am indebted to my parents, C. Robert and Maro Martin Ferris, who taught me to appreciate both the written word and the importance of families, and to Dorothy and Harold Motz, Cora Martin, Margaret Miller, Robert Ferris, and the other members of my own family network for their interest and support. Finally, I cannot begin to express here my appreciation for the unfailing understanding and encouragement offered by Timothy Allen Motz, my husband, who has learned more about nineteenth-century women than he ever wanted to know.

Introduction

As daughter, sister, wife, mother, and friend
She new her duties and she performed them

Тнеsе are the words inscribed on the tombstone of a woman who died in 1834 at the age of 24.[1] Daughter, sister, wife, mother, and friend—the nineteenth-century woman defined her duties in life according to these terms. She was simultaneously not only wife and mother but also sister, daughter, and friend. Women's domestic lives in nineteenth-century America involved, as do women's domestic lives today, the juggling of a number of often conflicting obligations. A woman's lifelong responsibilities as a sister and daughter remained basically unchanged by the new duties she assumed as a wife and mother. While nuclear families were fragile, destroyed by the death of either parent, threatened by financial disaster, the female family remained relatively secure, providing the central and lasting family unit that was indeed woman's sphere.

Much current concern about the decline of the family in the twentieth century is built on common misperceptions about the nature of the nineteenth-century family, misperceptions based on the assumption that the family was essentially a male-centered institution in which husbands exerted total authority over their wives while wives devoted all their energies to serving their husbands. Such an assumption makes nineteenth-century women's acceptance of home and family as their proper sphere appear to be merely a recognition of male dominance and a withdrawal from the practical concerns of the world. However, for a woman in the nineteenth-century, home and family represented a sphere much broader than the nuclear family. Based on her studies of nineteenth-century domestic literature, Nina Baym has suggested that home meant to women "not a space but a system of human relations," in other words a network of kin that extended well beyond the confines of the individual household.[2]

The correspondence of women in nineteenth-century Michigan suggests that they maintained lifelong intimate relationships with female relatives. Sisters, mothers, and daughters helped one another with domestic work and provided companionship, in many cases on a daily basis. Even those who lived in different regions of the country often corresponded frequently and gave one another minor financial assistance. Women also interceded with their husbands to provide more substantial loans and gifts to those in need. Women took nieces, nephews, and grandchildren into their homes, for the convenience of the adults involved or so that the children could receive better schooling or medical care.

In the frequent cases in which a husband traveled for business or pleasure or to establish a new home for his family, his wife and their children commonly lived temporarily with the wife's sisters or parents. Women who were deserted by their husbands or left as young widows turned to their relatives to provide homes and financial assistance until they were able to remarry or become self-supporting. The financial support of a kin network also enabled women to divorce husbands who neglected or mistreated them. Elderly women, often left widowed, similarly turned to kin for assistance. The laws of inheritance in Michigan in the nineteenth century left a widow only the use of a third of her husband's property, which she was responsible to maintain in good condition for her husband's children to inherit on her death. She would inherit any of the property gained during the marriage, even that produced through her own efforts, only if her husband willed her that property. And many widows were left with businesses heavily in debt but without the ability to continue to operate and thus discharge these debts. Women thus realized that they stood a good chance of requiring financial assistance from kin at some point in their lives.

Women also felt a need to rely on female kin in the event of their own deaths as young mothers. They commonly expressed a fear of leaving their children to be raised by stepmothers or to be "given away" to an unrelated family to whom the child would provide domestic service in return for room and board, a practice commonly discussed by women. Women attempted instead to "will" their children to their sisters and mothers. Since sisters and mothers often assisted a young woman with care during pregnancy and childbirth, care of the newborn infant, and advice and assistance throughout the child's life, these women were, on the death of a young mother, simply taking full responsibility for a child they had already nurtured.

Women valued and encouraged close ties with fathers, brothers, husbands, and sons. Yet in a society in which the nuclear family was extremely fragile, it was the female-centered kin network that ensured lifelong security in what both men and women viewed as an essentially hostile world. While the nuclear family could be destroyed by the death of either parent and frequently was threatened by economic disaster, the female family provided a stable unit in which to rear children and care for the ill, elderly, and impoverished. In the absence of governmental assistance, kin formed a necessary cushion, particularly for the women and children who could not readily support themselves in the absence of a male breadwinner.

As Christopher Lasch has discussed, popular literature of the nineteenth century portrayed the home as a "haven" to which men could retreat from the crises of the world.[3] Yet the household was not a self-sufficient unit isolated from political and economic forces; it was affected by the condition of the local economy, by political decisions leading to war, and by business vicissitudes encountered by the breadwinner. Both farmers and small business owners lived with the specter of financial failure, and were conscious of the effect of inflation on the cost of the goods they bought. Others were at the mercy of the job market and the whim of the employer. The location of Michigan as a midpoint for westward migration contributed to the sense of instability brought on by economic pressures. Many residents had moved to Michigan from the East, and many families included members who had moved farther west or were considering doing so. Then as Michigan developed from a frontier to a region of settled towns and cities, families were forced to adjust to a more urban way of life. In addition to these environmental pressures, there were the more universal crises connected with the life cycles of family members—young men going off to live independently, the financial instability of newly-established households, childbirth, aging, illness, and death.

If the family was to be a refuge from the trials of the outside world, it was the duty of women to create and maintain this refuge. Women were thus not the protected but the protectors. In order to preserve the family as a shelter, women produced and prepared food and clothing, nursed the sick, managed finances, and exchanged goods and services with other households. But women were urged by domestic manuals to hide their sense of responsibility, to conceal their productive activities beneath a veneer of effortlessness. Catharine Beecher and Harriet Beecher Stowe devoted a chapter in *The American Woman's Home* to "The Preservation of Good Temper in the Housekeeper," advising women on ways to appear cheerful despite domestic stress.[4] And Harriet Beecher Stowe a few years earlier had described the ideal wife and mother as one who "takes on herself what all others refuse or overlook . . . so quiet are her operations and movements, that none sees that it is she who holds all things in harmony."[5] As *Godey's Ladies Book* informed its readers:

> A good wife, a true woman is a real heroine and an accomplished actress. She puts her own grievances out of sight to drive away with pleasant smiles the clouds that gather around her husband's gloomy brow . . . .[6]

The responsibility held by women was thus to be hidden from view. But this carefully crafted illusion of domestic ease fails to obscure the reality of the active role of women in nineteenth-century families.

In his comprehensive study of the history of women in American families, Carl Degler notes the confluence in the early years of the nineteenth century of a widespread acceptance of rhetoric proclaiming home and family as woman's sphere with a simultaneously increasing expectation of female autonomy within the family. Viewing the family as a unit consisting of mother, father, and minor children, Degler finds in these two trends an apparent contradiction.[7] In terms of the female family, however, the simultaneous existence of these two phenomena appears neither coincidental nor surprising. In a society in which women found little possibility of total autonomy, especially once they had children to support, and in which males still maintained authority within the household, networks of female kin provided women with alternative sources of financial, practical, and moral support. Under the aegis of what has been termed the "cult of domesticity," networks of female kin thus enabled women to develop a limited autonomy within marriage. By assisting their female kin, women could devote themselves to home and family while at the same time increasing their independence from their husbands. The existence of networks of female kin thus explains in part the coexistence of women's increasing autonomy within marriage with the belief, expressed in the letters and diaries of women as well as in prescriptive literature, that home and family constituted women's sphere. For a nineteenth-century woman, marriage and family were far from synonymous.

Women, then, were not, as Degler suggests, "at odds" with the family as they defined the family. Although Degler discusses the importance of kinship ties, he views the family of origin—the woman's parents and siblings—and the family of procreation—the woman's husband and children—as sequential rather than simultaneous obligations. Noting the difficulty of establishing just when in a woman's life this transfer of loyalties occurred, Degler suggests that such a shift might have taken place during the years when the woman was raising her children.[8] The correspondence of the families examined here suggests that for women this switch of obligations never occurred. Throughout their lives these women maintained close ties with a female family extending beyond their own households.

Studies of families in mid-twentieth-century England and America reveal extensive interconnections among nuclear families, with women often holding primary responsibility for maintaining these ties with kin outside the household.[9] Tamara Hareven has suggested that nuclear families in the nineteenth century usually acted according to their interests as corporate bodies, subordinating the desires of individuals to the well-being of the family as a whole.[10] Input in family decisions, I would suggest, came from outside the household as well. If decisions involving work as well as family were indeed collective decisions of the family rather than decisions of individual family members, then interaction of female kin must have played an important role in determining the outcome of family decisions on place of residence, job choice, family size, divorce or separation, financial investments, and health care.

Through correspondence and social visiting, women controlled the channels of communication within the family. Although some males, especially bachelors, corresponded with their kin, letter-writing was widely viewed as the prerogative and duty of women, serving to preserve and strengthen the family ties from which women expected to derive both emotional and material support. What little autonomy and power women held was achieved through manipulation of the interaction among family members. When men as well as women were dependent on the goodwill of their kin, then influence—the ability to determine through persuasion the actions of others—did in fact, as prescriptive literature suggests, represent a partial feminine counterbalance to the authority held by male family members. The manipulation of relationships through verbal skill, use of metaphor, reference to norms, and threat of collective action thus represents the attempt of the less powerful to gain some degree of autonomy.

A woman in the nineteenth-century United States grew into adulthood with her familial ties intact. Indeed, marriage seemed to strengthen bonds between a mother and her daughters and between sisters. In entering the state of marriage and particularly in assuming the role of mother, a woman reaffirmed her commitment to her familial duties and entered fully into the world of adult women, a vocation for which she had served an apprenticeship since early childhood. The married woman who broke the ties with her kin would be relegating herself entirely to the authority of her husband. By choosing to marry, a woman essentially eliminated the possibility of an independent life. The maintenance of ties with her mother and sisters served, then, to decrease her dependence on her husband. And if she were left without the support of her husband, a woman with young children would be forced to turn to her kin for help. By eliminating the option of self-sufficiency, marriage served to consolidate a woman's ties with her female kin.

In the middle of the nineteenth century many states, including Michigan, passed Married Woman's Property Acts. While women held little claim to the assets created during a marriage and were precluded from the independent accumulation of assets during the marriage, under Michigan's Married Woman's Property Act of 1844 women were able to inherit from their own parents and siblings. After 1855 this inheritance remained under the woman's sole control, even if she married. Furthermore, she could pass on this inheritance to whomever she chose. Thus some women held financial assets that they could make available to kin. Furthermore, those women who owned inherited property could maintain some degree of financial autonomy from their husbands and could even, in some instances, exert pressure on a husband who had few financial resources of his own.

Ideology combined with practicality in reinforcing a woman's desire to maintain her familial ties. Prescriptive literature urged women to check their selfish impulses toward autonomy in favor of devoting themselves to family duties. Even those women who were unable to marry or chose not to marry often devoted themselves to surrogate families composed of single women. The adolescent break with the family, whether geographic or emotional, was essentially a male phenomenon whose occurrence was neither expected nor condoned in women. A woman depended on her female kin, rather than on her husband, sons, and friends, to protect her from loneliness and provide her with lifelong emotional and financial support. With few exceptions, the nineteenth-century woman never conceived of herself as autonomous. Since she derived security and satisfaction from her familial relationships, she failed to imagine an independent existence except in terms of loneliness and powerlessness. As mother, daughter, sister, and wife, she expected to live a life centered on her relationships with others.

These kinship ties were sometimes beset by conflict and ambivalence and were in many cases merely antidotes to a system of male dominance, ameliorating the condition of the woman without altering the fundamental underpinnings of her subordination. The nineteenth-century American woman was indeed urged to devote herself to home and family. But this family seldom consisted solely of husband and children; it included parents, siblings, and other kin as well. While these additional familial responsibilities added to the woman's burdens, they also broadened her sources of emotional support, enabling her to avoid the isolation experienced, we assume, by many twentieth-century women.

Nancy Cott and Carroll Smith-Rosenberg have discussed the importance of bonds among women in nineteenth-century families.[11] The term "sister" denoted an ideal of feminine intimacy and mutual support, as Cott reports, suggesting that the relationship among sisters was indeed valued, even serving as a model for other relationships. Through their affiliation with female kin, women could achieve a degree of autonomy within marriage while providing for their own security and that of their children. In recent years, anthropologists have disputed the theory that men are instrumental and women are emotive—in other words, that men act and women feel. For example, Carol Stack's examination of urban black families in the 1960s reveals women acting in strategic and instrumental ways to serve their own needs and those of other family members in an unstable environment.[12] The correspondence and visits of female kin in nineteenth-century Michigan served similar practical as well as sentimental purposes. Through their family networks, women were able to shape family actions with the assurance that they were acting within the domestic sphere and fulfilling their kinship obligations. In this way, women strengthened and preserved family bonds, reaching beyond the household to create a network of female kin, a female family that would provide lifelong security and emotional support.

In suggesting an alternative view of nineteenth-century family life, this study focusses on delineating a pattern of interaction common to the families examined. Despite differences in education and economic status as well as changes in attitude between generations of women, the clear outline of a female-centered family network emerges. Further examination of closely controlled sample groups could doubtless reveal changes through time, distinctions between urban and rural households, and other variations in the general patterns set forth here.

This study examines white, Protestant, native-born American women living in Michigan between 1820 and 1920 and the kinship networks to which they belonged, networks that often extended east to New England and the Middle Atlantic states and westward as far as California. The Bentley Library at the University of Michigan has compiled collections of the correspondence, diaries, photographs, and other documents of numerous family groups, each including many households. These documents provide the primary resources for this study. Many collections of correspondence span most of the writers' lifetimes and many include the letters of both participants in an exchange of correspondence. Numerous collections include the correspondence of several generations and all include male as well as female correspondence. While at least one household in each of the networks examined lived in Michigan, the collections include letters to and from relatives in other states and territories as well as correspondence with unrelated friends and business associates. Thirty collections of family correspondence, each including several nuclear families, provide the data for the study.

These data are particularly applicable to the study of women in families. By focussing on personal interaction within the family, we find women playing an active role that is not suggested by observation of residence patterns, household composition, or distribution of legally sanctioned authority. Correspondence reveals women's use of language to maintain personal relationships, to persuade and manipulate, and to obtain support. Thus the power base of the woman, her informal networks based on personal interaction, persuasion, and sense of obligation, becomes visible. These letters indicate that women's influence was not merely a fabrication of the literature of what has come to be termed the cult of domesticity but was a reality within many nineteenth-century families.

Of course there are limitations to the use of correspondence as a historical source. The collections of letters in archives are seldom comprehensive. Some letters, perhaps those containing particularly confidential information, may have been destroyed by their recipients. Heirs of the correspondents may also have removed letters before donating a collection. Some correspondence doubtless has been lost by random chance through the years. Thus it is important to keep in mind that the absence of correspondence in a collection does not necessarily indicate that the letters never existed. The correspondence which has been preserved must be viewed as pieces of a puzzle never to be completed but nevertheless revealing the contours of the whole.

Although this study focusses on female networks, the collections were examined in their entireties, including male as well as female correspondence. The collections studied were limited, however, to those in which significant amounts of female correspondence have been preserved. While this may skew the study towards those families in which women played an active role, it is impossible to determine whether some family collections lack female correspondence because such correspondence never existed or simply because it was not preserved.

In any method relying on written sources, the sample is limited to, or at best biased toward, those who possess at least minimal skills of reading and writing. In the case of letters, the sample is also biased toward those who used their literary skills to communicate with absent relatives and friends. The collections examined represent a disproportionate number of highly educated people. This may be due, however, not to the fact that the highly educated wrote more letters but to their greater inclination to value and preserve correspondence for an expressive and artistic as well as purely practical purpose. Furthermore, the family papers of well-known individuals are more likely to find their way into archives, since they seem to the heirs of these correspondents to have a greater intrinsic value. Probably families who, in the twentieth century, value literary expression and are sympathetic enough to a university to donate their family papers account for a disproportionate number of archival collections.

While the study includes a large number of families with at least one well-educated or highly successful member, the percentage of such individuals out of the total is small. Most of the family groups examined include no notable individuals and encompass wide ranges of education and wealth. Even in families including educated and

affluent males, the social, educational, and economic status of the
women who entered the family through marriage often varied greatly.
Of course many men and women attained a higher level of education,
wealth, and social status than that of their parents. Many letters
included in the study were written in phonetic spelling, often without
punctuation, and in a few instances letters were dictated by those
unable to write.[13]

It becomes apparent in reading the correspondence of these
nineteenth-century families that many individuals with only a ru-
dimentary education gained in a country school possessed not only
facility with spelling and punctuation but also great verbal skill.
Many letters are copied from drafts, some of which have survived,
and show great care and diligence in their composition. Even farmers
and their wives who possessed only an elementary education often
were able to express themselves eloquently in writing and practiced
this skill regularly with their relatives. The range of social and
educational levels represented by family correspondence therefore is
broad. Unlike modern America, this was a society which relied on
the written word for much of its intimate as well as formal communication and which assumed that competence in writing was
expected of all who aspired even to what we might term lower-middle-
class status. Thus, while the study includes only a few people who
could be considered less than middle class, a relatively wide range
of occupation, wealth, and education is encompassed. The families
examined include members who were old and young, college-educated
and illiterate, single and married, rich and poor, urban and rural.

The study is limited, however, to white, Protestant, native-born
Americans living in Michigan between 1820 and 1920, and their
relatives in other states and territories. White, Protestant, native-
born Americans represented the vast majority of Michigan's population in the nineteenth century.[14] Because of the relatively small
number of families examined, it would be impossible to include
adequate numbers of foreign-born Americans to represent their appropriate share of the population while still presenting a large enough
group to draw comparisons based on ethnicity. Therefore, this study
excludes those of foreign birth and those families who consciously
expressed a sense of ethnic identity. Of course, white, Protestant, native-born Americans are an ethnic group, precisely the group
at which the literature of the cult of domesticity was directed.[15]
Furthermore, white, Protestant, native-born Americans are the group
whose family life provides a commonly used, and often misused,

model applied to twentieth-century Americans as well as to the family life of other ethnic groups in the nineteenth century.

It is important to keep in mind, however, the limitations of the sample. The experiences of those who left their families behind to travel to a new continent doubtless differed from those of the families examined here. Ethnic groups which maintained distinctive cultural patterns may have reacted in very different ways. Certainly the lives of black Americans may have been divergent.

Aside from the variables of race, ethnicity, and religion, there remains the less tangible variable of social class. Most of the family networks examined include a notable diversity of wealth and education among family members. Was this diversity a common condition of nineteenth-century American families, as women married husbands of higher social status and individuals raised themselves above the economic and educational level of their parents? Or did these upwardly mobile individuals write or preserve letters while those families who remained in poverty did not? Did upwardly mobile men and women provide an uncharacteristic amount of assistance to their less fortunate relatives? While diversity within a family, especially between generations, makes it impossible to classify families by social or economic class without ignoring the differences among individual members, the families discussed here should not be assumed to represent all white, native-born, Protestant Americans—and certainly not all Americans.

One of the difficulties of research involving personal documents such as letters is determining how typical of their location, era, ethnic group, and social class were the individual people who created the documents. Since comparable studies do not exist, it is impossible to determine to what degree the female family networks examined in this study were typical of white, Protestant, native-born families. It is possible, however, to compare some of these families in their household composition, location, and occupation to the total population of southern Michigan. A study undertaken by Susan Bloomberg and others uses data from the 1850 and 1880 United States Census to examine the composition and age structure of households in southern Michigan. Of the families included in this study, 25 households appear in either the 1850 or the 1880 Michigan manuscript census. These families can be compared to Bloomberg's sample of southern Michigan families to determine to what extent they are representative of the total population.[16]

The households studied were close to the average geographical distribution of the population of the state. All but three of the households were located in the southern third of Michigan's Lower Peninsula, where 98.3% of the state's population lived in 1850, and 85.1% in 1880.[17] In 1850 approximately 62% of the sample lived in rural locations, a figure the Bloomberg study found to represent the percentage of the population then located in rural areas. However, in 1880 less than 17% of the sample was located in rural areas, compared to 46% of Bloomberg's sample.[18] While the families in this study include a relatively small number of Detroit residents, this percentage reflects the small proportion of Michigan's American-born citizens living in Detroit.[19]

The families examined here represent a wide range of wealth in real estate. Although data on wealth were not collected in 1880, of those households appearing in the 1850 census, five held less than one thousand dollars of real estate, six held between two thousand and four thousand dollars' worth, and two owned more than eight thousand dollars of real estate. The Bloomberg study does not provide data on average wealth in Michigan.

In household composition, the families studied were close to the average for the sample examined by Bloomberg, both in total household size and in number of children, with the distribution of both clustered closely around the average figures found by the Bloomberg study. Average household size for the sample was 5.5 in 1850 and 5.6 in 1880, compared to the state average of 5.5 in 1850 and 4.9 in 1880, according to the U.S. Census Bureau.[20] The percentages of households including a parent of the household head or his spouse (8.3% in 1880) or a boarder (8.3% in 1880) were also close to the southern Michigan averages as determined by Bloomberg.[21] The distribution of age of household head follows closely the distribution of age among Bloomberg's sample.

In some respects, however, these households differed from the norm. In both 1850 and 1880, a disproportionate number of household heads were professionals, managers, and proprietors, while very few were laborers. The households studied included more servants than was usual for southern Michigan, although most of the households examined here did not include servants. These two factors may indicate a higher than average educational and socio-economic level among the families examined. The other factor in which the households studied deviate significantly from the sample examined in the Bloomberg study is in the range of their children's ages, with sample households representing a smaller difference between the ages of the oldest and youngest child than was found in Bloomberg's study. Since the total number of children per household was close to the average for the state, this may indicate a closer than average spacing of children among the families examined.

The families studied thus represent a middle-class, white, native-born population including a large number of professionals but also many farmers, with a wide range of wealth. In composition and age, these households are representative of the patterns of the population of southern Michigan, with a larger than average number of servants and a tighter than average spacing of children, which may be representative of the group's ethnic, educational, and social level.

The experience of settlers in Michigan who wrote to absent kin may, of course, have differed from that of families who remained in the East. Indeed the unusual pattern of development of Michigan may have caused the family relationships of its settlers to vary even from that of families who settled in other regions of the West and Midwest. A ballad about "Michigania" reflects the rapid settlement of the territory:

What country ever grew up so great in so little time,
Just popping from a nursery right into life its prime?[22]

When the land was first opened for settlement around 1820, Michigan was a wilderness territory isolated by the Great Lakes to the north, east, and west and by the Great Black Swamp to the south. By the 1840s Michigan was a settled state, accessible through the Erie Canal and by steamship travel on Lake Erie, with many of its towns connected by rail. A large percentage of the population of the state in the middle and late nineteenth century were recent settlers who maintained close ties with relatives in the East and with family members who often proceeded westward to other territories. Except for a brief period after the land was opened for settlement around 1820, good postal service and transportation allowed settlers in Michigan to maintain extensive contact, by means of letters and visits, with kin in the East.[23]

Studies of other frontier regions would establish whether this pattern of family interaction was characteristic of the impact of westward migration on American families or whether the belated and rapid development of the territory created a unique situation. The disruption of family networks and the subsequent attempt to maintain them through correspondence was certainly typical of many families during the settlement of the West and Midwest. While the ideal was that all kin live near one another, separation of family members represented a common, perhaps even prevalent, experience for American families in the nineteenth century.

This study begins with the first large influx of settlers into Michigan after the territory outside Detroit was opened for settlement in the 1820s and ends with the general cultural changes following the First World War, particularly the emergence of the telephone as a means of family communication. Since telephones were found on half of all farms in the state by 1920,[24] it is impractical after the early years of the twentieth century to use collections of correspondence to study family networks. But until the use of the telephone became widespread, letters provided a crucial link among family members separated by westward migration. The development of communication and transportation networks in the nineteenth century enabled residents of Michigan to maintain ties with kin living further west, as well as with those in New England and the mid-Atlantic states.

The isolation experienced by families on Michigan's frontier in the 1830s lessened rapidly in mid-century as the agricultural regions of the state were linked to New York and New England by reliable and regular postal service and convenient transportation. Thus women who moved to Michigan did not sever ties with their kin. They not only communicated frequently by correspondence but also made extended visits, often of several months' duration, with the relatives they had left behind.

While these women felt a sense of loneliness for their kin, they looked forward to visits every few years, to regular correspondence, and to frequent exchanges of household goods. Most important, they expected to rely on these kin for support in times of financial distress, illness, widowhood, desertion, or their own deaths while caring for young children. Similarly, women living in Michigan maintained ties with kin who moved further west.

Thus, female kin networks proved to be viable and stable family units even in the face of geographic separation brought about by the settlement of the West. For women, female kin provided a sense of community, a community transcending even geographic isolation.

ONE

Into the Gulf of Matrimony: Husbands and Wives

Daughter, sister, mother, wife—these roles defined the familial obligations of women. Yet only one of these relationships, that of wife, was freely chosen. Only in this decision could most women shape their own futures and even here the choices were severely limited. While a man was free to search for a woman who would fit his ideal, a woman could only say yes or no to a particular man, without knowing what other options would remain should she decline. A man could choose to marry; a woman could choose only to marry a particular man. This situation caused a great deal of anxiety on the part of young women. While a man's life could certainly be made unpleasant by the wrong choice in a wife, a woman's entire future, financial as well as emotional, was determined by the decision of whom to marry. Yet in this choice, which was so crucial to her future, a woman held only the right of refusal, not the freedom of selection.

Women expressed a strong sense of duty to marry any man who met certain standards of decency, was an adequate provider, was moral and religious, and could be expected to treat his wife kindly. Isaac Demmon, later to become a professor of English at the University of Michigan, repeatedly wrote in his diary of his intense and growing love for Emma Regal, the young daughter of a traveling minister. Yet when he proposed to her, she wrote her father:

> I respect him and have some affection for him but his presence is not essential to my happiness and my love for him compared with

that I have for the members of our family seems little. I do not know what I ought to do under such circumstances. Will you tell me, please, what you think? I should be glad if I should not be asked to decide yet; but if I am I shall try, God helping me, to do what is right.[1]

Uncertain of the outcome should they agree to marry and equally uncertain of their future alternatives should they refuse, women sometimes turned to God to help them decide, believing that God would direct them to the appropriate husband. Elizabeth Gurney noted in her journal that she felt called by God to marry a minister. Since her own minister was unmarried, she feared that if she told him of her calling he would misinterpret, or perhaps correctly in-

1. Wives and relatives of University of Michigan Faculty. *Standing—left to right*: Mrs. Morris, Louise Pond, Mrs. Waldron, Mrs. Harry Hutchings, Mrs. M.C. D'Ooge; *seated—left to right*: Mrs. Pettee, Mrs. I.N. Demmon (Emma Regal Demmon), Mrs. James B. Angell, Mrs. Lombard, Mrs. B.A. Hinsdale, Mrs. Palmer

terpret, her intentions. When an older widower with several children, a missionary in the Upper Peninsula, proposed to her, she accepted, although she found him personally repulsive, believing that this was the will of God. "I do not look upon this as a mere love matter," she wrote, "but a matter of *duty* or *not duty*."[2] Harriet Johnson, although she was unhappy as a schoolteacher, expressed great anxiety over whether to accept a proposal of marriage, praying to God as well as asking her father for guidance.[3]

While many women married the first man to court them, Harriet was particularly cautious since she had nearly married a man she later came to believe had deceived her. For several months before and after her engagement, Harriet described in her diary her indecision. "What *is duty*? Am I old and staid enough to marry?" she wondered.[4] Harriet felt torn between her ambition to be a writer and the desire to be loved and taken care of, deciding that her higher duty was to give up her worldly ambition and pride, making herself subservient to her husband. "O that I might be willing to sacrifice *self* upon the altar of *right*," she wrote[5] in her diary, describing the sacrifice she was preparing to make:

> The 'distaff & wheel' will take the place of the pen.—My wings are clipped, and like the sober *goose* I'll plod along life's even way, never venturing to gaze upon the proud eagle's flight who, with eye fixed upon the burning 'king of day' soars up, higher, higher, and still higher, above earth born grovellers. My humble sphere is fixed, . . . and at last welcome the sober, matronly duties of the wife and mother—welcome all their unaspiring hopes and unassuming responsibilities. . . . To think of my being willing to settle down to the humdrum life of married folks and mending coats and patching breetches.[6]

To Harriet, as to many other women, marriage was a sacrifice rather than an opportunity.

Harriet wrote of newlyweds "full of hopes which are to be crushed," whose "fair brows would be lined with care & trial."[7] She described a woman whose "husband seems to look upon her as an inferior being, and she evidently is not *herself* but a crushed woman, tied to domestic servitude, a perfect slave to her children, and such, I suppose is *woman's sphere*."[8] Harriet expressed her own anxiety about her upcoming marriage, from which she would sometimes "tremble and shrink with almost horror," with a "shrinking dread; an almost shuddering fear."[9] She wrote:

> Tonight I feel as though I never *could* marry—much as I love H— there seems to be such a conflicting of desires—such a fearful shrinking from that last, final step—Oh: how *can* I take it?[10]

Harriet particularly feared losing her sense of herself as an independent person, writing that she "would not wish to lose my own identity and settle down into one of your dull characterless persons— who have no original thoughts—in short a mere nonentity."[11]

Harriet was torn between her fear of remaining forever single and her fear of marriage:

> My mind has been restless and unsettled—I feel that I love Henry, and yet I dare not *yield*—There is such a shrinking from the thought of marriage—of binding myself indissolubly—of *forever* pledgeing myself to him—I cannot—O *I cannot!* I cannot forego all the proud hopes that have bouyed my spirit from my youth up—I cannot become one of your homespun, commonplace characters, & settle down to household drudgery—No, no—I *cannot,* and yet I cannot cast from me a true, noble heart that loves me—I cannot resign myself to an unloved solitude.[12]

Harriet felt that she had only two choices—household drudgery or unloved solitude. With the role of a wife closely defined and the life of a single woman equally circumscribed, most women felt that they could only choose between total submission to the wishes of a husband and the needs of children and, on the other hand, the life of a "spinster" with no emotional or sexual relationships with men, with little chance for economic independence and security, and with the social stigma of assumed rejection by the opposite sex.[13]

Other women also expressed the fear of remaining unmarried.[14] One woman wrote at the age of eighteen that she was the last of her friends to marry and feared becoming "an old maid."[15] After several years of joking about the advantages of being single, a twenty-eight-year-old woman wrote to her friend of "that *awful* fear of living and dying 'old maids'."[16]

While women feared being left "old maids," they also feared marriage. Young single women frequently joked about the advantages of remaining single, with the unspoken understanding that eventually they would marry. One young woman wrote that she disapproved of "girls, being hasty, and getting married so young, for if they ever do, they will then see trouble enough."[17] Another woman explained to her cousin who was about to be married:

> No husband's frowns and baby's gowns
> My hart is fancy free
> Ill sing my song my whole life long
> An old maid's life for me.[18]

One woman jokingly told her sister of "the Holy Bonds of Padlock,"[19] while another woman warned that she considered her friend "altogether too innocent and *good* to take the final leap into the gulf of matrimony."[20]

Women wrote of their fears of abandonment by newly married women. One girl told a friend, "I suppose I ought to be cautious what I write, for now you are a married woman."[21] Another young woman wrote her cousin:

> If I had another Sister, oh if I only *had*—but if she *thought*
> of getting married I'd disown her. I don't believe in this marrying
> system, do you? its nothing but cares & forever after.[22]

Young women felt keenly the loss of the companionship of their sisters, cousins, and friends who married, the comradeship of the feminine community threatened by the intrusion of a male.

Older women sometimes advised single women not to marry at a young age. One girl reported that her aunt had told her, "Mary dont you get married yet this good while, you've got a good home . . . good Parents, have no care, no trouble & have nothing to do but enjoy yourself."[23] One woman wrote of a recently married woman:

> I am preparing my mind to see her return to us not in the full
> enjoyment of single blessedness but entangled with a double yoke
> of bondage which generally increases in heaviness every year till in
> many instances the grave is looked upon as a quiet resting place
> and scores of our sex sink therein long years before He who pro-
> nounced the "twain one flesh" designed they should.[24]

While the bitterness of her emotions is unusual, this woman expressed the negative feelings many women held towards marriage.

Some women found forming households with other women to be a viable alternative to the choice between the perceived loneliness of the single woman and the demands of a traditional marriage.[25] These emotional and in some cases sexual relationships provided women with domestic comforts, companionship, and independence within a wider kin network but without the necessity of submitting to the wishes of a husband. One young woman wrote to another that it would be "splendid for you and I to set up housekeeping together, wouldnt we have splendid times with our books and music, and our cats."[26] Two young women, who may have been related, wrote of traveling to California, where they bought land and planned to live together.[27]

Both Jessie Phelps and Abby Field established households based on intense emotional relationships with other women.[28] The close female friend with whom Abby bought a house referred to her as her "loving partner," while Abby's sister referred to their household as a "family."[29] Jessie wrote in her diary of taking "for better or for worse" and then later "divorcing" the woman with whom she maintained a long-term friendship that satisfied, she wrote, both her "sense of aloneness" and her "unfulfilled desire to mate."[30] While still maintaining ties with other kin, these single women formed close bonds with women outside the kinship network, bonds which substituted to some extent for the nuclear family. And these households often were accepted by the female kin network as alternative family units. The camaraderie of female friendship became a replacement for marriage, a familial world of domesticity without men. These female households, like those of married couples, however, could not provide the life-long security of a kin network.

But most women chose to marry. With marriage, a woman assumed the role of wife, a role perceived as universal in its definition, for which there existed no male analogy. Marriage truly joined "man and wife," the role of husband undifferentiated from that of man, while the woman attempted to fill the role of wife, the highest role to which a woman could aspire but one not all women could adequately perform. The marriage relationship itself was viewed as a given set of duties assumed by a man and woman rather than as a personal and unique relationship whose form would be determined by the two individuals involved. A woman who would be a good wife for one man would be a good wife for another, and a woman upon marriage could expect to follow the same path as had her mother and sisters. With marriage a woman took on the common duties and responsibilities of a wife; she assumed a well-defined role of work and behavior common to all married women.

One woman wrote that she "took upon me the responsibilities of a wife,"[31] while a man wrote his newly-married sister that he hoped she would prove "worthy of the station which you hold ever be mindful of your duty and always endeavor to promote the happiness of your husband."[32] A female friend told the same young woman that she trusted she would be "inabled to maniage with proper energy and correctness in all cases and in all circumstances that you may be cauled to act much is depending on the propriety of our conduct."[33] Harriet Johnson, the schoolteacher who gave up her ambitions as a writer for marriage, expressed concern that she be able to "perform the duties of a wife . . . love on forever . . . be a cheerful assistant in adversity . . . ever sustain and encourage . . . be a counselor—a never failing friend—in short a faithful, devoted, loving wife."[34] An unattributed poem written "to a young lady on her leaving School," and copied into an autograph book, advised the girl,

> To act, as you proceed through life,
> As daughter, mother, friend, and wife.[35]

A woman considering marriage was concerned that she marry a man who would treat her kindly; beyond this her concern was her own ability to perform her domestic duties as wife, mother, daughter, and sister.

If men felt such anxiety over the performance of their domestic roles, they failed to express these concerns in their correspondence. As males, in the absence of overt cruelty, they were by definition adequate husbands. They directed their attention instead to the ability of a woman to perform the duties expected of a wife. One man praised his fiancée's "decision, prompness of character," and morality, yet still wondered if she could "fill the wife's place."[36] Men sometimes devised lists of the characteristics they expected in a wife. Judson Bingham, the son of a missionary in Michigan, told his sisters that he required "1st piety 2nd Health 3rd affection 4th Industry 5th Will she have me?" A year later his expectations were apparently unchanged, since he wrote his sister of one girl who was both industrious and healthy, but was of uncertain piety and affection.[37] And when Maria Bingham Seymour suggested a friend of hers as a wife for her brother, he asked her height, the state of her health, and whether she was interested in missionary work, his chosen career.[38]

Just as men sometimes made a calculated search for a woman who met their qualifications, women often weighed quite calmly the financial and emotional advantages of marriage. When Frances Hall told her friend about her bachelor cousin and the house he had built, the girl replied by asking "if there were blinds, etc."[39] One young woman whose fiancé had died shortly before their wedding, wrote a year later of her plans to marry another man:

> I have received an offer of marriage from one whom my friends approve of and as I am probably ever should be dependent upon my own hands for my support—I have consented to the offer of what is best for me to do & the time is set for our union.[40]

The choice of a marriage partner was for both men and women a sober decision, to be made on a rational basis with advice and assistance from kin. Whatever affection and intimacy existed or developed, the decision to marry remained a practical one involving also the exchange of a woman's services for a man's financial support. The mutual obligations a couple assumed were understood and upheld by their kinship network.

Once married, women voiced their expectations concerning the behavior of their husbands, using the limited means available to them to ensure proper treatment. The mutual obligations of husband and wife were defined by law as well as custom. A husband owed his wife financial support, sexual fidelity, and freedom from cruel treatment. A wife owed her husband sexual fidelity, her time, her earnings, and her services.[41] These obligations were to some extent enforceable by law. In addition to allowing divorces for misconduct, the law provided for criminal prosecution for some offenses involving familial obligations. Adultery was grounds for divorce after 1819 and was punishable by fines and jail sentences as well.[42] A woman was entitled to a separation or divorce from her husband if he treated her cruelly or if he neglected to support her. By the early twentieth century the failure of a husband to support his wife and children was made a felony, punishable by three years in prison.[43] Thus a woman could claim a legal as well as moral right to her husband's financial support, fidelity, and kind treatment, while a man could claim his wife's services on his behalf.

While unmarried adult women held essentially the same legal and financial rights as their male counterparts, a woman assumed upon her marriage a legal status ancillary to her husband. This dependent status was partially alleviated by Michigan's Married Woman's Property Act of 1844 which, like many such laws in other states, gave married women the right to own property under some circumstances.[44] Before the passage of this act, a married woman had no right to own property in her own name and, in fact, no legal existence apart from that of her husband. Any property she owned at the time of the marriage, inherited during the marriage, or earned during the marriage belonged to her husband. Before 1844, the only situation in which a woman could regain the property she had brought into a marriage was in the case of a divorce awarded to her on the grounds of her husband's adultery. Even after her husband's death, a wife did not regain the property she had brought to the marriage unless it was willed to her by her husband. She was entitled only to the use during her lifetime of some of her husband's real estate and to a part of his personal estate.[45]

The Married Woman's Property Act of 1844 gave a married woman limited control over property owned before her marriage or inherited during the marriage. The act provided that:

> Any real or personal estate which may have been acquired by any female before her marriage, either by her own personal industry, or by inheritance, gift, grant or devise, or to which she may at any time after her marriage be entitled by inheritance, gift, grant or devise, and the rents, profits and income of any such real estate, shall be and continue the real and personal estate of such female after marriage, to the same extent as before marriage; and none of said property shall be liable for her husband's debts, engagements or liabilities. . . .

A woman could not, however, "give, grant, or sell" such property without her husband's permission. Nor could she remove the property from the premises of her husband.[46] In 1855 the act was amended to allow a married woman's property to be "contracted, sold, transferred, mortgaged, conveyed, devised or bequeathed by her, in the same manner and with the like effect as if she were unmarried."[47] The money earned by a woman during her marriage was not covered under this act, however, but belonged to her husband.

The Married Woman's Property Act protected a married woman and her children from the seizure of her property for her husband's debts and protected the state from supporting a woman whose husband had squandered her inheritance. It also provided a mechanism by which an inheritance could be passed through a woman to her children, ensuring that property bequeathed by a man to his wife would not be appropriated by a future husband.[48]

The basic responsibilities of husband and wife remained untouched by the Married Woman's Property Act. A husband was still required to support his wife and children, a wife still obligated to give her time, services, and earnings to her husband. Only after 1911 was a married woman entitled to her own earnings, and then only if her husband chose to allow her to use her time for her own benefit. A married woman could sue or make contracts only concerning her own property.[49]

The Married Woman's Property Act benefited the husband as well as the wife. Since a wife's inheritance was not liable for her husband's debts, a woman with inherited property was ensured of some financial security even in the face of her husband's business losses, a provision which benefited the family as a whole. A husband could legally favor his wife over other creditors in repaying loans, providing the husband as well as the wife with a shelter from creditors. After 1911, when a woman became entitled to her own earnings, a husband could work for his wife's business in preference to working on his own behalf, with the profits untouched by his creditors.[50] The Married Woman's Property Act thus was intended not to give greater power and autonomy to the wife but to give strength and security to the family.[51]

The Married Woman's Property Act, however, enabled a woman to inherit from her parents, retaining sole control of her inherited property. Thus some women owned property apart from their husbands'; this property and the income such property often produced gave these women a degree of leverage in the marital relationship since they could sometimes determine their husbands' actions by withholding, or threatening to withhold, monetary support. In practice, therefore, the Married Woman's Property Act served to strengthen the bond between a woman and the parents from whom she would inherit while simultaneously weakening the control a husband held over his wife. After passage of the Married Woman's Property Act of 1855, some women also held financial resources that they could make available to kin even without their husbands' consent.

Sarah Regal informed her evangelist husband on one occasion that she would pay his way home only if he intended to remain at home permanently. "I can collect some of my dues from a certain gentleman in the West," she wrote.[52] Presumably this money came from an inheritance since she appears to have had sole control over it, control she used to affect her husband's activities. Edmund Hall's cousin, who cared for Edmund's father in his old age, wrote Edmund for assurance that she would inherit her uncle's farm. The property left by her first husband, she wrote, had been "embarrassed" by her second husband, but she was controlling the interest with the help of her children and wanted to ensure that she would inherit additional property to provide her own financial security.[53]

For most women financial power through inherited wealth was unavailable. Women did, however, maintain expectations of a minimal standard of behavior on the part of their husbands, using moral suasion to attempt to reform husbands they viewed as failing to fulfill their duties. Within a few months of her marriage to a young professor of sociology, Elsie Cooley, a former schoolteacher, spent several months with her husband's parents, where, she wrote her husband, she felt needed and appreciated. After a few months of negotiation by mail she returned to a lifelong and apparently happy marriage.[54]

Many women objected to the absence of their husbands. Eli Regal, a traveling evangelist, was away from home much of the time. His wife sometimes lived alone with her young children, sometimes with various relatives. She repeatedly urged him to return home, once telling him she only wanted "a little pleasant home and live together and enjoy ourselves with our dear children."[55] Her sister wrote of her own husband whom she saw only every seven or eight weeks. "I am getting tired of living so," she complained.[56] Lucy Parker frequently asked her husband, an attorney and land speculator, to return home to help her care for their children. Sometimes her sister-in-law made extended visits to assist her, but usually she lived alone with the children.[57] These men were kept from home by business concerns. While the letters between spouses appear affectionate, the absence of their husbands was a source of distress to the wives. Both Sarah Regal and Lucy Parker received assistance from their kin, and through the years both women became increasingly financially and emotionally independent of their husbands.

One middle-aged woman was quite articulate as to her expectation of mutual concern and companionship within a marriage. Harriet

2. Family portrait in Charles and Elsie Cooley's home in Ann Arbor (1906). *Standing— left to right*: Rutger Horton Cooley (b. 1893), Charles Horton Cooley (1864–1929), Margaret Horton Cooley (1897–1926); *seated*: Elsie Cooley holding Mary Elizabeth Cooley (1904–1978)

Whittemore complained of her husband's failure to sympathize with her numerous illnesses and of the attention and financial resources he devoted to his lumbering business, located in a remote region of the state. She wrote to her son of her husband's failure to write while he was attending to his lumbering concern, claiming her right to his attention:

> God has very wisely implanted a *peculiar* interest between man and wife . . . this peculiar interest and true hearted friendship cannot be kept warmly alive in the heart without mutual interchange of feelings. It should be reciprocal, I think I do not claim anything

more than what reason and justice, would allow. I am peculiarly sensitive on this point. I can see no earthly happiness where this mutual friendship among friends does not exist.[58]

Shortly thereafter she wrote her husband, suggesting that he had a moral obligation to live with her:

I hope the coming year we can arrange matters so that you and I may remain at the same place and enjoy each others society If our lives should be prolonged. We need to be together for our spiritual as well as temporal good.[59]

Aware that she was unable to control her husband's behavior, Harriet attempted to persuade him of his obligation to her.

Sometimes persuasion could overcome a husband's legal authority. Several correspondents discussed the influence women sometimes held over where the family would live, although the husband maintained the legal authority to make the decision. "I suppose Olive Densmore has started for Missouri," one woman wrote, "but; I think he will not get there before his wife decided to go no further."[60] In his autobiography, Josiah Littlefield claimed that his father "had, no doubt, been induced to leave the farm and move to Flat Rock and Gibralter because my mother's relatives lived there."[61] Lovicy Cooper, sister of Harriet Whittemore, the woman who reminded her husband of his obligation to live with her, explained to Harriet that her husband had purchased a new house in Detroit two miles from their current home. She wrote her sister:

I wont tell you yet whether we shall move there or not I require great deliberation before I can consent to leave a place where I have resided thirty-four years, and especially at my age I am not [moving] against my will . . . . I hardly think he would be contented to live there himself but when we determine what to do we will inform you, but I think you will visit us here before we move.[62]

In spite of her legal obligation to follow her husband, Lovicy insisted on her right to participate in the decision.

Other women took unilateral action. One woman whose husband had allegedly mistreated her for years established herself in business when her husband moved west and simply refused to join him when he sent for her. When he eventually married another woman, she returned to New England to "his friends and hers."[63] Another woman decided to leave her common-law husband; she took their five children and traveled to Michigan to join her parents and siblings.[64]

While women held little power within a marriage and were quite aware of their vulnerability both within and outside marriage, they did expect to receive a minimal level of consideration, time, and affection from their husbands. Women were quick to remind their husbands of any deficiencies they perceived, although often in submissive language. Women did in fact claim the right to the respect, protection, and affection which the ideal of a patriarchal family assured them was their due. Furthermore, female kin sometimes insisted on the proper treatment of a mother or sister, aligning themselves against a male related by marriage.

Kin sometimes urged a reluctant woman to divorce her husband. Marilla Turrill advised her mother to sue for divorce from her second husband, Marilla's stepfather, after he had left her with his elderly father and their two young sons to support. Marilla wrote to her brother that her mother "does not write to me any more because I told her she ought to get a divorce and be freed from Bailey and the old man too."[65] She told her brother that their mother's second marriage had deprived them of money that would otherwise have been theirs and had forced them to support her second family.[66] Marilla viewed her stepfather and his kin as outsiders who were draining the family's resources.

In the Smith family, several sisters aligned themselves against a brother-in-law, advising their sister to divorce him and offering her financial assistance. May's husband, who, May's sisters believed, had beaten her, and also threatened her and berated her publicly,[67] told May's sisters to address all future correspondence to him since May was ill.[68] Soon thereafter, he wrote of a fire in their house and his arrest on grounds of arson for insurance fraud.[69] When Will was convicted and their property seized, May tried unsuccessfully to raise the money to pay her husband's fines and release him from jail. One sister wrote that she would give May money only after May's husband went to jail.[70] When May threatened suicide if her sisters did not provide the money to pay his fine, one sister wrote another that she had written May, "Do you think if he goes to *Prisen* that he can take this greate big world with him & all the *lovely* men that are in it," saying that nothing would please him more than her death. Another sister, she explained, "wrote May a good letter & told her he wasnt worth her life and brace up and come home & she would do all she could for her and so would Larry."[71] May replied that Will was a good, kind husband and her sisters were trying to wreck her home.[72]

Thus female kin sometimes advised women to sue for divorce and even attempted to assist them financially in divorcing their husbands. Divorce was the only way for a woman to regain the legal ability to control her own earnings or to free her kin from the responsibility of supporting her husband's family, as well as a way to avoid emotional or physical abuse. Among women, then, divorce apparently was viewed as an unfortunate necessity in some instances, a means of rectifying a situation in which a woman was exploited. Divorced women often returned to their kin, permanently if they were elderly, temporarily if they were young.[73]

In spite of the advances in the legal protection of women and children within the family, women remained largely under the legal domination of their husbands into the twentieth century. Women in Michigan, as in many other states, were granted some legal rights in the nineteenth century, including the ability to inherit and control property and to divorce a cruel or neglecting husband. Those women who owned property inherited from their families could maintain some degree of financial autonomy from their husbands. Furthermore, by threatening to sue for divorce, women theoretically could exert some control over the behavior of their husbands.

But since most women could not support their children alone, they had, in actuality, little hope of true autonomy. The ability to turn to kin for assistance, however, enabled women to exercise, or threaten to exercise, the legal right to divorce their husbands for mistreatment. Such autonomy as a woman had, then, was of necessity backed by her kin network, from whom she could inherit and to whom she could turn for alternative support. In a study of wifebeating in nineteenth-century America, Elizabeth Pleck has found that in the absence of legal sanctions on wifebeating, the community or the victim's family informally punished the offender.[74] Similarly, women attempted to balance their lack of authority within the nuclear family with the collective moral, social, and financial pressure of their kin networks.

The system of laws governing the family in the nineteenth century made viable, then, by omission as well as commission, the maintenance of extended kin networks centered on female family members. As patriarchal control was weakened and married women were granted some autonomy, while still for the most part unable to support families through their own efforts, they turned to their female kin to provide stable family groups for nursing the ill and elderly, for child-rearing, and for the sharing of financial support and household labor.

In most marriages, of course, both partners fulfilled at least their minimal obligations. Indeed, many husbands and wives attempted to achieve a personal intimacy far beyond that required by law or custom. Josiah Littlefield and his wife Nellie discussed before marriage the importance of frankness, forbearance, and forgiveness on the part of both husband and wife and the desirability of a husband's assistance with the housework.[75] Their correspondence indicates that they did indeed maintain a happy and intimate relationship from the time of their marriage until Nellie's death in childbirth less than a year later. When Nellie was caring for her ill sister shortly after her own marriage, her husband Josiah wrote of his mishaps in making biscuits, saying that he would prefer a housekeeper of two or three months' experience sitting across the table from him "with the sunshine in her hair and in her face too."[76] Another man wrote that he had made his young wife his confidant in business matters so that she would be able to carry on the business in case of his death. On her death as a young mother he wrote that he had lost not only a wife but also a business advisor.[77] Many women deeply mourned the loss of their husbands. "We were all the world to each other only God knows how we loved each other," one young widow wrote.[78]

Such intimacy continued and even deepened in many long-lasting marriages. After many years of marriage, Eli Regal, the traveling evangelist, wrote his wife, "I have sympathized with you in your cold, hatmakings, fire making, and would have felt it a great treat to have kept you warm all night, and then to have warmed the kitchen for you in the morning and in company with those pledges of our love, have partaken of *your* 'fare', which you know has, so long, been necessary to my health & happiness."[79] Charles Horton Cooley and his wife Elsie attempted throughout their courtship and long marriage to communicate honestly and respect one another's individuality, negotiating the financial, sexual, and emotional aspects of their relationship.[80] Yet even in the most intimate and lasting marriages some crises required the help of kin outside the household: childbirth, nursing the ill, caring for the elderly and for orphans, financial support in emergencies. And in virtually all marriages one partner would at some point be widowed, perhaps in need of assistance

3. Josiah Littlefield (c. 1870)

4. Picnic at North Lake (c. 1888). *Seated—left to right*: Ed de Pont, Agnes Leas, Mrs. P.C. de Pont, Elsie Jones (later Mrs. C.H. Cooley), Prof. de Pont, Charles H. Cooley; *standing*: Dick de Pont

from relatives. Female kin provided support in the day-to-day tasks of raising a family as well as in times of crisis.

Duties to one's kin and duties to one's husband sometimes came into conflict. Women often were forced to mediate between their nuclear family and their kin network, justifying the actions of one group to the other or seeking assistance for one group from the other group. Since the roles of sister and daughter as well as those of wife and mother were viewed as essential aspects of a woman's domestic responsibilities, women had some flexibility in selecting which obligations were of greater immediate importance, justifying their choice on the grounds of familial duty.

Usually, however, the various roles performed by women did not conflict. Female kin recognized the importance of the marital relationship in introducing financial resources into the kin network and in rearing as well as producing children. Furthermore, the duties a woman owed her husband were believed to be ordained by God, to be accepted as a religious burden. Husbands, for their part, recognized the importance of kinship networks. Women as well as men would inherit from their kin. And, more important in most cases, men as well as women expected to rely on kin for nursing care and childcare as well as emergency financial aid. Since women's domestic roles were, for the most part, interchangeable, a man could expect to rely at some point on the services of his wife's kin when they assisted her or substituted for her. Thus female kin networks usually were not subversive to nuclear families but were, instead, essential to their operation.

The various possible relationships between nuclear families and kin networks can be described in terms of descent groups. Kinship systems are thus viewed as institutionalized authority structures regulating the transfer of power and wealth from generation to generation and governing relationships among nuclear families. In brief, anthropologists divide descent groups into categories of patrilineal, matrilineal, and bilateral. In societies with patrilineal descent groups, both property and authority pass through the male line from father to son. A female in such a society generally severs ties with her own kin at the time of her marriage, entering fully into her husband's kin group. Matrilineal descent groups are more rare and somewhat more complex. Although property and authority descend through the female line, they are generally held by males, creating a situation in which a woman's brother wields authority over and transfers property to the woman's son rather than to his own son.

In both types of society, membership in a particular kin group is clearly defined by birth, and lineage is traced either through the mother's kin or the father's kin but never through both sets of kin. Thus each person belongs to a bounded kin group with an established line of authority.

In a bilateral kinship system, such bounded descent groups are absent. Since each person traces his or her lineage through both parents, solidarity of kin groups is an impossibility. And since each individual and each household belongs to more than one kin group simultaneously, lines of authority cannot be established. In nineteenth-century America, a bilateral descent system necessitated the establishment of positions of authority anew for each generation. Instead of a transfer of authority from father to son, both father and son maintained authority simultaneously over their own households. Relationships between households therefore were devoid of institutionalized authority. Descent groups as bounded entities were nonexistent; instead, each individual was part of an infinite network of kin relationships, expanding to encompass the kin networks of those who married into the group.[81]

Primogeniture was the legally prescribed method of inheritance in Great Britain until well into the nineteenth century, a system establishing a chain of authority and a passage of property from one generation to the next within a hierarchical family structure. From the colonial era, primogeniture was discouraged in America,[82] a factor which encouraged the establishment of independent nuclear families unfettered by relationships of authority.

Since studies of American families before the nineteenth century have focussed on the passage of authority and property through males, little information is available on relationships between women and their kin. We do know, however, that in the nineteenth century inheritance by daughters as well as sons was encouraged by law.[83] Thus a married couple could expect to inherit from both sets of parents. They were therefore involved simultaneously in two separate lineages, neither of which could they afford to alienate, yet neither of which could exert total control over their actions. The institutionalized chain of authority within the family was replaced by the simultaneous claims of "in-laws." The married couple was no longer under the authority of a patriarch but was faced instead with balancing the claims of different kin groups on its resources, assistance, and attention. In such a situation the role of mediator was taken by the wife. While the husband held authority within the nuclear

5. Four generations of the Cooley/Angell family. *Standing—left to right:* Mary Horton Cooley (1830–1890), Thomas McIntyre Cooley (1824–1898), James Burrell Angell (1829–1916); *seated—left to right:* David Horton, Betsey Carey Horton, Fanny Cooley Angell (1875–1934) holding Thomas Angell (1885–1896), Alexis Angell holding Sarah Angell (1883–1928), Mme. Angell, Sarah Caswell Angell (1831–1903)

family, the wife maintained ties with her kin network and often with her husband's kin as well.

These simultaneous claims on the nuclear family allowed for a great deal of flexibility in kinship relationships. While claims of familial obligations coming from all sides involved some conflicts over scarce resources and some moral dilemmas over priorities accorded to the needs of various individuals, they also allowed a large degree of leeway in selecting which obligations would be met. Nearly any course of action could be, and was, justified on the grounds that it fulfilled a familial obligation to someone. The individual could therefore balance and play off against one another the claims as well as the assistance of the nuclear family and the two families of origin.

For women, claims of obligation provided a justification for helping kin outside the nuclear family. Until 1911 in Michigan, a husband legally owned his wife's time and services. A woman's time and services were therefore not hers to give.[84] In custom though not in law, however, a woman's kin network held a right to some of her services, allowing her to claim an obligation on her time other than that made by her husband. References to obligation may have been used in some instances to justify assistance that was actually given out of a genuine desire to help. A woman lacking the autonomy to give her services freely could justify her decision to help her kin on the grounds of familial obligation. Some references to familial obligations must therefore be viewed as rhetorical, reflecting women's inability to overtly direct their actions according to their own wishes. Women found it necessary to see themselves always acting in response to the needs of others, to justify their own decisions on the grounds of obligation. While norms of familial obligation provided women with a rationale for maintaining ties outside the nuclear family, they also reflect the inability of women to assert their own needs, desires, and choices as the basis for their actions.

While the demands of these kin groups were sometimes unwelcome, they did provide material and emotional support, important especially to women who were neither economically nor legally self-sufficient. Richard M. Emerson has examined the role of networks in power allocation, finding that in a relationship between two people, a person without power can gain power by either of two methods: first, by finding other sources of obtaining whatever benefits were derived from the initial relationship, in other words, by developing other potential options to that relationship, and second, by mobilizing the collective power of a group of people to influence the more powerful person to accede to the wishes of the less powerful person.[85] For nineteenth-century women, networks of female kin fulfilled both of these functions. First, by providing alternate sources of emotional and material support, they lessened a woman's dependence on her husband. Second, by their collective reinforcement of norms, they protected a woman from violations of what was considered proper treatment within a marriage, bringing social rather than legal pressure to bear. A network of female kin thus provided a woman with a lifelong source of support which she could use to balance her dependence on her husband as well as to provide assistance for her nuclear family.

For women, the sphere of home and family included female kin as well as husband and children. This network of female kin enabled a woman to maintain some autonomy in her marriage while at the same time devoting her attention to childcare, nursing, and domestic tasks, the domain of the female family. Women balanced the long-term security, openness, and understanding they shared with female kin against the loyalty, sense of dependence, and, in most cases, affection they felt for their husbands. While sometimes held in precarious balance, the two sets of relationships were by no means necessarily contradictory or competitive. While female kin did, in some cases, urge women to divorce their husbands, as long as a wife was treated with a minimal level of consideration, her kin network supported her fulfillment of the role of wife and mother, seen as her duty to God as well as to her husband, standing ready to assist her should she be left without male protection.

TWO

A Sister's Privilege—Perhaps Her Duty: The Female Family

WOMEN commonly assisted their mothers, daughters, and sisters with the day-to-day tasks of managing a household and raising children. They provided this assistance within the context of a kinship network that included male as well as female relatives. For men as well as women, kinship ties extending well beyond the nuclear family were an important source of assistance as well as obligation. In nineteenth-century Michigan, all relatives were, in theory, potential members of a kin network. One young man wrote to another that he had discovered both shared a common relative. "Being of common ancestry—we must be kindred to each other—and being kindred to each other we should be acquainted and familiar with each other. There is no doubt in this respect." In this instance, the letter-writer wanted to marry the sister of the man to whom he wrote; yet his justification for writing was the claim of common ancestry.[1]

In practice, kin networks were limited to one's parents, siblings, nieces and nephews, while aunts, uncles, cousins, and grandparents were more tenuously included. Until their own marriages, women generally adopted the kin networks of their mother and father, that is their own aunts, uncles, grandparents, and first cousins, as well as their parents, siblings, siblings' spouses, nieces and nephews. With marriage, and more specifically with motherhood, contact with aunts, uncles, and cousins (particularly those with uncles and male cousins), often became infrequent. Single women, however, maintained relationships with aunts, uncles, and cousins throughout their lives. Interestingly, married women without children also maintained similar kinship ties.[2] Presumably these kinship ties were dropped, then, not because of marriage itself but because of the demands made by young children on a mother's time, as well as the belief that the birth of the child marked the creation of a new, independent household.

While some unmarried adult males remained out of touch with their parents and siblings for years at a time, especially when their mothers had remarried,[3] contact with kin usually was reestablished on marriage. A woman maintained lifelong contact with her kin, perhaps sometimes initiating her husband's reunion with his kin network. While men who experienced social and economic mobility may have tended to minimize their contact with relatives, for women such changes in status failed to disrupt kinship ties.[4] In achieving upward mobility through marriage, women avoided the drastic changes in roles experienced by upwardly mobile men; all women performed the same tasks as wives and mothers. Services of nursing and child care could be exchanged regardless of differences in financial and social status. In addition, while a man's occupational and financial status presumably would remain stable throughout his life, a wife who derived her higher status from her husband could experience a sharp drop in status if widowed or divorced. Thus no matter what her current financial or social status, she might need to rely on the support of her kin network in the future. Regardless of differences in social and economic status, then, female kin could offer one another both assistance and security.

Membership in a kin network began at birth and continued even after death. Members of the kin network who were no longer living were still regarded as part of the family and the services and support provided to the children of deceased kin were viewed as gifts to the deceased relative. Religious belief in the reunion of kin in an afterlife fostered the sense of kin ties extending beyond a temporal lifetime.

References to joining kin in heaven were frequent and served as a consolation for separation on earth. One woman, for instance, wrote to her aunt: "If we never meet on Earth again may we all meet in Heaven to join the loved ones that has gone on before us is the Prayer of your Neice."[5] Another woman wrote of her sorrow at being separated from her kin, consoling herself that "it is very sad & very hard to part with dear friends but we hope to meet them again where parting is no more." "Dear Sister," she wrote, "if we never meet in this life I hope to meet you in that better world."[6] Rhoda Buckland wrote to Harriet Mack, later to become Harriet Whittemore,

"I think sometimes when I git to think about the folks that I shall never see them agin but I dont alow my self to think so enny more then I can help fore I now it dont do enny good I am in hopes that you will come and see me next winter." Rhoda wrote that she wished she could see Harriet even for an evening but took comfort in the thought that they would meet in heaven.[7] "If I see you not here," one man wrote his brother, "the expectation will at least be a comforting one, that I shall see you soon hereafter."[8] Geographic separation thus was accepted as merely a temporary break in the kin network. The family itself was eternal.

It was particularly important for kin to be present at the time of death. Both men and women expressed a horror of dying alone; death was a family as well as an individual experience. When a mother of young children died unexpectedly, her mother-in-law, Mary Cooley, commented that she had died so suddenly that "not a child was called to the bedside."[9] After her father's death in a buggy accident, one woman wrote that she was glad that all his children were present, wishing that other kin could have attended also "to mingle our tears together."[10] Another woman wrote her son that she realized "what your feelings must have been to see your poor Father suffer and die without one relation to weep with you."[11]

One hardship of the frontier was the possibility of dying away from home, among "strangers." One man notified his brother of their brother's death in the West. "We have reason to feel thankful that he was with Friends that Friends (not strangers) performed the last sad offices for him which we was denide the privilege of doing," he wrote.[12] Henry Parker Smith wrote of a friend who died on the frontier "without a relative to close her eyes and very few sincere friends."[13] Elnathan Phelps wrote to his son, Edwin, who was searching for gold in California, of his desire to live nearby, "where you can close my eyes when I sleep the sleep of death,"[14] while Lucy Smith's sister wrote that "sister A has come up to day she cannot hardly be reconciled to think [Lucy] died away from her friends."[15] Since Lucy's husband was with her at the time of her death, the friends referred to presumably were Lucy's mother and sisters.

Women presided over the rituals of death, often preparing the body for burial,[16] sometimes recording in great detail the deathbed scenes of their relatives. These accounts reveal not only concern for the religious salvation of the deceased, but also the affirmation that the family would be reunited in heaven. Florence Pomeroy Raab wrote a detailed description of her mother's death, to be sent to her relatives.

5 a.m. Wednesday

Mother: Do you want to tell me that I'm going to die tonight?

Irving: No Mother, we think you'll live until tomorrow when Father is coming.

Florence: You're not afraid to die, are you dear?

Mother: No, not afraid,—not afraid at all.

Florence: You'll meet grandma, and Aunt Mary and so many there.

Mother: Yes——yes——yes.

Florence: We all love you so much, everybody loves you. Father writes every day, and Aunt Helen and Aunt Amie and so many have sent love to you.

Mother: Yes, I know, I know.

(Kisses Margaret, Irving & Florence)

Florence: Death doesn't really separate us; (Mother: No.) we'll always love you, and you'll be near us, always, won't you, dear?

Mother: Yes, I will—I will.

Irving: We're going to live in Detroit, Mother, and Margaret is going to live with us. Won't that be nice?

Mother: Lovely.—I'm glad.

Mother: Will you preach my funeral sermon, Irving?

Irving: Yes, Mother, if you want me to.

Florence: I've asked Dr. Spencer to come, would you like that?

Mother: Yes, very much.

Florence: And the funeral will be held in Adrian at Aunt Amie's house . . . .

6. Frances Pomeroy (c. 1900)

7. Hannah Bingham (1794–1868)

Wednesday 2 p.m.

Mother: So glad Henry was here, so glad you all were here. So glad,
    repeated again and again.
Margaret: Goodbye darling.
Mother: Goodbye.
Margaret: The love of your dear girls goes with you.
Mother: Yes, every where, everywhere.[17]

Here family relationships are described as continuing even after the
deaths of family members.

The Gates Ajar, popular with women in the late nineteenth
century, consists primarily of a reassurance that those who have died
are still conscious of all that happens on earth,[18] that, as Florence
Pomeroy Raab reassured her mother, "death doesn't really separate
us." Harriet Johnson Smith, whose ambition it was to become a
writer and who read extensively, wrote of her deceased sister as her
guardian angel, her advisor and confidant.[19] Heaven became, in wom-
en's fiction, the scene of cosmic family reunions, the location of the
ideal family unit. In *Uncle Tom's Cabin*, St. Clair's salvation is
assured when he glimpses his mother beckoning him to heaven as
he says the single dying word "Mother."[20] It is little wonder, then,
that heaven in its domesticated guise came to be viewed as women's
domain.[21] Death marked the reunion of kin who had been separated
on earth, the creation of a perfect world of domesticity and unbroken
family ties.

While families were reunited spiritually in heaven, they were
reunited physically in cemetery plots. Family members attempted to
create family plots in which all kin could be buried.[22] If a family
member died elsewhere, relatives went to great lengths to return the
body for burial at home. Although Kate and Eugene Cooley were
themselves living elsewhere, they sent the body of their newborn
infant to Ann Arbor for burial in the family plot. "We felt the little
one belonged in Ann Arbor," Kate wrote her mother-in-law. "I could
not lay such [a] one to rest all alone with strangers."[23] A woman
whose husband died during the long sea voyage to California lamented
particularly that he had been buried at sea.[24]

The graveyard served as a concrete symbol of family solidarity
and heritage. When Juliana Caster wrote Harriet Whittemore that
her "fondest hopes of spending my remaining days in New England
and making my grave by the side of my fathers are blasted," she
chose the cemetery as the symbol of the family ties she was reluctant

to break. She would, she continued, join her husband in Michigan, taking "my last leave of my beloved friends, my native village and the graves of my beloved parents and others near and dear."[25] She was leaving a family consisting of dead as well as living kin, joined in their physical as well as spiritual presence.

When Juliana Caster referred to her "beloved friends," she doubtless included her family in her definition of "friends." While modern usage of the term "friend" specifically excludes kin, the word was used in the nineteenth century to describe anyone with whom one was linked by ties of affection, obligation, and concern. While casual acquaintances were excluded from the category of friends, as were kin with whom a close bond was lacking, both kin and non-kin with whom an intimate relationship existed were termed "friends." Marilla Turrill wrote to her brother, "I have no friends here, not even Mother." She was at that time living across the street from her mother but was not on speaking terms with her.[26] Friendship thus implied more than merely a blood relationship. Yet the term clearly included kin. Marilla Turrill wrote to Myron Buck: "Some of our friends have been to see us among them is Uncle Dayton & Aunt Electa—Father and Mother are coming this week."[27] Another letter stated, "I was thinking today of the many friends and so many of them my relatives."[28] Ideally, then, kin were linked with close bonds of friendship, bonds which could only rarely be formed with those outside the family.

These kinship ties were based on custom, sense of obligation, and affection rather than on legal requirements. The earliest territorial law of Michigan regarding relief of paupers, passed in 1805, does not specify any obligation to support one's kin.[29] The 1825 law, however, stipulated that:

> The father and grandfather, mother and grandmother, children and grandchildren, and the brothers and sisters, being of sufficient ability, of every pauper, shall respectively, at their own charge and expense, relieve and maintain every such pauper, in such manner as any two justices of the peace on application being made on behalf of such pauper, shall order and direct.[30]

This law was amended in 1827 to eliminate the liability of brothers and sisters.[31] After 1846 only the father, mother, and children were liable for a pauper's support. Furthermore, support was required only if the pauper was "blind, old, lame, impotent, or decrepit, so as to be unable to maintain himself," and was collected only from those who were of "sufficient ability." The father of the pauper held primary responsibility, followed by the children and then by the mother.[32] Thus by the middle of the nineteenth century only parents and children were responsible for one another's financial needs, and then only when the individual was unable to provide his or her own support.

Although such aid was not legally required, kin commonly did provide one another with financial assistance in times of temporary need as well as permanent disability.[33] While this aid usually originated from males, its distribution might be directed by women. Mary Cooley, for instance, provided financial assistance for her parents and brothers. Although she arranged for the aid, the funds presumably came from her husband's earnings.[34] Mary also insisted that she and her husband provide their daughter-in-law Kate with an allowance for personal and household expenses, money Kate would be led to believe came from her husband. Mary thus provided assistance to Kate so that, she wrote, Kate would not need to ask her husband for money.[35]

Requests for financial assistance were sometimes channeled through women. When Mary Louise Miles needed money to continue her schooling, she wrote to her mother, asking her to convince Mary's father to borrow money to send to her.[36] And when May Smith's husband was jailed for arson, she wrote to her sisters for money to pay his fine and release him from prison, threatening suicide if she could not raise the money. One of her sisters informed a third sister that she had told a male friend or relative not to send the money but to give to it May after her husband was jailed, saying that "he had confidence that I would tell him whether to send it or not."[37] Women thus sometimes provided access to financial resources controlled by males.

Sometimes women directly provided one another with minor financial help. Abby Field once thanked her married sister for a small loan.[38] Hannah Bingham, a missionary's wife, wrote her daughter Maria that she and Maria's sister Lina were sending her two dollars, fifty cents of which she had earned by knitting. "We sent it to do you good," she wrote, "fearing you might be needing something very much and might be cramped in your feelings—hope this little mite will be laid out to the best advantage as it was our own laborious earnings."[39] When Philamena Loomis Brown was left a penniless widow, one sister solicited financial help from her other sisters, reminding Ann Gennette Loomis Preston of the assistance she had received from her sisters when she was widowed.[40] Thus with the limited resources under their own control and with the influence they sometimes wielded over the expenditures of their husbands' funds, many women were able to provide one another with financial assistance. Women also exchanged help with childcare and household tasks, sewed for one another, bought clothing and household goods for one another, and sent each other sewing patterns.[41]

In addition to such assistance, relatives frequently offered advice. Women, as might be expected, gave advice to their children. They also advised brothers and sisters on financial and career decisions as well as domestic matters. Marilla Buck, for instance, responded to her brother Myron's request for her opinion by advising him against becoming a doctor.[42] Mary Cooley provided her brothers with financial advice as well as assistance. Her husband, Thomas Cooley, a prominent attorney, urged her to provide financial and personal advice to their sons as well as her own brothers, saying that he would "leave all matters of advice on business or family matters where they belong. You know I have always thought you should be advisor and not I."[43]

Young men living away from home provided particular cause for anxiety. Betsey Phelps wrote her sister-in-law, Harriet Whittemore, to inform her of her son's "wild Conduct," adding that she hoped she was not a busybody.[44] Martha Hall advised her daughter, Mary Littlefield, that Mary's grown son should not live alone lest he be driven to matrimony or "that horrible station" for companionship.[45] Aunts, brothers, and sisters as well as parents provided advice and moral guidance. Ann Gennette Loomis Preston worried about her son who was living alone in Chicago "where noone cares for you or to advise you for your own good." She hoped he might avoid the "many temptations in a city for young men without home or friends" to offer moral guidance.[46]

Indeed, giving such advice was an obligation. Elizabeth Chandler, abolitionist and poet, attempted to convince her brother not to run a tavern. She wrote:

> Do not my dear brother accuse me of an unwarrantable interference in thy concerns. I do not wish to assume the grave aspect of a counselor . . . the idea of thy being engaged in it is very painful to me Thee must not feel offended with me brother, for having spoken so plainly, it is a sister's privilege—perhaps her duty; and

8. Elizabeth Margaret Chandler (1807–1834)

> I love my brother dearly to regard anything that concerns him with
> feelings of indifference.[47]

Stephen Mack informed his sister, Harriet Whittemore, that he had
tried to persuade their mother not to accompany another daughter
on a Mormon migration to the West, writing:

> I have endeavored to point out to her the difficulties and suffering
> attendant on such a journey and the improbability of her even living
> to get through it—I have also endeavored to show her the necessity
> of adopting the judgment of her children in a matter of such
> importance to her future welfare and to their peace of mind—
> Whatever the result may be I feel that I have discharged my duty
> in the matter with such ability as I possess.[48]

The apologetic tone of these comments suggests that such advice
was sometimes unwelcome.

A consensus opinion may have been more influential. Mary Louise Miles wrote to her mother asking whether she should go to live with her brother or return to the parental home. "I desire to do that which my friends think best that I should," she wrote.[49] Jane Howell wrote from Philadelphia to advise her adult niece in Michigan, Elizabeth Chandler, that "thy friends all approve of thy keeping a school provided thee can have one at home."[50] The newly married Hannah Bingham wrote that she would stay with her ailing mother if her friends thought she should.[51] Since the kin networks referred to as "friends" included by definition those who were concerned about the welfare of their relatives, both men and women felt a strong obligation to follow such advice. Acting individually or collectively, members of a kin network could thus enforce norms and influence behavior.

Males as well as females offered and sought advice on potential marriage partners, whom they viewed as future members of a kin network as well as future husbands and wives.[52] Martha Hall hoped that her nephew would delay marriage, since the local girls were unsuitable as wives, while Henry Parker Smith's sister cried on learning of his engagement to Harriet Johnson, saying that he would never find another woman who loved him as she did.[53] Yet most women welcomed the addition of congenial women to the family. Female relatives sometimes suggested to males that they look for wives. Often they tried to introduce eligible women, thus influencing the selection of the women who would be included in the network of female kin.

Harriet Whittemore told her son James of eligible women that he might consider as potential wives.[54] Jane Howell advised her nephew to marry after the death of the unmarried adult sister with whom he lived. "Marriage," she wrote, "when properly entered into, contributes greatly to earthly happiness."[55] As Judson Bingham approached thirty, much of his correspondence with his sisters involved his search for a wife. He wrote one sister that his mother thought a girl in Detroit "was about the right one." Judson was less enthusiastic about the prospect, writing that "I care not much except for mother's sake whether I am married or not."[56] His sister wanted to introduce him to a friend of hers, an offer he declined. Josiah Littlefield's cousin wrote him that she knew a girl who needed a husband, a girl who was "not pretty" but practical, who played the piano and raised plants.[57] The two were married after a courtship consisting largely of correspondence. When women suggested to their male relatives friends who they thought would make good wives, the potential brides participated at least indirectly in the selection process and may in some cases have instigated the suggestion.

Women wanted their sons and brothers to marry women who would be desirable members of their kin networks. Mary Cooley wrote of a young woman she hoped any one of her sons would marry, although she feared the girl was already engaged.[58] And when her son Ed announced his engagement, Mary wrote to another son that the girl was "very quiet and unassuming, a good housekeeper, and altogether a very desirable person to have in the family."[59] When her son Eugene decided to marry, he wrote his mother that he did not "wish to bring into the family anyone who would not be perfectly acceptable to all members of it."[60] Thus a man ideally married a woman who would be a congenial member of the kin network as well as a good wife.

With marriage, a woman accepted a wide range of familial roles, including those of daughter-in-law and sister-in-law. Before her marriage to Henry Parker Smith, Harriet Johnson, the young woman who expressed such anxiety over giving up her ambitions as a writer, noted in her diary her concern about her ability to fulfill such obligations.

> In loving him I would wish to love *his*—I would wish to be a child of those parents—a sister to that lovely girl, who says fondly, that she hopes Henry will never *marry* . . . . And can I be *all* this—can I fill all these spheres—can I perform the duties of a wife even . . . . I would spend my life in gloomy solitude . . . rather than to bring the grey hairs of those fond parents down in sorrow to the grave.[61]

In nineteenth-century Michigan, as elsewhere in America, married women, in spite of differences in social class, economic circumstances, and education, performed essentially identical duties. Either alone or assisted by hired help, usually unskilled young girls, they were responsible for the daily tasks of cooking, cleaning, and childcare, as well as the occasional duty of nursing the sick. The similarity of the daily work of all married women, and the definition of these tasks as "women's work," led to the belief that only other women could share and sympathize with a woman's experience.

Indeed, it was considered the duty of a sister, mother, daughter, or friend to provide comfort and sympathy as well as practical

9.   Cooley brothers (c. 1890). *Left to right*: Edgar Cooley (1852–1914), Thomas Cooley (1871–1903), Eugene Cooley (1849–1938), Charles Horton Cooley (1864–1929)

10.   Four generations of Horton/Cooley/Angell women. *Back row— left to right*: Mary Horton Cooley (1830–1890), Sarah Caswell Angell (1831–1903); *front row—left to right*: Fanny Cooley Angell (1857–1934), Sarah Angell (1883–1928), Betsey Carey Horton

assistance. Fanny Cooley Angell, a mother and the wife of a young lawyer, wrote to her own mother after the visit of her sister-in-law in 1890:

> I am quite desolate without her. I had never realized before what a comfort 'twould be to have another woman in the house, to talk matters over with and to feel that there was someone upon whom one could call in case of emergency. It makes me quite impatient to have Sarah grow up, tho' bless her heart! She is a great deal of comfort and company already.[62]

In 1869, a 21-year-old woman asked a young female friend of her brother-in-law, a woman she had never met, to come to California to live with her. "I am very lonely sometimes," she wrote. "I have no mother nor sisters nor brothers only my father and husband and two little boys."[63] Apparently she felt only another woman could provide true companionship.[64]

The nature of emotional support, companionship, and practical assistance provided by female kin varied according to geographic proximity. The degree of proximity of most family networks changed through time as family members moved away either temporarily or permanently. Many people expressed a feeling of "home base," a location in which most family members were located, or where a few kin remained within a community known to many members of the network. While this home base was likely to be the community in which at least one generation of the family was raised, in some families it was the area in which several of their households had settled as a group. Young adults were not always the ones to leave; sometimes adult children remained behind in the home community while their parents moved west.[65] The composition of households also varied as children, adolescents, and unmarried adults lived for months or years with brothers, sisters, or aunts.

Those living apart from their kin sometimes formed close bonds with neighbors who fulfilled some of the functions of kin, providing companionship, advice, help with daily tasks, and emergency assistance.[66] Some women felt, however, that friends could never take the place of family members. One woman wrote that she had come to live in Florida nearly four years before and was "still bound by ties no dearer than at that time." "One can scarcely be expected to feel the same kindred for adopted people that one does for their very own," she wrote.[67] Kin, even when unable to provide companionship

and assistance on a daily basis, could be counted on for short-term
or long-term aid in case of emergency.[68] Thus geographic distance
did not eliminate the major function of a kin network—providing
financial and emotional stability.

Among kin, absence may indeed have made the heart grow fonder,
or at least have eased the tensions inherent in a daily relationship.
One's best side could be presented in letters to kin. Relationships
consisted of such communications surrounded by the fantasies built
around absent kin. And since distant kin were unable to engage in
unwanted participation in one's daily affairs, people may have been
more willing to confide in kin who were geographically distant than
in those who lived nearby. Distance itself thus served to protect
privacy and independence, perhaps allowing for a greater expression
of emotions and a deeper verbal intimacy than would be achieved
among kin living in proximity. Geographic separation thus decreased
the amount of daily reliance on kin for assistance and companionship
but may in some cases have increased the degree of verbal intimacy
and allowed for a greater idealization of kinship ties.

When kin were living in close proximity, they talked with one
another and communicated with gestures and eye contact as well as
non-verbal expressions of affection such as unsolicited help or gifts.
Kin living nearby related to one another within the context of a
community. Kinship interaction thus involved what a person told a
friend about a relative as well as direct conversation between the
two relatives themselves. When Abby Field contemplated moving to
Big Rapids to teach school, she wrote that she could live with her
cousins and "go in society just as much as I liked, being a cousin
of theirs."[69] For a newcomer, membership in a kin group provided
both a sense of identity and a means of establishing social contacts
in a new community.

The social ritual of formal calling served to separate the informal
and intimate nature of kin ties from the more formal and superficial
contacts outside the kin network. Close female kin frequently made
calls as a group, two cousins or a mother and daughter discharging
their social obligations together. Harriet Johnson wrote, after an
afternoon of calling on nine households with her aunt:

And now our calls are over and I can act myself—this smiling and
talking smooth things is *so* fatiguing to rough nature . . . one must
sit just so, and go through the same ceremony at every house,

speaking of the weather, and your great anxiety to call before, hoping
they will remember you &c &c . . . .[70]

Kin living in the same community thus maintained relationships
with other members of the community as members of the kinship
unit.

Kin separated by geographic distance kept in contact through
letters and visits, as well as through information received from mutual
friends and relatives. Even between families in Michigan and their
relatives in New England, visits were exchanged every few years.
These visits lasted several weeks or even months.[71] Unmarried brothers and sisters frequently made extended visits to their married
siblings, often for as long as a year. And married women made visits
of several months' duration to their relatives, usually taking their
children with them. In addition to renewing ties among close kin,
these visits served to preserve ties with more distant kin and with
friends. Visits helped those who had moved away from the family
home to continue to feel that they were members of the home
community. Visits made to those who had moved away helped people
to visualize their relatives' new environment and learn to know their
new friends.

Aside from periodic visits, letters were the primary source of
contact among kin. While written communication is inherently different from face-to-face interaction, letters were an alternative method
of keeping kinship ties active, allowing kin to learn of one another's
health and activities, to reassure one another of their continued
affection, and to offer and ask for advice. Letters also linked close
relatives with a broader network of kin and friends. Elizabeth Chandler wrote from Michigan to her aunt, Jane Howell, in Philadelphia
that it was a

> great satisfaction that our dear Aunts continue so well; and it is
> pleasant to hear of their visiting thee frequently, it seems to approach
> the nearest to participation in their society, and then we at least
> have the satisfaction of thinking that you frequently talk of us.[72]

Women who had left the family home thus could feel a part of the
lives of those they had left behind.

Those who remained could hear about the new friends of their
relatives, friends who were sometimes accepted as substitutes for
absent kin. Jane Howell wrote from Philadelphia to her sister Ruth

Evans on Michigan's frontier: "Remember me to Aunt Sally and Ann Comstock, I feel that I love them altho I have never seen them, for such disinterested kindness to you, strangers in a distant land, has knit them close in my affections." She wrote later: "Give my love to Aunt Sally and Ann Comstock. I expected before this to have been personally acquainted with them. Thy friends feel to be my friends and I love those who have treated thee kindly."[73] Letters thus preserved kin ties and enabled them to adapt to new circumstances.

In daily visiting, in visits to distant kin, and in letter-writing, women served as conduits of information, advice, and assistance. Through their partial control of the channels of communication, they could to some extent determine the nature and level of assistance given to kin. The provision of advice and assistance to kin was indeed viewed as an important aspect of the "woman's sphere." Since women were the primary correspondents, the burden of requesting aid for the nuclear family usually fell to them. The responsibility of a woman for managing the resources of her household thus included negotiating with kin in other nuclear families to spread familial resources to best advantage, mobilizing the network to come to the aid of those in need. The allocation of resources, of money and goods as well as services, was one of a woman's domestic duties, requiring her to maintain close contacts with kin outside the nuclear family. Women, through their connections with their kin, held potential access to resources beyond those of the nuclear family. Their verbal skill and ability to manipulate norms of kinship obligation to support their cases could result in assistance to themselves, their children, and their husbands.

THREE

A Letter Traced By a Friendly Hand: The Context of Correspondence

NINETEENTH-CENTURY Americans viewed letter-writing as a suitable task for a woman, indeed as a characteristically feminine occupation. But correspondence was more than a genteel and innocuous pastime; women used letters to preserve the cohesion of the extended family, providing a source of tangible and emotional support for family members. The letters examined here were written by barely literate servants and seamstresses, by wives of farmers and tradesmen, as well as by affluent, college-educated women. Many of these letters were the result of great effort by women who wrote only with difficulty and who sometimes could not afford the cost of postage. A few correspondents dictated their letters because they could not write, and several women used phonetic spelling. Even among educated women, letter-writing involved a considerable outlay of time taken from housework, childcare, and employment.

For family members separated by westward migration in nineteenth-century America, letters were the only direct means of communication. During the period in which literacy was widespread and the postal system reasonably efficient, but before the common use of the telephone, letters flourished among the middle class as a means of intimate as well as formal communication. The language used in these letters, it should be remembered, is not a direct transcription of daily speech, but follows the formal grammatical structure and vocabulary of written discourse, producing a style to a great extent unique to personal correspondence. Recognizing written text as a poor substitute for speech, women nonetheless attempted in letters to their kin and friends to create a style of writing amenable to intimate communication.

Nineteenth-century periodicals devoted much attention to proper and improper modes of correspondence, frequently noting differences between male and female styles of writing. In practice, however, men sometimes used a style considered feminine, women a style regarded as masculine. To understand these gender distinctions, it is necessary to examine such discourse within its social context, distinguishing modes of writing and looking at the various factors involved in the act of communication. Who, for example, received letters, and who wrote them? What was the role of the communication in the context of a personal relationship, as well as its immediate purpose? Examining correspondence within families, we can view language in the context of continuing and intertwining relationships, discussing the uses of language in personal communication.

Language style varied, then, not only according to gender but also according to the context in which language was used. In his study of sex roles among westward migrants on the Overland Trail, John Faragher suggests that men and women used different writing styles in their diaries and that these different styles reveal divergent perspectives created by gender distinctions in nineteenth-century American society.[1] These distinctions appear, however, to be in large part the result of the immediate context of the migration experience rather than the broader context of gender distinctions in American society as a whole. The writing styles used by men and women in their correspondence varied according to the relationship for which letters were written, the age of the writer, and other factors. Courtship letters, for instance, obviously differ from business letters in style as well as content.

The nature of family relationships in nineteenth-century America affected the writing styles employed by men and women. Women used their control of the channels of communication, their traditional role as correspondents, to persuade kin to provide aid and also to maintain relationships on which they might later need to rely. They also attempted to replace the conversation and rituals of the female family with written descriptions of their daily lives and with verbal expressions of affection. In letters to absent husbands, women reflected their relative lack of power in the use of persuasive but submissive language. While single men for similar reasons used descriptive and persuasive language styles, married men, for the most

part, relied on a direct, matter-of-fact, unemotional tone in correspondence with family members.

Letters exchanged among family members reveal the use of language to create and manipulate networks of kin. Letters differ from
diaries in this respect. A diary may be intended only for the writer,
shared with select friends, written for the author's descendents, or
designed for publication. While these different uses of the diary call
forth different styles of language, all diary forms differ from letters
in representing an expression of the author's thoughts designed for
an indeterminate audience, a style ostensibly if not actually written
for the author alone. Like speech, however, letters are directed to a
particular audience, often a single other individual, the writer choosing
from a range of possible styles one appropriate to the relationship
of writer and reader.

While there was a woman's style appropriate to the female-
dominated world of family and female friendship and a man's style
appropriate to the world of business, the use of these styles was not
limited by sex. Males, too, used a "female" style in courtship letters,
in letters to children and female kin, and sometimes in sermons and
diaries, while women used a "male" style for business letters and
sometimes for diaries. In 1904, for example, *Harper's Bazar* advised
women of the different styles required for various types of correspondence, categorizing business letters, formal social letters, personal
letters, and courtship letters. Business letters were to be clear, condensed, and brief, without ambiguity, personal letters ideally to rely
on suggestion rather than explanation of emotion.[2]

Correspondence to Abby Field, for instance, included letters regarding her work for the Woman's Christian Mission Association.
Although most of these letters were written by women, they reveal
a formal, businesslike style:

My Dear Abby:

Your card came to hand this morning and Mrs. Ford suggested
that we might be able to obtain rates for you from Grand Rapids
here by way of the Grand Rapids and Indiana road that comes
through Richmond, Ind. For that reason I went this afternoon to
the office of the Pennsylvania Lines. Mr. Freeman whom I desired
to see is in Chicago and will not return to the city until the middle
of next week. I left word for him to call here as soon as he returns.
I thought more could be done in this way than by any certificate
from here when you were desiring to make so long a journey away

from Michigan . . . . I shall, however, try to have Mr. Freeman obtain by way of the Pennsylvania Company that courtesy which I have before described. If you get good results from both I shall be glad. It is not likely that I can send you word from Mr. Freeman until Thursday at the earliest and possibly much later next week.

Your much appreciated letter from Milwaukee was heard in Board meeting in that part which related to our work at the Head of the Lakes. Bro. Lane had previously written us that he must know early in September what we would do about making an appropriation to that work another year and we replied that we could not make our appropriations for the new year until after we were able to see the outcome of the closing year and our probable resources for the future. We are therefore paying him up to the first of October and letting him go . . . .

Lovingly your Sister in Christ's service,
Lois A. White[3]

By contrast, bachelor Newton Buck wrote a detailed and personal letter to his brother and sister-in-law:

Myron and Susan

A hearty "thank you" for your compound letter of June 1st.— compound because made up of three parts. Thank you Susie for not allowing any paper to run to waste: I always like to see the whole sheet filled out especially when it can be done to so good advantage and with so much pleasure to my self. Dealia's health is tolerable good. She is just emerging into womanhood being 20 this summer and what is due to her age shows some womanly traits. Proves a great help to her mother in doing housework, a business in which she shows no little activity. As is the case with Albert she still remains single and for ought I know without a beaux. The next on the programme is cousin Vincent—5 ft 9 in. high and as slim as a boy perhaps as you ever saw. His recent growth has been somewhat like that of a potato sprout in a damp cellar, though unlike it I think will come out into the sun of manhood without withering. May be said to be the man of the house as he is farmer by himself. Has about 2 acres planted this year a sufficient amount perhaps for a boy of 18 yrs.

* * * * *

Thus ends the list of this family circle—a circle which has been rendered incomplete by death. Two links are gone—perhaps the strongest in the chain. It is yet rather a happy family & one in which you may pleasantly spend a week. Have visited the grave of Sarah Ann. She fell asleep just in the bloom of life to bloom forever above. Give my best regards to——there is no kind of use to commence mentioning names for pray tell me when and where would this letter close if I should? Just insert everybody as the word is sufficiently comprehensive if New Boston has not grown beyond all account for the past two years. Good morning brother and sister. Hope to be on intimate terms of epistolary correspondence with you till steam, that great annihilator of time and space, enables us to correspond verbally.

> Yours fraternally,
> Newton[4]

Edwin Phelps sent an intimate letter to his young children shortly after the death of his wife:

Tell Grand Ma that I think of her and in fact of you all many times evry day and evry night. . . . Now Dear little little Family *all* goodbye and know that you are more to me than all the world beside. Give my love to G Ma Aunt Helen Uncle H Emily and all the rest. . . . God bless you my little motherless ones is the prayer of your Father.[5]

As these letters suggest, writing style was determined as much by the content of the correspondence and the relationship between writer and recipient as by the gender of the writer.

Rather than two distinct categories, male and female writing styles represent a continuum from which a writer could select a style appropriate to a specific situation, one reflecting the sex of the writer and the recipient as well as the nature of the relationship between the correspondents. At the feminine end of this continuum were letters exchanged between female kin, letters between female friends, and courtship letters, as well as letters written between unmarried males and their female kin and letters written by fathers to their young children. Letters between husbands and wives, between unmarried males, and between married males and their female kin contained elements of both a male and a female style. At the masculine end of the continuum were letters written by married men to male friends and relatives and business letters, especially those written by men.

Letters exchanged between men and women differed from those written for an audience of the same sex. In a nineteenth-century article on letter-writing, Edith Schel claimed that women's letters to men were more condensed, less personal, and less revealing than those written to other women, while "men write best to women, for women alone have power to draw out their tenderer side—to make them most themselves."[6] According to this writer, both men and women moderated their writing style when corresponding with the opposite sex, changing to a more neutral style combining both male and female elements. A young Michigan woman, for example, wrote her male cousin: "I am not much accustomed to writing to gentlemen and don't know what will interest them." "I can write most anything to the girls the first thing I can think of," she commented, indicating her belief that a different style and content was appropriate when writing to a man.[7]

The fact that two persons were related to one another was considered justification for correspondence. Many letter writers commented that kin ought to correspond with one another or ought to do so with greater frequency. One letter addressed to "cousin Mary" stated, "I agree with you that correspondence should be kept up with or between all known relatives of the Ela family. It is a shame that no one knows the residence of every one of them."[8] Letters written to people whom the writer had never met were sometimes prefaced by the comment that the author felt free to write because he or she was a relative.[9]

Outside the family, the choice of correspondents was, except where related to business concerns, apparently dependent on the personal intimacy of the parties involved. Single women, and to some extent single men, corresponded frequently with members of the same sex. Some single women mentioned with dismay the expectation that upon marriage correspondence with female friends would diminish. One young man wrote to his sister: "Miss Levantia says that she has given up ever hearing from you directly again, since you are married." "I very seriously doubt whether friendships (real) are broken by mere marriage," he added.[10]

Correspondence between unrelated males and females was acceptable only under certain circumstances. Custom required a single man to request a woman's permission to correspond with her, correspondence that was to constitute a formal and exclusive courtship relationship. In the collections of letters examined here, correspondence almost always led to marriage, although this may perhaps reflect only a tendency to dispose of letters from former suitors. Correspondence between a single man and a single woman was, in any case, considered a serious courtship, while correspondence between married persons of the opposite sex was considered improper.[11]

Women commonly shared among themselves the courtship letters they received. After reading the courtship letters written to a female friend by the man her friend had since married, Harriet Johnson wrote in her diary: "She has read to me some of the love laden epistles sent in courtship's sunny day and again those later, but dearer missives from an absent husband. Shall I ever receive such? F— says they will be more precious than any that can spring from a lover's pen." Another young woman wrote to her newly married friend: "I wish I could see one of your love letters, I don't believe you ever wrote any for I know I should have seen them." Angelina Bingham told her sister Maria that she had found two courtship letters from Maria's husband. Since Maria had always shown her his letters, she had read them and found them "very good indeed."[12]

Within the family, most correspondence was carried on by women, who often conveyed messages from their husbands. Fanny Cooley, who usually corresponded with her sister-in-law, Kate, informed her brother on one occasion, "You will perhaps be somewhat surprised to find this letter addressed to you."[13] A long letter written by a woman to her mother, mother-in-law, or sister would often contain a few brief sentences from her husband to the husband of the recipient of the letter. While unmarried men wrote to their mothers and fathers jointly, and wrote to sisters as well as brothers, married men usually relied on their wives to communicate with their mothers and sisters, and thus indirectly with male kin as well. If a married man wrote a letter, it was usually directed to male kin concerning business or political matters considered outside the domain of women, or to inform relatives of his wife's illness.

After writing her sister a letter describing her loneliness, saying that she felt "sometimes like one nearly forsaken, by my never forgotten friends," Electa Phelps added that she would leave "the other side for Dar to write the election particulars to Ed."[14] Charles Horton Cooley, writing to his parents as a young unmarried man, described details of farming operations and economics in the southern states in which he was traveling. "I know Father likes to have me make my letters the vehicle of useful information," he wrote.[15] Males tended to use letters to convey factual information, often information about the society at large or about business matters, while women usually focussed on the family, the immediate community, and their own emotions. "To be sure one can write the news," Lucy Smith wrote, "but the real feelings of the heart I want separately."[16] For women, letters not only communicated news, they also expressed and preserved emotional bonds.

The letters of Lucy Smith and her husband, Morton, provide an interesting contrast in both style and content. Lucy's mother and Morton's father had married one another after being widowed. Therefore when Lucy and Morton wrote a letter to their parents, Lucy addressed her own mother, Morton his own father. Morton's portion of the letter deals primarily with matters of business. The style is terse and direct.

> Dear Father
>
> We Rec[d] your letter the fifth day after it was mailed was happy once more to hear from home I finished my Harvesting about two weeks ago I have some as pretty wheat as you ever saw I have made a contract to have it thrashed and Ready for Market the 15th of this month I thought if you Would advance me a hundred dollars I would send you forty barrels of flour of the best quality and the remainder of what it is worth apply on wheat I owe you & Townsend wheat is on the rise in this place they are offering 58¢ but little bought You Wished to Know how much corn & potatoes I have on my farm I have about six acres looks as well as any but the extreme dry weather has dried it up some and unless we have rain soon our summer crops I am afraid will come out minus Our Business this summer is very good our sales amount to about one thousand dollars a Month you need not feel uneasy about me I am on pretty safe footing I can leave the concern any time I Choose and draw wages or one fourth part of the profits We Shall be able to meet our demands this fall in New York the net profits of this store have been from two to four thousand dollars a year I shall remain until spring . . .
>
> > in haste OM Smith
> > Love to All

Lucy, in contrast, devotes much attention to her own emotions and describes herself in the act of writing the letter. Although she discusses the health of family members, Lucy's main concern, even writing under pressure of time, is to establish a sense of intimacy rather than to convey practical information.

My dear Mother

Morton has given me an opportunity to say a few words if I will do it in great haste, and this is the way above all others that I do not like to write (in a hurry) but, however I can say a few words now and more at another time. your kind letter reached us sooner than ever one has before. that is one advantage in living here it seems to bring you nearer to us. O if I could only see you as well as hear from you. your letter lies before me it looks so natural, those letters *your hand has traced*, it brings home and friends near though I do not always wait for a letter to be reminded of dear ones. How sorry I am to hear of Jane's poor health hope she will do every thing that can be done to restore it. What a blessing is health I often think of it but do not value it as I should. It is generally healthy here no prevailing disease, but dysentery and bowel complaints are quite common. The measles have raged here ever since we have been until now, little sis has been exposed a number of times but did not take them they seem to have left the village now and are visiting the country all that have them recover no deaths. I presume you have seen accounts of Eyresypelos in Michigan there has been a great many cases in adjoining towns none here it goes by the name of black tongue, generally commences in the throat. I have thought it could not be the same as at the East.

How gladly dear Mother would I accept your advise with regard to our keeping boarders and live in a more quiet and retired way. it was never my wish and I am heartily sick of it I tell you frankly for who can I if not to a Mother . . . Mother dont you think

11. Lucy Ann Wyman Smith (d. 1847)   12. Eli Regal (1810-1872)

Morton has sold that Vermont buggy I could hardly give it up. then last week sold his last horse so that I feel quite shut up here he thought they were no profit to keep them here. he knew best about it I know. Well Mother the stage has come and I expect M. will be in every moment for this letter do write very soon and accept the love of your ever affectionate daughter Lucy Ann
Love to Father Jane and all
next time I will write more[17]

A reluctance on the part of males to write letters was accepted, perhaps even expected. Jane Howell, whose sister, niece, and nephew lived together in Michigan, wrote that she understood why her nephew couldn't write, since "his time is more profitably employed" in other activities. She later suggested that Thomas, her nephew, should excuse his brother for failing to write. Jane wrote her sister that a male friend had intended to write the family but "he says it is a task he seldom undertakes unless he has urgent business."[18] After adding a short paragraph to a letter composed by his wife Lucy, Morton Smith noted that writing was "quite a task" for him.[19] One woman wrote that her uncle "thinks it a dreadful task to write even a postal."[20]

Women, in contrast, valued correspondence as a substitute for personal contact. "Next to a personal intercourse with friends," a friend wrote Mollie Phelps, "there is nothing that I prize more than a letter traced by a friendly hand, dictated by a friendly mind." Elizabeth Chandler wrote of her aunt's desire to see her new home: "That will be better than all this letter writing—good as it is in the want of a better mode of conversation."[21] For women, letters were indeed a form of intimate conversation. "As soon as you receive this sit down and write a real long letter just exactly as you would talk," Lucy Smith wrote her mother.[22]

Many articles appearing in British and American periodicals, especially during the last decade of the nineteenth century, commented on the superiority of women as correspondents. Letter-writing, according to one author, was "an art especially invented to suit the talents of women." Another author wrote that "ladies also write to old friends of their own sex: men never write to each other if they can help it." An article published in 1869 proposed that "letters, when they are real, are usually pervaded by this play of feeling and affection, hence it has been said, that a man can rarely write a good letter; it is eminently woman's forte and function."[23]

Several nineteenth-century writers claimed that women's letters were more spontaneous and less constrained than letters written by men. These writers believed that women expressed greater warmth and affection, were more witty and playful, while letters written by men were, in the words of one writer, "dull, trite, trifling epistles." According to the commentators, men's greater reserve and propensity to write in a methodical and reasoned manner led them to produce ponderous, weighty missives, while women's reliance on intuition produced letters which were light and ingenuous, "the off-hand effusions of warm affection, undoubting confidence, sweetness, gaiety, fancy, wit, pleasantry, playfulness." According to these critics, women included greater detail in their letters, describing "personal occurrences, not objectively, as parts of history, but with reference to themselves and their own affections."[24]

These writers claimed that women's superior style arose from what they viewed as innate characteristics of the feminine personality such as warmth, openness, lack of logical ability, and lack of objectivity. Yet some of these writers also suggested that women's style may have been due to social conditions, one author proposing that women turned to letter-writing as an artistic expression because correspondence was adaptable to the many interruptions they experienced in the course of their domestic duties. This factor, rather than a lack of logical capability, the author suggested, accounted for the lack of cohesiveness in women's letters. Another writer proposed that because of the boredom and isolation of their daily lives, women could divert a greater proportion of their intellectual and social energies into letters. As the author quotes James Russell Lowell, "their ordinary employments do not suck them dry of all communicativeness—I can't think of any other word—and their writing is their play, as it should be." One writer attributed women's skill at correspondence to "a 'feminine' desire to please" one person or a small group of friends and family, the woman's letter thus directing "all its artillery at the capture of an individual" while men were prone to seek for their writing more public praise.[25]

While these commentators obviously reflected stereotypical views of masculine and feminine characteristics, they confirm the existence of widely held concepts of male and female writing styles as well as a belief in the primacy of women as letter-writers. According to these writers, the letter became a typically feminine form of expression only in the nineteenth century; previously both men and women of the upper classes had engaged in correspondence. Many nineteenth-century British articles reprinted in contemporary American journals bemoaned the demise of the genteel tradition of letter-writing, publishing examples of the lost art. While this hallmark of education and aristocratic heritage, the witty personal letter was, according to these authors, seldom exchanged among European and American men by the nineteenth century, it remained extant among American women with even an elementary education and, according to the nineteenth-century commentators, among British women as well.[26]

In nineteenth-century America, publicly supported local schools provided, even in rural areas, a basic education to young women as well as young men, and many women continued their education at female seminaries.[27] Even those women with only an elementary country school education were often fluent and even eloquent in their writing; many who lacked the requisite skills in spelling and punctuation improvised a genteel style of writing. Women adopted the writing style of the upper classes of earlier generations much as they attempted to follow what they believed to be genteel styles of dress and entertainment. The adult male culture deemed such styles effeminate, appropriate only in certain relationships with women and children. Thus the genteel letter, once the mark of a gentleman, became tagged as feminine, a part of the cult of domesticity.

This emotional, witty, yet formal style served a dual function for women. In their correspondence with other females, women used language to cement ties, to create a sense of solidarity; in correspondence with men, they used a similar language style to persuade and influence while at the same time concealing the fact that any attempt to influence was occurring. Lord Byron, a more astute observer than many of the nineteenth-century commentators on women's writing, noted the instrumental use of a feminine style:

> The earth has nothing like a She-epistle,
> And hardly heaven—because it never ends.
> I love the mystery of a female missile,
> Which, like a creed, ne'er says all it intends,
> But full of cunning as Ulysses' whistle,
> When he allured poor Dolon:—you had better
> Take care what you reply to such a letter.[28]

The politeness, euphemism, and indirection frequently noted in the language of women today and evident in the correspondence of women in the nineteenth century represents an attempt by women to use language to convey their opinions and desires without seeming to do so. As well as a tool for cementing ties with female kin and identifying oneself as a genteel lady, feminine language style represents a strategy for gaining at least a persuasive influence in situations in which women held little real power.[29]

In their letters women adopted a tone of politeness and formality, with frequent use of circumlocution and euphemism. Metaphors were used frequently, both as physical description and, in more extended form, as anecdotes with messages for the reader. The physical environment was recreated in detail, with both the writer and the reader frequently placed in specific settings. Women often wrote that they wanted their readers to visualize their activities, to share their lives vicariously. Some even sent objects such as leaves and stones as well as baked goods and samples of cloth and wallpaper. Events were recorded in detail, the letters frequently discussing activities of other people in the community, expressing opinions as to their judgment and moral standards.

Male correspondence was more terse, expressing desires and opinions directly rather than through anecdotes or suggestion. Detailed physical descriptions were seldom presented, males infrequently placing themselves in a setting or commenting on that of their readers. Men seldom wrote of the activities of those in the community and were less likely than females to discuss their emotions or their opinions of other people. They did, however, often discuss political or economic issues.

These distinctions between feminine and masculine style and content were not universal; unmarried men, again, writing to their female kin and their fiancées, and men writing to their young children often closely approached a feminine style of expression. Differences in writing style thus arose not only from gender distinctions but also from the dynamics of interaction within the family. Within a marriage, males learned to express their opinions and desires directly in the expectation that their intentions would be carried out; women learned to express opinions only indirectly, often as universal principles rather than as their own desires and ideas. Hence there was in women's letters a prolific use of euphemism, metaphor, and circumlocution as well as frequent reference to moral standards and moral obligation.

Women learned to couch their attempts to influence others, especially men, in the language of politeness. They had the power only to persuade and then only by indirection, using language to obscure as well as express their intentions. The letters written by Sarah Regal to her husband Eli, a traveling evangelist, reveal persistent attempts to influence his decisions while appearing to defer to his judgment. This strategy represented a sense of ambiguity rather than sheer manipulation since she held, as she wrote to her sister, "a desire to be willing to yield to his better judgment."[30] Sarah had, in fact, some degree of financial autonomy, although she seems to have had little authority in making family decisions. She apparently had inherited some land which yielded income and also, in Eli's absence, conducted farming operations and borrowed money on the strength of her own credit.

Eli often lived away from his family for months at a time while conducting religious revivals. Sarah followed one of her repeated suggestions that Eli either return home or allow his family to join him with the comment, "I name it now merely as a suggestion without any desire to use authority if I had any or have you think I thought it infallible for I do not but on the contrary I can see difficulties in the way." Yet she informed her husband in the same letter that she would pay his fare home only if he would agree to stay permanently.

On another occasion Sarah approached the same subject:

> You ask me what I think we had better do I cannot tell you for I know you would not agree with me and I do not know what to propose that I think would meet your approbation. I confess my heart sinks when I think of going through what I have years back of living alone in cold winter carrying in wood and water and having everything to see to but if you think best to remain there without your family I am willing to try and do the best I can I had hoped to not have to keep house alone this winter.

Eight years later she wrote, "whether you come home or stay longer and that I cannot know what will be best. If I should consult my feelings, it would not take long to decide. But you have said so much against being governed by feeling that I dare not urge it now." Here, then, was a woman who had learned to express her desires clearly though indirectly.[31]

Indirection apparently was wise in Sarah's case, since in a sermon on "The Marriage Relation" Eli wrote that "God made the woman *for* the man." "On the other hand," he continued, "the woman should consider that the man was not made *for* her, but she was made *for* the man, and derived under God; her being from him. Therefore the wife should see, that she reverance her Husband."[32] Answering a letter in which her husband told her, "Do not chide me for I have done the best I could to get away," Sarah Regal described a friend whose husband "is coming home this week to take his family with him. I think he has staid away long enough to try the strength of their attachment for each other if that has been his object I hope he has not staid long enough to break the cord." Lest her husband miss the point, Sarah urged him to come home, apologizing then for offering her opinion and claiming that she only wanted to know his plans in order to find proper clothing for the children.[33]

As Sarah's description suggests, women used anecdotes and gossip to communicate opinions they could not express openly. Gossip provided a mechanism for confirming standards of behavior and justifying one's own actions, as well as indirectly communicating opinions and desires. For example, Hannah Bingham, the wife of a missionary in Michigan's Upper Peninsula, wrote to her adolescent daughter describing the local "trash" society, a group of young girls who met in a sewing circle "more for society than charity" to be joined by young men for dancing, behavior she clearly hoped her young daughter would not emulate.[34]

Weltha Field wrote her unmarried daughter, Abby, of a neighbor who gave birth only three months after her marriage. Although Weltha wrote that she had helped the girl with her washing, she commented that "some of the neighbors think it would be disgrace even to go there." While describing her own charitable attitude toward the girl, Weltha also conveyed to her daughter the disapproval felt in the community toward premarital sex and the social ostracism suffered by those women who transgressed the moral standards of the community.[35] Nell Whitehead's sister, Lottie, wrote her of mutual friends who visited a dying man. The visitors apparently were told that they would "eat [their hosts] out of house and home" and went elsewhere for their meals. This inhospitable behavior, even under the burden of serious illness, was repeated as an example of an inexcusable breach of manners, if not of ethics.[36] Women's discussions of the activities of other people, their comments on the judgment and moral standards of others, represented a means of establishing mutually accepted standards of behavior. Since women in particular were judged on the basis of their conformity to standards of propriety, gossip served an important function in female correspondence.

Women sometimes attempted to influence the actions of others through references to kinship obligations. Electa Loomis wrote to her daughter Ann Gennette Loomis Preston:

> We should be glad to see you Mary & Elizabeth I never expect to see again they have not the means but you who have your thousand I should think would come once more & see how lonely and desolate every thinghs looks about home will you not be so good as too answer this letter.[37]

Many elderly mothers, like wives writing to husbands, were in positions of little power, depending on their persuasive abilities while avoiding direct personal appeals. They relied instead on references to filial obligation intended to provoke a sense of guilt.

One young widow used a similar technique to convince her brother to help her care for their aging parents. She wrote that their mother "is dying by inches about you and Nell and your unsettled state . . . if you want to send her to her grave go to Kansas or Nebraska." She asked him to heed "the petition of your only sister who in her lonliness and sorrow appeals to you to come and help her prolong the life of *your* parents as well as *hers*."[38] Jane Howell similarly appealed to her nephew's sense of duty. She wrote:

> I have been counting the days, weeks, and months which have elapsed, and have now almost come to the conclusion that thee cares nothing about me: be that as it may, it does not in the least, lessen the love I feel for thee, I almost wish sometimes that I could think less about thee: it would relieve my mind of a great deal of anxiety, but that is a thing impossible.[39]

Where they lacked power, women often attempted to invoke guilt.

Female letters, however, were not merely persuasive and manipulative. Women used letters to preserve emotional bonds, to establish a sense of solidarity, and to create intimacy in spite of the great distances which often separated families and friends, writing long and detailed letters to female kin.[40] One male correspondent ended his portion of a letter with the closing comment: "As there are two more of your friends that wish to have something to say to you in this sheet (& both women) I must conclude by wishing you health and happiness."[41]

Women used detailed description to preserve a sense of community with absent kin, frequently urging one another, as well as their male correspondents, to write of their activities. Sarah Regal's mother wrote to her daughter, asking her grandchildren to "write every opportunity and to write peticula for I want to hear from them often and every thing relating to their Health and Circumstances." Jane Howell asked her niece to write one letter which could be passed around to their friends and another to her personally "with everything in it let it be ever so trifling in domestic concerns as I feel anxious and interrested to know all and everything about you." In another letter she urged her sister to write so that they could spend their evenings reading her letters if not visiting with her, since "everything respecting you, even to the most trifling of your concerns, is interesting and you may be certain we will be gratified by the most minute particulars." Josiah Littlefield's mother told him she was "interested in everything you do and would like to have particulars," while Mary Cooley wrote to her unmarried son, "You must write me all about it—what your work is, who are your fellow boarders, how you spend your evenings, and in short everything you can think of; everything that concerns you interests me." Frances Pomeroy wrote to her daughter, "No, my darling girl your letters are not *too* long to please your mother—I don't know what your father said, but I am glad of every detail of your life." Separated from their kin, women attempted to recreate the lost closeness through a knowledge of the details of daily life.[42]

Sometimes this desire for detail focussed on physical surroundings. Women frequently wrote that they wanted to be able to visualize their friends and relatives in their new environments, one young woman writing to her mother about her absent sister, "I can hardly bear to think that I have never seen Hatties new home and cannot, I suppose imagine very correctly, how she looks in it, or rather how it looks, for I can think just how she looked when I last saw her."[43] Jane Howell wrote her relatives in Michigan:

> I often think that you have greatly the advantage over me, for when my imagination pays a visit to Hazelbank, it no doubt deceives me grossly . . . but you have only to turn your thoughts to No. 477 North Second street and there you may see us just about as you left us, except that we have our middle room painted and papered.[44]

13. Elsie Cooley's kitchen (1906)

Sometimes women sent one another scraps of fabric from dresses or wall paper they had recently bought so that their relatives could visualize them in the new clothes and surroundings.[45]

Often women attempted to maintain contact by sending small gifts of domestic goods. Sometimes these presents were of practical benefit, as when candy, sherry, and other purchased goods were sent to isolated families by their eastern relatives. But goods were also sent from Michigan to the East, even such commodities as flour. Temperance Mack expressed the psychological importance of such objects when, before she joined her daughter's family in the Mormon migration west to Nauvoo, Illinois, and finally to California, she wrote, "I want all my children to send me a little keepsake that I may have it to look back upon and think of them when I am far from them."[46] When a friend returned from a visit to Jane Howell's sister, niece, and nephew, Jane expressed the desire to receive tangible objects:

> I told him that I had heard a great deal about Michigan, but I had never seen anything that was produced on the soil and asked him why he did not bring me something that I could see and handle . . . he immediately took out a hazelnut from his pocket and told me he picked it up off of Thomas' land. I set a high value on it; it proves you *really* live on Terra Firma.

Later, Jane's niece wrote of sending pound cake, sausages, and hazelnuts from her home in the Michigan wilderness to her aunt in Philadelphia. Several months later, Jane wrote:

> Whilst I was reading thy letter my dear sister, which I received by post, after Samuel Lovett left you, and my spirits highly elated, and my imagination actively employed in dividing the cake, distributing the nuts, and in shewing the specimens of flour, onion, etc., etc., among my friends, interested in your welfare; how grievously I was disappointed when thee informed me that Samuel had taken his departure without seeing you . . . To see, to taste, and handle, are real realities and which I thought I had realized until I came to the cross lines in thy letter,—and then how shockingly provoking it was, to find it all vanish just like waking from a pleasant dream, and leave nothing but disappointment.[47]

Hannah Bingham sent her daughter a cake and some stockings, telling her: "I don't know but you might prefer sugar but I thought you would love to eat a little bit of Mother's cake made at home by her own hands." She wrote that another daughter was sending "a comforter that she and I knit."[48] Lucy Smith's mother in Vermont sent her a package of apples she had dried, while Jane Howell sent candy to her relatives in Michigan.[49] Even the letter itself could become a cherished object, to be handled and saved not only for what it said but also because it had been held and indeed created by the absent writer. In telling her mother how "those letters your hand has traced . . . [bring] home and family near," Lucy Smith expressed the importance of the physical presence of the letter she set before her, a letter that looked "so natural."[50]

Before the introduction of parcel post service in 1910, packages could be carried only by travelers, making their delivery infrequent

and uncertain. Nonetheless, by overcoming these difficulties to exchange domestic products, particularly baked goods, women were able
to foster a feeling of tangible presence. Duplicating as nearly as
possible the sharing of domestic tasks carried out before separation,
such gifts created an illusion of physical closeness among women
living in different parts of the continent.

Focussing their attention on personal relationships, women usually avoided discussions of political issues or national events. Although
Elizabeth Chandler published anti-slavery poetry in William Lloyd
Garrison's paper, *The Liberator*, and was a close associate of the
abolitionist Benjamin Lundy, she infrequently discussed national
issues in letters to her family. Jane Howell, Elizabeth's aunt who
was, like Elizabeth, a Quaker, justified a comment on the subject of
slavery by claiming the right to express her "feelings" if not her
political opinions:

> I have always detested female politicians and of course will bridge
> my tongue, altho I cannot my feelings for who can remain in a
> state of apathy when the country's rights are trodden down.

In a later letter, however, she discussed both politics and the United
States Bank.[51] While women occasionally described prices and wages
in their region, generally they failed to connect these concerns with
national politics or economic policy. Similarly, while many women
discussed the unfortunate situations of women of their acquaintance,
they seldom connected the misfortunes of individual women with
legal constraints or suggested that women's suffrage might alter
women's position in society. For instance, although Nellie Hart replied
to her fiancé's inquiry, "yes I could like to know what the decision
of the November election will be in regard to woman suffrage," she
expressed no great concern about the matter.[52]

The Civil War was the one national issue that elicited frequent
comment from women, who discussed the war in terms of its tragic
impact on their own communities and families. In 1863 Sarah Regal's
mother wrote her: "O when will this cruel barbarous war come to
an end." As an adolescent, Abby Field discussed her relatives who
were fighting in the war. "I wish there was no war," she wrote. Abby
expressed in her diary her personal, though naive, reaction:

> Heard bad news in the paper that the rebels have come over into
> Indiana. I hope they may none of them get hurt. I'm afraid they

are not all ready to die [referring to religious conversion] if they were it would not seem so bad.

In letters to her daughter, Ann Gennette Loomis Preston's mother described the deaths of boys they knew and urged her grandsons not to join the army. Philamena, Ann's sister, wrote of the sorrow of women sending their husbands to war. She expressed concern over the possibility that Ann's son would enlist in the army. "I have often felt that it must be like burying a loved one alive to say goodby when they leave for the war," Philamena wrote her sister. When Mary Littlefield's son enlisted in the army, her mother wrote: "My dear daughter I need not tell you how deeply I sympathize with you in this time of trial."[53] Women viewed the war as an unwelcome intrusion of national events into the family, and thus into the domain of women, a "cruel barbarous" threat to family unity and security. Even in their discussion of the war, women expressed their concerns in terms of their own families.

One of the most frequently noted characteristics of nineteenth-century women's letters to other women is the use of affectionate language which would today be considered appropriate only between lovers. As Carroll Smith-Rosenberg has suggested, such expressions of affection were common not only among female friends but between sisters as well.[54] A series of letters written by Ellen Regal to her older sister, Emma, during the weeks following Emma's marriage, while written in a romantic style, appear to be a genuine expression of intense love for her sister and sense of loss occasioned by her sister's marriage. She wrote:

> I thought about you the moment I woke and saw you so plainly lying in your little nightdress as I have so often seen you as I lay beside in the morning before you were awake. Sometimes you come before me so vividly and I almost *feel* you in my arms. God Bless my sister!

In another letter she told her sister:

> My darling . . . I never wanted to see you so much in my life. It seems to me a year since I left you—I *never* will go away from *you* again, my lamb, my precious little one.

Shortly after Emma's marriage, Ellen wrote:

14. Regal children. *Left to right*: Ellen Regal, Abel Regal, Emma Regal

15. Frances Pomeroy (1840–1904)

What can I say to my darling this morning? Only that I love her, sweet one, you have been the blessing, the happiness of my life . . . . I have never loved any one as I do you—I never can. You have always been good. I think you the loveliest of human beings. I thank God for you and I thank you for loving me so. I would give my life to make you happy. While I exist I shall love you. May God keep you!

These affectionate letters continued even after Ellen's own marriage, when she again wrote to Emma:

I never could love anyone more than I love you. It seems to me there is nothing I would not do or suffer to make you happy. I kiss your hands and your sweet face.[55]

Angelina Bingham told her newly married sister, Maria, that she wished she had chosen to live with Maria and her husband so that she could have been with Maria while Maria's husband, a ship captain, was away. "We could have comforted each other in all our troubles," she wrote. "It seems as if I could be happy anywhere with you," she told her sister, calling her "my guardian Angel."[56]

Such expressions of affection were not limited to women; they also occurred between brothers and sisters. Marilla Buck wrote to her brother, Myron, telling of her engagement and asking his opinion of her fiancé. "I want to tell somebody something about myself and I have selected you—being as I love you. H. says he believes if I were separated from you and him both for some length of time, that I would be ready to give you the first kiss." Judson Bingham wrote to his younger sister Angelina that he had dreamed of her:

You were in my thought, your countenance oft refreshed my sight, your image was on my heart. This sounds a little like the language of love, and affection. Cold hearted as I think I am sometimes, I know I love you, and some other ones for I think of you and them not only during the night shades, but when my most sober judgment rules the thoughts of my mind.

He continued to tell his sister that happiness comes only through the love of friends and virtue, and particularly, the love of Jesus.[57]

While the mores of genteel society in the nineteenth century prohibited discussion of sexual feelings and strictly limited their expression, both verbal and physical signs of emotion and affection were often allowed a wider range of expression than in contemporary American society. This was true within the family as well as between female friends. The expression in writing of close, loving, familial bonds was considered not only appropriate but desirable, and certainly not defined as sexual behavior. For women at least, the relationship between husband and wife and that between mother and young child were not expected to provide the sole source of emotional support. Intimate bonds between sisters and, to a lesser extent, brothers and sisters, provided lifelong companionship and affection.

Feelings of affection among family members were expressed freely in letters, perhaps more freely than in conversation. One nineteenth-century commentator wrote that letters "enable friends to understand those sentiments and motives of action which proud modesty never could otherwise reveal."[58] Letters were thus a unique form of inter-action, different from speech and daily contact, different also from diaries and other forms of written expression.

In a study of twentieth-century British speech patterns, Basil Bernstein has proposed that different socio-economic backgrounds give rise to different language codes, middle-class children learning an elaborated code in which emotions and opinions are explicitly stated, working-class children a restricted code in which emotions are conveyed implicitly, often non-verbally. The elaborated code, according to Bernstein, allows the speaker to differentiate the self from others, emphasizing personal opinions. The restricted code, in contrast, minimizes individual differences, emphasizing shared values and group solidarity.[59]

The restricted code is characterized by brief, simple phrases, direct commands and requests, a lack of adverbs and adjectives, and a tendency to deal with concrete facts rather than abstract ideas and symbols. The elaborated code characteristically expresses emotions and attitudes, explaining the reasons for a request rather than giving a simple command, with relatively detailed descriptions and free use of adverbs and adjectives. The user of the elaborated code is more likely than the user of the restricted code to speak in abstract, metaphorical, or symbolic terms, and to move from an example to a more general principle. For the speaker of a restricted code, these principles are assumed to be shared by the listener and need not be reiterated in connection with a specific incident.

These language codes seem at first impression to correspond to male and female styles of writing in the nineteenth century, with women writing in an elaborated code and men in a restricted code.

In most correspondence, this distinction holds true; yet in their diaries, many rural Michigan women used a restricted code while many educated men used an elaborated code. Gender, therefore, was not the determining characteristic in the choice of language code. Nor was social class alone a determining factor. Bernstein argues that different language codes arise not from innate class differences but from the different types of family interaction typical of the middle-class and working-class home. The working-class family, according to Bernstein, tends to be authoritarian while the middle-class parent relies on persuasion as the primary method of child-rearing. If, as Bernstein suggests, different patterns of family relationships give rise to different language codes, then we would expect that in nineteenth-century America, with clearly defined roles for males and females, different experiences of interaction within the family would lead to the development of different styles of expression for males and females. Furthermore, these styles of expression would be altered throughout the lifetime of an individual in response to changes in family dynamics and different contexts of language use.

In his examination of men's and women's diaries on the Overland Trail, John Faragher found that women's diaries conformed to Bernstein's model of an elaborated code while male diarists wrote in a style similar to Bernstein's restricted code. However, the presence of men's and women's diaries in both language codes in nineteenth-century Michigan suggests that this difference in codes was determined by immediate social context as well as by gender. Women on the Overland Trail may have been describing their activities for either a future reader or an imaginary reader, much as women in settled areas wrote letters in a similar style to their distant kin. As Faragher points out, women on the trail were more isolated than males; they also probably were more isolated than the women on Midwestern farms who produced diaries conforming to Bernstein's model of the restricted code. The women's sense of isolation and the men's sense of solidarity which Faragher sees as the basis for the difference in writing styles may therefore be unique to the experience of the trail rather than a reflection of sex roles in society as a whole.[60]

The diaries of many rural Midwestern women were, like those of their brothers and husbands, terse accounts of weather and daily activities, with little commentary on emotions or reactions. Metaphors were seldom used, with even modifiers infrequent. These diaries were seldom in sentence form; instead, minimal phrases were juxtaposed on the page. This is the entry for April 14, 1883, in the diary of Julia Slayton, wife of a Michigan farmer:

> Cloudy & warm   some rain & hail   Pleasant evening   baked 3 apple & one custard pie   fried cakes   swept dining room & kitchen   made my bed   ate my dinner & went to Mrs Donovan's to help lay out Priscilla   she died about Eleven O clock   came home at 5 o clock Aut & Mans went to Jessie's   Dave took F. Slayton to S. Davis.

Her husband described the same day in the following words:

> Wind South West   Some cloudy   very warm   had a shower of rain with some hail   cleared off pleasant at noon. We done chores & I weighed out a tone of hay for Mr Knap & in the afternoon went with Roch to buy a cow   Austin & Mansel went down to Mr Welches & stayed all night. Priscilla Donovan died at 11 O clock to day[61]

These diaries, close in form to Bernstein's model of the restricted code, were the product of an integrated rural society, their authors, male and female, defining themselves in terms of their relationship to both the natural environment and the community. There was little need to differentiate the self or to make explicit values which were generally accepted by the community.

Letters written to absent kin represent a response to a break in this community, a splitting of the family that was perceived as both unnatural and unfortunate. When kin were separated geographically, the only means of maintaining the familial ties which formed such a crucial aspect of the woman's sense of self was through correspondence. Yet writing was felt to be a poor but necessary substitute for speech. Bernstein writes that the elaborated code was used primarily by those who viewed themselves as separate individuals rather than as part of a social unit. These women, in writing to their absent relatives, expressed a sense of isolation and loneliness, a desire to unite with their female kin. Instead of the metonymic, restricted code found in rural diaries, these women used a metaphoric, elaborated code in which they expressed emotions and opinions, described events and scenes in detail, and in general attempted to recreate for the reader the texture of their daily lives.[62]

Shared attendance at church and social events, sharing of farm work, housework, and childcare, reliance on one another for emergency help, daily interchange of support and advice—these non-verbal expressions of affection, camaraderie, and support could no longer form the basis of a relationship once families were separated. Instead, women were forced to "take pen in hand," attempting to recreate on paper analogous emotional ties. One woman wrote to her daughter: "It is greivous to have to resort to pen and paper to converse with my dear children it does not remove the greivous loneliness which has for more than two years overpowered mind."[63]

Women attempted to lessen their loneliness by articulating emotions which would otherwise have been expressed through daily contact and mutual assistance. They attempted to reconstruct for their readers the sights, sounds, and even scents of their lives, including the reader vicariously in the domestic activities in which she also would have been a participant. The language used by these women cannot therefore be taken as a transcription of the usual interaction of female kin living in proximity. Women's letters represent not a reflection of a "female world of love and ritual"[64] but rather the creation of a world in which both love and ritual were of necessity articulated in writing rather than expressed in deeds. The translation of emotions, speech, and actions to written language was seen as a handicap to communication, a panacea designed to lessen the estrangement among kin until the break in the family could be healed and its members reunited.

While males suffered similar separations, social conditions made the break with their families less traumatic. Faragher argues that in most instances men had chosen to move westward either to improve their economic status or to join family members or friends. While some women departed willingly, most left their families with great reluctance, following their husbands out of devotion and duty mixed in varying proportions. Males apparently formed close ties with their male neighbors with greater rapidity than women formed ties with other women.[65] While a man found companionship among the community, a woman's central emotional ties remained with her family. Indeed, these relationships formed the center of her world, her primary reason for existence.

Behind these differences lies a dichotomy inherent in a patriarchal family structure. Adult males were, at least in theory, independent from their families, supporting their wives and children through their own efforts. Except for initial parental assistance in establishing them in a trade or on a farm, married adult males were economically self-sufficient. Married women, on the other hand, were dependent on their husbands for their subsistence. If their husbands ceased to support them due to death, illness, desertion, or neglect, they were forced to turn to kin for assistance. To support themselves and their children, they could look neither to the government nor to their own ability to earn a living. Furthermore, women expected to rely on their female kin for help in childbirth, child-rearing, and nursing the sick. While married or widowed men would in some cases ask their female kin to aid in nursing or childcare, such assistance was more likely to come from the wife's kin. The expectation of future need thus led women to exert great effort to maintain ties with their kin. Married males lacked the same sense of reliance on their kin and therefore did not feel such a need to preserve kinship ties.

Any cursory examination of family relationships reveals that mutual reliance for emergency and daily support does not preclude emotional attachments; in fact such reliance often strengthens emotional ties. Thus kin relationships were not only emotional but also instrumental, providing lifelong security to married women who could seldom achieve total self-sufficiency.

The relationship between the structure of the family and the nature of language used among family members explains the use of "feminine" language by men in some instances. Males used this language style most frequently when they were in positions of relatively little power, when they were not fully established as independent adults, when they were attempting to persuade. The feminine style was used by men in courtship, when a male found it necessary to persuade a woman, and by single men still attached emotionally and financially to their kin. These men, like women, found it expedient to use politeness, euphemism, metaphor, and gossip. Married men relied on their wives to preserve emotional ties with kin, sending one another primarily practical information or requests for assistance. Thus as males gained power within the family, they dropped the feminine style, composing direct "masculine" letters or leaving correspondence to their wives.

The feminine style of writing typical of nineteenth-century women's letters was more than an expression of trivial domestic concerns or sentimental feelings. Women used this language of domesticity to forge bonds with their female kin and to attempt to exert influence on their husbands and other family members. Without real power to control decisions within the family, women learned to manipulate words to persuade without seeming to persuade and to create for themselves an illusion of community out of the reality of their isolation.

FOUR

The Valley of the Shadow of Death: Motherless Children

With little private insurance and no governmental aid available, women who were widowed or left by their husbands were dependent on the support of their families, neighbors, or charitable organizations for their basic means of subsistence. In times of illness, the nursing care provided by kin could become a matter of life or death. And if a woman was raising young children, she would want to ensure that in case of her death her children would be competently and lovingly raised, preferably within her own family. While any individual would hope to avoid being widowed or deserted, having a serious illness in the family, or dying as a young mother, these were likely enough possibilities to be sources of real concern to women.

By the aid she gave to other family members, a woman could hope to ensure future assistance for herself and her children. A woman could, of course, never predict whether or not she would need to rely on her kin for the care of her children after her death, for financial support, or for other emergency assistance. As one might today make payments on an insurance policy to ensure security in case of personal disaster, an individual in the nineteenth century would consider assistance to family members as an investment in the availability of aid should it be needed in the future.

Parents sometimes discussed the expectations that their children would repay them with money and care in their old age. One man, whose mother had left her common-law husband to raise her children alone, gave his elderly father only monetary support since he felt this was the only type of care his father had give him.[1] The reciprocal nature of exchanges of services within the family is shown by the expectations of Josie Smith's brother-in-law. After Josie Smith's sisters nursed her through her terminal illness, she left a will naming her employer as sole beneficiary. Her brother-in-law angrily sent the employer a bill for the room, board, and nursing provided by his wife, demanding payment for services which had not been repaid as expected. Had Josie left much of her undoubtedly small estate to her sisters, both Josie and her sisters would have been viewed as fulfilling kinship obligations, motivated by affection rather than norms of reciprocity. Only Josie's failure to fulfill what was viewed as her obligation reveals the underlying reciprocal nature of the exchange.[2]

Assistance might be returned by a different person than the one to whom it was given. Florence Pomeroy wrote her mother that her maternal aunt had told her that she was glad to have her visit and "would do that much for your Mother's sake, if I didn't care for you at all."[3] People were expected to contribute to kin in need and in turn would receive assistance from those able to help at a time when they themselves needed aid. When Philamena Loomis Brown was left a young widow, one of her sisters wrote to another sister, Ann Gennette Loomis Preston, "I hope you will be disposed to contribute your mite you must remember when you was in the like straithtened circumstances . . . . 'Give and it shall be given unto you.'"[4] Thus an individual helping a relative could expect this assistance to be returned by some relative at some future date.

Delays in repayment caused little anxiety because a woman never knew when she might need to call for major assistance. Since kinship ties were lifelong, she could safely assume that eventually she would receive a return on her services, perhaps in her old age. Or the assistance might be returned to her children, particularly if she were to die at a young age. Even the death of the person receiving the assistance would not preclude repayment of the favor since someone else would feel an obligation to help a relative who previously had helped others.

Carol Stack writes in *All Our Kin* that the contemporary black women she studied loaned or gave objects to one another in an attempt to create obligations that could be called back at will. Even if the recipient wanted to discharge the debt, to be free of obligation, the donor would prefer to maintain a cache of outstanding debts.[5] The same dynamic occurred in nineteenth-century white families. Some individuals gave assistance to kin who would not be expected to repay the debt until much later, in the meantime maintaining an obligation to the donor. By providing services to kin, a woman could assure the return of such assistance in the future.

A woman could assume that her assistance to kin would be returned, if necessary, through the care of her children were she to die at a young age. She could rely on her sisters and mother to take her children into their own homes, thus protecting them from what were viewed as the potentially disastrous consequences of care by strangers, whether a stepmother or an unrelated family. Female kin thus assumed a significant role in child-rearing in nineteenth-century families. While marriages could be, and frequently were, broken by death and desertion, kin networks provided stable units within which to raise children.

Any woman would have realized the real possibility that she might die before all of her children were old enough to live independently. One study has found that 8% of all white children born in the United States in 1870 and 6% of all white children born in 1890 lost their mothers before they reached the age of 15. Of all white women born in the United States in 1870, 23.5% died before they reached the age of 50, as did 17% of those born in 1890 and 9% of those born in 1910. A study of Massachusetts women found that 31% of all mothers born in 1830 died before the age of 55.[6] Of course a woman needed only to perceive early death as a reasonable possibility in order to feel concern about the welfare of her children should they be left motherless. Although less than 1% of births resulted in a maternal death in Michigan between 1860 and 1900, women faced the possibility of impending death with each new pregnancy, realizing that they might leave behind at least one dependent child.[7]

The families examined in this study included 12 motherless households with young children. Five of these groups of children were taken in by a sister of the deceased mother, one family by the father's sisters, two by the maternal grandmother, and two by the paternal grandmother. In one instance, a daughter was old enough to keep house for her father and care for her younger siblings, but in another instance the child was sent to live with an unrelated family when the father remarried shortly after his wife's death.

While individuals devised various solutions to the problem of caring for motherless children, the mother's sisters were most frequently chosen, followed by either the paternal or maternal grandmother. In the only instance examined in which the father's sisters took the motherless children, the sisters complained that the father would not take his children even though he was remarried.[8] In none of the instances studied did a married or unmarried brother or father of the deceased mother take over the care of her young children. None of the widowed fathers attempted to care for children without the assistance of female kin and none hired a housekeeper to care for the children. The care of motherless children was thus a female responsibility. While the father was expected to exercise judgment in the placement of his child, he was not expected to care for the child himself.[9] Indeed, he would have found it nearly impossible to do so while earning a living. The care of motherless children was therefore the duty of the deceased woman's sisters and of the child's grandmothers, although the age of the grandmothers sometimes precluded raising a child to adulthood.

A woman sometimes selected a member of her kin network to care for her children in the event of her own death. Frances Pomeroy wrote on her daughter's sixth birthday, "Will Mamma be here to celebrate her seventh? If *not*, to my precious and noble sister Helen I commit the care of my darling."[10] Although a father held legal custody of his children, maternal aunts and grandmothers nevertheless felt a right and obligation to care for motherless children. One judge complained that maternal grandmothers frequently attempted to gain control of their deceased daughters' children, not understanding that a father held the legal right to the custody of his children.[11] In the families included in this study, legal rights to custody were never mentioned and apparently were not a factor in determining who would raised motherless children. Regardless of the lack of legal sanctions, female kin networks claimed the right to raise motherless children and mothers assumed the right to "bequeath" their children to relatives.

Sometimes, of course, a woman's husband was the stepfather of at least some of her children. A woman would realize that her husband also might die at a young age, leaving their children alone or under the care of a stepmother. It was highly unlikely, in contrast, that all of a woman's female kin would die before her children were raised. One woman who was widowed at a young age wrote that her husband's children from a previous marriage were sent, on his death, to live with their paternal grandmother and their mother's relatives.[12] Thus even if a father maintained custody of his children after his wife's death, the children might at any time be orphaned, in need of the care of their relatives.

Within a kinship network, responsibility for motherless children was often shared or shifted from one person to another as circumstances required. On the death of Flora Palmer in 1833, her mother, aided by Flora's 13-year-old sister, Fiona, took over the care of Flora's baby. At the age of 17, Fiona married her former brother-in-law, filling, she wrote, her sister's place as wife and mother.[13] After Lucy Smith, whose mother was married to Lucy's husband's father, died in Michigan in 1847, her mother and sisters discussed the fate of her young children. One of Lucy's sisters wrote her mother, "I should think you would like one if not both." Another sister wrote that she would take one of the children. Lucy, however, had requested that her husband take the children to their parents' family in Vermont, and her mother apparently raised both children.[14]

In another instance, a young widow with children went to live with her brother; on her death a few months later, the brother took his orphaned niece and nephew to live with his sister, the children's maternal aunt. She herself was widowed within the following year and, with no means of support and with children of her own, could no longer support the orphans. She wrote to her own maternal aunt, who was, she said, the same as a mother to her, and who had in fact taken care of her as an orphan, to inquire whether the aunt could find a home for both children together among her relatives in Michigan. The widow herself eventually found a home for her sister's children with a childless couple who were raising their own nieces and nephews and who were near enough to be under the aunt's watchful eye.[15]

Networks of female kin acted not only on the death of a mother but whenever it could be mutually agreed upon by the women concerned that child-rearing should be temporarily or permanently transferred to another member of the network. Mary Cooley's granddaughter, for example, spent a winter with her to attend school in Ann Arbor, and Josiah Littlefield spent a winter with his grandmother so that he could do chores for her while attending a local school.[16] Lucy Smith wrote to her mother in Vermont in 1839 that she wanted one of her younger brothers to live with her and her husband in Michigan for a few years.[17] An anonymous letter written from Jackson in 1864 expresses the acceptability of such exchanges, commenting on a woman who took an orphan girl "to keep awhile." "I really thought if she took anyone it would be one of her numerous nieces. Didn't you?" the writer remarked.[18] In 1889, Kate Cooley wrote to her mother-in-law of her guilt over not sending her school-age daughter to the girl's widowed maternal grandmother. "I feel so guilty when I deny my lonely mother Edith's company," she wrote. Two months later she again wrote, "I feel guilty whenever I contrast my large family with her loneliness and still can't lend her one." Kate felt an obligation to share the services and company of her daughter with her own mother; the child belonged not only to her parents but also to the network of female kin.[19]

The decision to take a child to raise was apparently made by the wife alone. While she was considered a substitute mother, her husband was not necessarily viewed as a substitute father. Harriet Whittemore's niece, Mary Ann, who was raised by her aunt, referred to Harriet as "Mother," but to Harriet's husband as "Uncle Olin," and to her own father as "Father."[20] Thomas Cooley discussed his wife's decision as to whether to care for her brother's son as a choice in which he played no part. "Mrs. Cooley is considering whether she will have her mother take the child back or take it herself," he wrote in his diary.[21] Since Cooley compiled the laws of the state of Michigan in 1857 and was one of the state's leading jurists, his familiarity with the laws of child custody can be assumed. Yet, in his own family, the custody of a motherless child was divided among and determined by the child's female kin.

The sexual division of labor in nineteenth-century American society, and particularly the designation of motherhood and domesticity as the role of women, created a cultural climate in which only women could serve as the primary nurturers of children. The separation of males and females into different work roles, modes of behavior, and even patterns of verbal expression began in early childhood and was accentuated with marriage, when the male took on the role of breadwinner and the female that of housekeeper and mother. The common experiences of women, determined both by biology and by the sexual differentiation of work roles, thus provided women with the sense of a shared destiny as wives and mothers. At the same time, since tasks were clearly differentiated by sex, women were forced to turn to one another for support in childbirth and child-rearing as well as for assistance in their daily work. In this cultural context, only women could be mothers or surrogate mothers, providing emotional nurturing and physical care of children.

Women shared with one another the experience or expectation of pregnancy and childbirth. Women frequently discussed in their correspondence the births occurring among their acquaintances. Pregnancy, no matter how welcome, was greeted with concern, and the pain and danger of childbirth, viewed as woman's duty and destiny, created a bond among women from which males were excluded. Assuring a safe pregnancy and childbirth, the first step in the care of the child, was the responsibility of the woman's female kin, and was, in fact, excluded as a proper topic of discussion between males and females. While Charles Horton Cooley was visiting his father, Thomas Cooley, and his sister in 1892, it was his wife Elsie who, writing to her sister-in-law, advised her of her pregnancy, which was apparently a matter to be discussed between female kin rather than between brother and sister.[22]

A woman's mother and sisters provided advice and assistance in prenatal care and childbirth, especially with her first pregnancy, when she joined her own mother and married sisters in their common role as mothers. Nellie Littlefield, who was shortly thereafter to die in childbirth, wrote to her newly-married sister in 1875: "if you take after your mother and your married sisters you need not have any of the fears you expressed. They had three months of grace and then found themselves traveling the old road. To be truthful, I cannot say it is an easy one, although the end may bring the coveted prize."[23] Another young woman wrote to her mother-in-law shortly after the birth of her baby:

> It was comforting to know that you had always had a hard time when your babies came. I guess that is the usual experience of mothers. Certainly the suffering is indescribable and I guess not to be comprehended by those who have not passed through it.[24]

The suffering of pregnancy and childbirth, emphasized more than the joy involved, thus formed a bond among women.

Older women offered comfort. "Be sure I understand and sympathize with you dear expectant mother," Florence Pomeroy Raab's mother-in-law wrote.[25] They also expressed concern for the danger of childbirth. Ellen Whitehead wrote her sister-in-law, Nellie, that her mother "says she has got a double portion of anxiety now you and I both to think of but we will leave it all in the hands of the Lord."[26] Mary Cooley wrote her daughter-in-law, Kate, that she was glad Kate was "safely and comfortably through your trial and hope the little daughter will live to be a great comfort to you."[27] Childbirth was a trial not only as a time of suffering to be endured but also as a time of mortal danger for the mother.

Women expressed to one another the fear of their own imminent deaths. Ellen Regal, daughter of a traveling evangelist, wrote her brother-in-law, Isaac Demmon, that "it is not strange [Emma] should tremble and shrink at the thought of the Valley of the Shadow of Death which she must so soon enter."[28] Another woman wrote that her pregnant cousin was "awful blue for she has an idea that most of folks die at such times."[29] Women were aware of the risk of puerperal fever. Nellie Littlefield wrote her husband that her sister had developed a fever, "as sometimes makes its appearance in such cases," on the fourth day after childbirth.[30] Ellen Regal wrote her brother-in-law, Isaac, that his wife Emma had "escaped the fever we feared" after the birth of her first child.[31]

At this time of uncertainty and anxiety, women turned to their female kin for practical advice and assistance as well as reassurance. Jennie Keal's grandmother advised her shortly after the birth of her baby to get a good nurse, stay in bed, and be careful not to take cold.[32] Nellie Littlefield's mother made clothes for the baby, brought food to her daughter, and traveled to her daughter's home to assist with the birth.[33] Susan Buck's unmarried sister, Abby Field, stayed at Susan's home to assist during and after childbirth.[34]

A young bride frequently returned to her parental home for the birth of her first child, often leaving her husband for several months. In 1844, Maria Bingham's mother wrote her that: "Mrs. Church says you would of course wish to come home and be with Mother if you expect any family troubles—you know what a healthy plan this is and how much better it would be to be at your own home when you should be confined." This was no small undertaking, since Maria was living in Detroit at the time and her mother was living in Michigan's Upper Peninsula at a missionary outpost accessible only by boat and only during the summer months.[35] Emma Regal traveled from Ohio to Michigan, spending several months with her mother and sister to await the birth of her first baby.[36] One woman informed her mother-in-law and sister-in-law that she preferred to have her baby in the hospital for economic reasons, although, she wrote, "the worst feature is the loneliness." She urged them to travel from Michigan to Pennsylvania, however, to be present for the birth.[37]

Thus even before the birth of a child, the female kin network assumed responsibility for the child's welfare. It was a woman's mother and sisters who provided the baby's earliest care, assisting the new mother and taking over the baby's care if the mother was unable to attend to the baby's needs. Since it was customary for women to remain in bed for several weeks following the birth of a baby, female kin must have helped care for even a nursing baby.[38] When Mary Phelps developed what was to prove a fatal illness, she traveled to her parents' home where she could remain under the care of female relatives who weaned her baby and nursed Mary until her death.[39] Nellie Littlefield and her sister Emma both returned to their parental home for the birth of Emma's child. When Emma developed puerperal fever a few days after the birth and apparently became temporarily mentally ill as well, Nellie and her mother assumed care of the child.[40] When a mother of young children died, and the children were raised by the woman's female kin, these relatives often were merely assuming full responsibility for children in whose care they were already involved.

Women claimed a right to and a responsibility for their sisters' and daughters' children, not only because they were females and therefore capable of nurturing children, but also because of their specific kinship relationship. As women, a brother's wife or a female cousin could have taken over the care of motherless children, but in none of the families studied did any female kin other than a sister or mother of the child's parents take the child. Although a mother-in-law often provided advice and assistance to a young mother, a woman's mother and sisters maintained primary responsibility for her children. Circumstances surrounding the care of motherless children in the Palmer family attest to this distinction. When David Wheeler Palmer's wife and sister died at nearly the same time, each leaving a young child, David took his child to his mother-in-law, while his own mother took her daughter's child.[41]

In some instances a conflict arose between the maternal and paternal grandmothers, with the maternal grandmother claiming priority in matters of childcare. Abby Whittemore's mother-in-law, Harriet, wrote that she agreed with Abby's decision to spend the winter of her pregnancy with her own mother rather than with her mother-in-law. "It is natural and right," she wrote, "to give her the preference and no doubt she is much better qualified for such a responsibility than myself."[42] When Nellie Littlefield died in childbirth, her mother, who had assisted with the birth, insisted on her right to raise the baby. The father argued that he should keep the child, with his mother as housekeeper and surrogate mother. This decision was apparently influenced by Nellie's sister's opinion that her mother was too old and impatient to care for the child, and probably also by the fact that the maternal grandmother was poor and nearly illiterate. Nellie's mother acquiesced reluctantly, writing that: "I feal as if I had ought to have her. it seams very hard for me to not see her indead it seams almost mor than i can bear." She insisted on receiving letters concerning the child once a week and on frequent visits, thus maintaining her right to the child's company and affection and her responsibility for the child's welfare.[43]

A mother's reliance on her sisters and mother to care for her children in case of her death arose in part from a fear that the children would be subject to neglect or abuse from their father, stepmother, or father's kin, a concern apparently supported by enough instances to give credence to the fear. Since a father could not himself raise a child, he was forced to turn the care of the child over to a woman—his new wife, his female kin, or someone outside the family. Even relatively conscientious fathers sometimes casually or inadvertently left their children with caretakers who took advantage of the child.

If a father paid a family for his child's care, the money could be diverted to purposes other than the care of the child. When David Woodruff went to the California gold fields in 1849, he left his young son with a married couple who, he discovered two years later, had not properly clothed the boy or sent him to school but instead had misappropriated the funds intended for his support. The father later told his mother, in whose care he subsequently left the child, that he realized he should have taken more care in choosing a home for the boy but had not had time to do so.[44] Girls particularly were subject to exploitation, since they could be overworked by foster parents interested only in the domestic services they provided.

Stepmothers were sometimes criticized by their stepchildren for their lack of concern.[45] While this was probably not always a correct perception, a mother would doubtless have been concerned about her children falling into this potentially and traditionally vulnerable situation. In some of the families studied, children were returned to their father upon the father's remarriage, but the mother's sisters usually continued to assume some responsibility for the children and probably kept a watchful eye on their care.

In several instances a child was sent to live with an unrelated family upon the father's remarriage. When he remarried, Lucy Smith's brother-in-law sent his young daughter to live with another family for a number of years, after which she would be sent away to school.[46] One woman commented with disapproval about another such action. "Soon after his wife died he married a woman very much inferior to his first wife but not inferior to him. he has given his little girl away," a Vermont woman wrote to her aunt in Michigan.[47]

Many women had first-hand experience with raising an unrelated motherless child. The potential danger of their own children being similarly "given away" must certainly have come to mind. Lucy Smith took into her home for the summer the daughter of a friend who had recently died, leaving eight children under the age of thirteen.[48] Abby Field wrote that a friend had asked Abby's mother to take a child but she had refused.[49] Abby's friend Ellen wrote that "Carl's baby girl" had been put in a "Home." "If Carl does not care any more than that for it," the unmarried woman wrote, "I think he might give it to me. I can't bear to think of Lizzie's grandchild being cast off that way."[50] Mary Littlefield wrote that "Old Mr. Root" had asked her to take his nine-year-old daughter. "He does not expect us to give her anything of consequence but to have her well instructed and taken care of," she wrote.[51]

Even the father's kin were a potential source of neglect or exploitation. Thomas Cooley, a prominent Michigan jurist, recorded in his diary that his wife's brother, who had recently lost all his money in speculation, had left his son with her, "brought and left without our consent."[52] While the child was not in this case mistreated, these are hardly circumstances designed to ensure loving care.

Another instance indicates the practical motives which could underlie the provision by the father's relatives of a home for a motherless child. Harriet Whittemore gave a home to her brother's young daughter, Mary Ann. Although the girl was apparently treated affectionately, she was expected to serve as her foster mother's nurse. Her foster brother advised that she should "brush mother's hair and fix the pillows for her and keep the doors shut and not cry nor tease mother when she wants anything." At an age when she could be described as being no taller than a table, she was also baking biscuits and pies. When another sister of the girl's father lost her daughter, she wrote to Harriet asking her to send Mary Ann to "take Louisa's place . . . since you have other children and grandchildren on which to bestow your affection and property." Circumstances indicate that her concern, however, was not solely to fill the gap in their affections or provide for their property. She and her husband already had living with them a young boy, either their own son or Mary Ann's brother. They had lost the daughter they depended on, they wrote, and their other daughter "has chosen to leave." What they apparently needed was a nurse. Her husband, the woman wrote, was in poor health, and in fact Mary Ann spent several months nursing her aunt until the woman's death, when she took over the care of her elderly uncle.[53]

Michigan laws provided little protection against mistreatment of children. In the early nineteenth century, neglected children were placed in apprenticeships, a situation mothers would certainly attempt to avoid for their children. A law passed in 1809, for example, stated that children who were "living in idleness and indigence, and not in a situation to acquire useful instruction, or the habits of industry," should be removed from their homes and placed in apprenticeship under the care of a guardian appointed by the court.[54] An 1817 law provided for the care of neglected children while relieving the territory of the burden of their support by binding to apprenticeship those children whose parents were unable or unwilling to support them.[55]

Not until the mid-nineteenth century did the law penalize parents and guardians for failing to provide physical care and financial support for the children in their care. The first such law, passed in 1846, was extremely limited in scope. Any parent or other adult responsible for the care of a child under the age of six who left the child in a "street, field, house, or other place" with "intent wholly to abandon it" could be punished by a prison sentence.[56] In 1881 the law first stipulated limits of allowable treatment of children within the family, making it illegal for parents to thwart a child's moral development by allowing the child to beg, frequent drinking establishments, or consort with thieves or prostitutes.[57] Only in 1893 was the physical abuse of a child by a parent or guardian prohibited by law. It was then made a felony to torture, cruelly or unlawfully punish or wilfully, unlawfully, or negligently deprive of necessary food, clothing, or shelter a child under 16 years of age or allow the child to engage in dangerous occupations or morally corrupting activities.[58] In the absence of strong protective laws, a child was dependent on the kindness of the individuals who cared for him or her.

A motherless child was at the mercy of his or her foster parents, and, as folklore and popular literature suggest, was vulnerable to exploitation and neglect.[59] While many children were no doubt conscientiously and lovingly raised by stepmothers, fathers' sisters, and unrelated foster parents, it was impossible for a mother to predict the character of the woman her husband would choose to marry or select as the child's caretaker. She would therefore be uncertain as to the fate of a child left to her husband's protection, regardless of his conscientiousness as a father.

In contrast, a woman's female kinship network provided a relatively secure home for her children. These were women already known and trusted by the child, or at least women the child had heard his mother discuss. Since death was unlikely to destroy the entire network, other female kin could replace those who died or were no longer able to care for the children. Furthermore, a woman whose sister or mother took her children would be assured that the children would be raised by a woman who felt for them essentially the same responsibility and affection she felt for her own children. Frances Pomeroy wrote in her journal that she knew her sister's "loving tenderness will be equally shared between her own and mine," and indeed the two sets of children had spent much of their childhood together.[60] Another woman wrote that she would like to raise her deceased sister's children. "Cradled as they have often been with my own they are very dear to me and I do not like seeing them fall into other hands," she wrote.[61] A woman's mother or sister would usually raise a child with the same child-rearing practices the mother would have used, teaching the child a compatible set of values.

Indeed, a woman viewed herself as stepping in to fill the place of her deceased sister or daughter, becoming emotionally although apparently not legally the child's mother. The maternal aunt and grandmother viewed the child as a memento of a sister or daughter, a replacement for and a gift from the deceased mother. The bonds involved in the female kinship network thus continued even beyond the lifetime of a woman through the care given to her child. While a woman could be replaced in the affections of her husband, she could never be replaced as a sister or daughter. The female kinship network thus provided a stable family unit on which a woman could rely to assure the care of her children in the event of her own death.

The delineation of home and family as the "woman's sphere," and motherhood as her primary role in life, both reflected and facilitated the ability of a woman to form close ties of affection and obligation to her female kin, particularly with the mother and sisters who were her partners in motherhood and domesticity. A woman was expected to be not only a good wife but also a good mother, sister, and daughter, relationships involving the performance of certain duties and responsibilities throughout her life. A husband who demanded his wife's withdrawal from her kinship network would be forcing her to abdicate the familial responsibilities which were central to her life and essential to the care of her children. He would also

16. Florence Pomeroy (1875–1955) holding Margaret Pomeroy (c. 1883)

17. Kate Taylor Cooley (1850–1931) and children. *Standing—left to right*: Edgar L. Cooley (b. 1882), Edith Cooley (b. 1873), Fanny Cooley (b. 1875); *seated—left to right*: Eva Cooley (b. 1882), Kate Taylor Cooley holding Adaline Cooley (b. 1884), Elizabeth Cooley (b. 1878), Frank Eugene Cooley (b. 1880)

alienate himself from kin upon whom he might later need to rely to care for his offspring.

The existence of female kinship networks that were responsible for continuity of childcare within the family suggests that nuclear families were not isolated from their kin. Furthermore, parents were not solely responsible for the rearing of their children. In spite of geographic separation, female kin acted as a family unit in the care of children, providing stability and continuity in child-rearing despite financial and medical setbacks experienced by nuclear families or even the dissolution of a nuclear family unit. The concept of a woman's children as the joint asset and responsibility of her female kin was not uniquely characteristic of black families, as has been suggested by studies of contemporary urban black kinship networks,[62] but was in fact a common pattern in nineteenth-century white, Protestant families as well. The fact that the kinship networks in which these Michigan women participated extended to the New England states suggests that this pattern of child-rearing may have been widespread in America in the nineteenth century.

A woman not only depended on her female kin for short-term assistance in childcare but also relied on her kin network to assume long-term responsibility for her children. Only through her female kin could a woman guarantee that her children would be reared according to her own values, within her own family. As a primary unit of long-range childcare responsibility, the network of female kin was thus of even greater importance than the husband-wife unit, continuing even after the dissolution of a marriage. A woman's ties to her own sisters and mother were lifelong; in marriage, she lived with a man who was, especially in the early childbearing years of the marriage, viewed as essentially a stranger, an outsider. In death, the woman showed trust not for this stranger but for her own female biological kin. These sisterhoods of female kin, networks not only of affection but also of obligation and trust, thus served the important function of ensuring continuity of child-rearing within the family.

FIVE

Woman and Nurse: Care of the Ill

Two of the best loved heroines of nineteenth-century fiction, little Eva in *Uncle Tom's Cabin* and Beth in *Little Women,* were young women whose illnesses and deaths provided images of feminine helplessness and resignation. Catharine Beecher noted the prevalence of female invalidism during the nineteenth century, as did many male physicians. Indeed, some doctors described women as inherently ill, their ailments arising from a reproductive system whose normal function as well as disfunction was viewed as a source of ill health. Historians have attributed the prevalence of female invalidism in the nineteenth century to the psychological dynamics of the patriarchal family in which women gained power only through the subterfuge of apparent weakness.[1] Yet the supporting role in the drama of female invalidism was the nurse, also female, usually a member of the family. While the invalid was helpless and weak, the nurse was strong and competent.

In the nineteenth century, most medical care took place within the home, the woman's domain. Women often assisted with childbirth and routinely advised pregnant women and young mothers on health care. The role of the housewife, however, also included nursing her husband, children, and other family members through illness, treating them with herbal cures and patent medicine. Indeed, women were believed to protect the health of their families even through the daily tasks of cooking and cleaning.

Medical beliefs held by physicians as well as laymen in the nineteenth century stressed the importance of the environment in preventive and curative health care. Before general acceptance of the germ theory of disease, doctors believed illness to be caused by an internal state of disequilibrium, usually brought on by unfavorable environmental conditions such as drafts, poor ventilation, unhealthy climate, improperly prepared food, and poor hygiene.[2] Disease, then, could be attributed to the neglect of a homemaker. Nineteenth-century domestic manuals devoted much attention to health care as the central function of the housewife. In cooking, in cleaning, in washing clothes, it was she who was to control the cleanliness of the home environment and therefore the health of her family. One domestic manual advised that "every housewife is necessarily, to a greater or less extent, a physician, in her own family."[3]

When illness did occur, women were responsible for nursing the sick family member. They prepared special food, attended to all the patient's needs, and administered medicine, creating a clean and quiet environment in which the patient could regain health. While some diseases responded to surgery or drugs, attentive nursing care was often the best treatment available, and female kin could be relied upon to provide careful attention to the patient. During her son's fatal illness in California, Lucy Parker, who was at the time visiting her relatives in Connecticut, wrote to her husband in Michigan: "You know we think so much depends on careful nursing and that I am afraid he will not get where he now is."[4] Networks of female kin provided this essential health-care service to both male and female family members.

For instance, when Susan Buck's son became ill with scarlet fever, she wrote asking her sister Abby to come and assist her as she had with the births of Susan's children.[5] When Edmund Phelps' wife became ill, she traveled to the home of her sisters, who cared for her and the baby she was nursing until her death.[6] Helen Elizabeth Miles went to New York as a young woman to nurse her mother's brother during a long illness.[7] Jessie Phelps and Olive Boyd both nursed their sisters in their terminal illnesses.[8] When Frances Pomeroy was ill for five weeks, her sister came to help her.[9] When Nellie Littlefield's sister became ill after the birth of a baby, Nellie remained to care for her sister and the baby.[10] When Weltha Field suddenly became ill, she sent for her sister, who treated her with home remedies and nursed her back to health.[11]

Nursing the sick was seen, in fact, as a central aspect of the woman's domestic role, not only within her own household but among other kin as well. Caring for the sick served both to express and to symbolize the role of the wife and mother within the family. The nurse was expected to be attentive, nurturing, and self-sacrificing, cheerful even when exhausted, willing to assume the most distasteful tasks. Yet the nurse controlled the patient while responding to his or her needs. Indeed, the role of the homemaker in providing a clean, orderly, cheerful environment assumed crucial importance in a life-threatening situation. Nursing the sick, then, was both an expression of and a metaphor for the feminine domestic role.

While men did sometimes care for the sick when necessary,[12] both men and women viewed nursing as women's work. Sarah Chandler lamented that her ailing aunt had only her brother to care for her, claiming that while "Thomas is everything it is in the power of a man to be, . . . his business necessarily calls him away, and it is not in his power to attend so closely as a female could."[13] Since Thomas was a farmer, he was probably outdoors much of the day. Yet many women also burdened with other responsibilities found time to serve as nurses. Included in the "power" of women were the skill and knowledge of nursing which were passed from woman to woman. Frances Pomeroy wrote, after her sister had come to nurse her, that "Henry did a great deal; but *men* havent a womans skill in the sickroom."[14] The importance of the woman as nurse extended beyond having the time available to devote to nursing and the skill of caring for the sick: nursing was equated with womanhood. Josiah Littlefield wrote his mother, "I am glad you have Miss Pollock to doctor you when you are sick. I have great respect for her as a woman."[15] Henry Parker Smith, caring for his ill mother and sister, wrote: "I am woman and nurse now."[16] Thus both men and women associated nursing with femininity itself.

Yet health care was viewed as the domain of women not merely by virtue of their gender. Nurses met difficulties in achieving professional status, while midwives were the objects of a campaign to regulate or abolish them in the late nineteenth and early twentieth centuries.[17] Indeed, nursing was the domain of women only within the family. While women frequently nursed their neighbors, especially during childbirth, such care was provided in a familial setting. A paid nurse assisting a new mother would live with her for a few weeks, assuming responsibility for domestic work as well as nursing and thus substituting for female kin who were unable to attend to the woman's needs. The ideal was to be nursed within one's own home, by one's own kin. When Abby Field became ill, a female friend expressed the hope that Abby could soon travel to her mother, writing that "it is good to have kind friends to wait upon us in illness: but who can take the place of her?"[18] Lucy Smith wrote from Michigan to her mother in Vermont, two weeks after the birth of her daughter, that a female friend and the minister's wife "have watched over me with all the kindness and tenderness of a Mother so many many times."[19] Mothers desired the same care from their daughters in illness and old age. One woman wrote, "I often think when I am sick if I could have one of my own girls with me how glad I would be."[20] Women wanted not only to be nursed by other women, but specifically to be nursed by their own female kin.

Women viewed childbirth, of course, as their particular domain. While male midwives and doctors took over much obstetrical care during the nineteenth century, even those women whose births were supervised by male doctors usually also were attended by female kin and friends.[21] Women often returned to their parental homes for childbirth, especially for the birth of the first child. Women advised one another on health care during pregnancy and on the care of infants. Laura Gibbs wrote in 1872 that "the old ladies say I must not wean [the baby] till she gets her teeth," taking as medical authority the advice of older women.[22]

The role of women as health care experts extended also to a knowledge of herbal cures. Some midwives distributed herbal medicine to the sick. Josiah Littlefield wrote that his grandmother produced herbal remedies for her neighbors in Michigan in the mid-nineteenth century.[23] A basic knowledge of herbal cures and other home remedies was available to most women through domestic manuals as well as information shared by female kin. Recipe books published in the nineteenth century commonly included, along with cooking directions, cures for illness. Lydia Maria Child's popular manual, *The American Frugal Housewife*, first published in 1829, presented recipes for medicines, most of which consisted of common household ingredients such as honey and milk to cure worms and a rind of pork wrapped around a wound to prevent lockjaw. Child recommends, for instance, "a stocking bound on warm from the foot, at night" as "good for the sore throat."[24] *The Southern Gardener and Receipt Book*, published in 1860, describes medicines for serious ailments such as cholera, consumption, whooping cough, and deafness, as well as less serious complaints like bee stings, colds, and minor burns.[25]

In family correspondence, women frequently exchanged medical advice, particularly regarding herbal cures and ingredients commonly found in the home. In 1875, for example, Mary Cooley advised her daughter Kate to cure her child's earache by placing a paper full of pepper in his ear.[26] Orpha White wrote her sister Nell Whitehead that her mother's medicine consisted of "two quarts gin or whiskey to one ounce each of [illegible] and black cabash." The dose was one tablespoon three times a day but, she noted, "ma wasent paticular she drinked out of the bottle."[27] Apparently for future reference, another woman noted in her diary, among her farming records, "what the Doc done for Wm when he was sick put Hot flanels on him and want him to take Olive Oil." She also noted "what Mrs. Wiart say is good for lumpy milk achanite."[28] Ellen Whitehead Gascoyne sent her sister-in-law "the receipt for liniment equal parts of sweet oil and ammonia."[29] Women recorded these cures and passed them along to others as they did family recipes.

Often, such treatment involved patent medicine. One mother, for instance, mailed her adult son a dollar to buy a bottle of "Constitution Water."[30] Patent medicines, often composed of herbal ingredients, frequently replaced herbal remedies concocted at home. Helen Elizabeth Miles told her brother that "Aunt Hannah thinks the medicine that Erastus Dodge is taking, Earles vegetable compound, will be good for him, she tried to get a bottle to send him by Mr. Henderson."[31] In their attempts to regulate the sale of patent medicine, some doctors claimed that by distributing such remedies to their friends and neighbors women were illegally practicing medicine.[32] In fact, these women were practicing a traditional form of feminine health care.

Many patent medicines were marketed as the secret recipes of women. In the late nineteenth century, Lydia Pinkham and her descendants capitalized on the image of the woman as health-care expert by advertising the popular Lydia Pinkham's Vegetable Compound, a combination of herbal ingredients in an alcoholic base, as a cure for various disorders of the female reproductive system. The advertisements prominently displayed photographs of the matronly Lydia, and readers were advised even after her death to write to Mrs. Pinkham. Attracted by advertisements stating that "The Doctor Did No Good" and "Woman Can Sympathize with Woman," those who asked for medical advice were told, in most cases, to avoid doctors and instead take Lydia Pinkham's Vegetable Compound.[33]

Various medical sects vied for popularity in the nineteenth century. While those doctors who formed the American Medical Association in mid-century and have since dominated American medical practice relied largely on "heroic" measures of surgery and medication, other medical sects particularly popular with women turned to herbal cures, diet, and hygiene. A women's medical college was the first institution to establish a professorship in hygiene.[34] Samuel Thompson, who gained a large following in the 1830s, promoted herbal cures which he claimed to have learned from a woman. Thompson opposed male midwives and believed in "women's superior capacities for the science of medicine." Furthermore, he believed men and women could control their own health if properly instructed.

Many women studied Thompson's system of health care and the lecture series which he inspired included talks for women as well as men. "Ladies Physiological Reform Societies" developed throughout the country, dedicated to teaching women principles of hygiene and anatomy. Eclectic medicine included female practitioners, while homeopathic medicine, which emphasized sanitation, diet, and fresh air, had many female adherents. While Thompsonian medicine and the popular health movement appealed mainly to rural and working-class women, upper-class women attended health spas to take cures based on frequent bathing.[35] Abby Field, for example, at times assisted an aunt on the East Coast who "doctored people" with a vegetarian diet and water cure.[36]

Health care, involving herbal and patent medicine as well as hygiene and nursing, was a traditional area of feminine expertise, an area in which male intervention was accepted only reluctantly. Women monitored with suspicion the activities of medical doctors. While some upper-class women in the late nineteenth century apparently idolized the doctor as a paternal authority figure,[37] many women expressed antagonism towards doctors and skepticism about their treatments. In 1836, an aunt warned her nephew, probably wisely, not to let the doctors give him mercury.[38] When Winnie Parker entered the hospital for an operation, apparently for cancer, her sister was dismayed at being denied entrance to the operating room. Although Winnie's husband did not attempt to join her, her sister believed it her right and duty to accompany Winnie even during surgery, an opinion not shared by the attending doctors.[39]

The claims women made to control health care arose from the perception that women were responsible for the welfare of all members of the family. If, as was commonly believed, disease was brought on by environmental deficiencies, then the housewife's duty to control the home environment included the preservation of her family's health. But the definition of health care as part of the housewife's role involved a less consciously recognized symbolic dimension as well. Considering nursing the sick as the role of female kin preserved the boundaries of the family unit from intrusion by strangers. Furthermore, in serving as nurses, women were able to consolidate positions of covert control within the family. As nurses, women acted out in exaggerated form the feminine domestic role: nurturing, purifying, protecting.

While historians examining Catharine Beecher's domestic manuals have looked primarily at her attitudes toward household skills,[40] Beecher actually devoted much of her attention to the preservation of health as the primary duty of the homemaker. One of Beecher's domestic manuals was entitled *Housekeeper and Healthkeeper*, the equal division of the text between the two categories emphasizing the importance of health care as part of the middle-class woman's domestic role. According to Beecher, the homemaker was responsible for providing healthful food, insuring proper personal hygiene among family members, and creating a clean home environment.[41] Beecher and Stowe, who devoted two chapters of their book, *The American Woman's Home*, to the responsibility of the homemaker in assuring proper ventilation, warned that "both the health and comfort of a family depend, to a great extent, on cleanliness of the person and the family surroundings." Beecher urged housekeepers to have "pure water, pure air, much sunlight, beds and clothes well cleansed, every arrangement for cleanliness and comfort, and all that tends to prevent disease or retard its first approaches," and she also advised against the use of medicine in the care of infants, preferring close attention to the child's food, air, clothing, and cleanliness.[42] Beecher, then, viewed preventive health care as an integral part of the housewife's domestic role.

If a woman was responsible for the health of her family, then illness could be attributed to the housewife's failure to perform her domestic duties. According to a popular nineteenth-century household manual, "it may be presumed that every housewife will be acquainted with those primary and fundamental laws of health which relate to food, clothing, ventilation, and cleanliness." The housewife was particularly responsible for digestive complaints and colds, the manual warned, since these ailments were caused respectively by improperly chosen or cooked food and by incorrect clothing.[43] Through their control of the domestic environment, women were believed to play a central role in the prevention and causation of disease.

When illness did occur, the housewife's role assumed dramatic significance. The homemaker attempted to alleviate disease by correcting environmental deficiencies, taking special care to prepare healthy food for the invalid, providing proper ventilation, keeping the sickroom scrupulously clean and free of the excretions from the skin which were believed to be carriers of disease. Furthermore, the nurse was expected to ensure absolute neatness and orderliness, creating a peaceful, harmonious, and quiet atmosphere in which the patient could recuperate. Nineteenth-century medical belief in America and Europe held that emanations from the bodies of the sick transmitted disease.[44] The bedding of the sick person, the air surrounding the patient, and the patient's eating utensils were believed to be carriers of disease which required cleansing by the nurse, a nurse who was also required to protect the patient from further contact with his or her own excretion. Here, again, the nurse followed the role of housewife in her daily tasks. One domestic manual advised that "almost the whole business of the housewife may be said to consist in providing for and disposing of the waste of the body" through ventilation, housecleaning, washing clothes, and bathing.[45] By disposing of these bodily wastes, the housewife protected her family from the pollution of disease.

The nurse was believed to be responsible for the moral as well as physical atmosphere surrounding the patient. Catharine Beecher wrote that the sick were particularly susceptible to the "moral atmosphere" about them, feeling "the healthful influence of the presence of a true-hearted attendant . . . while dissimulation, falsehood, recklessness, coarseness, jar terribly and injuriously on their heightened sensibilities." Beecher advised those who cared for the ill to "offer to read the Bible or other devotional books, whenever it is suitable." According to Beecher, disease itself was attributable to religious neglect since "laws of health are the laws of God, and when you disobey them you sin against your Heavenly Father."[46] Thus a virtuous woman would naturally follow rules of hygiene; a less religious woman would bring the danger of illness to the family. Both Florence Nightingale in England and Dorothea Dix in America emphasized the importance of moral purity, personal cleanliness, and orderliness in their hospital nurses, applying to the nineteenth-century hospital principles of hygiene understood by middle-class American and British women. Dix stipulated that the nurses she would accept to treat soldiers during the Civil War be over thirty, plain in appearance, and dressed in black or brown, without curls, ornamentation, or hoop skirts.[47]

In her study of pollution beliefs, Mary Douglas provides a conceptual framework within which the role of the nineteenth-century woman as nurse can be examined. Douglas believes that dirt, disorder, and sin are closely allied concepts, while cleanliness, order, and purity are similarly joined in the popular mind.[48] In stressing the importance of cleanliness and orderliness in the sickroom, Beecher associated dirt and disorder with disease. Furthermore, she claimed that moral purity on the part of the nurse was essential to the healing process. Thus illness was seen as the result of dirt, disorder, and moral laxity, while health and healing were the result of cleanliness, order, and moral purity. A woman was expected to protect her family from pollution by removing bodily excretions, purifying the atmosphere, rendering food healthful through careful preparation, and providing a proper moral atmosphere.

Women in Western culture have traditionally been viewed as holding unique powers to cause and cure illness, powers frequently associated with magic and witchcraft. In medieval Europe, there were both bad and good witches, bad witches causing harm, good witches curing the sick. Those witches who healed, it was believed, were as much the agents of Satan as those who harmed. The healing power of women, then, was feared as well as sought. As late as the seventeenth century, English midwives were forced to practice under the supervision of a bishop, promising to practice no magic.[49] An entry in Louisa May Alcott's diary, written while she served as a nurse for the Union army during the Civil War, suggests that the association of nursing with witchcraft still prevailed in nineteenth-century America, at least on a subconscious level. While ill with typhoid fever, Alcott dreamed that she was suffering persecution for witchcraft: hanging, stoning, and burning. She also dreamed that a doctor and two of the nurses with whom she worked tempted her to worship the devil. While Alcott describes nursing as a genteel occupation compatible with, indeed a metaphor for, the Victorian ideal of womanhood, her dreams suggest an association of feminine healing power with witchcraft.[50]

It becomes clear, then, why it was so important to be nursed by female kin. The strange woman was a figure to be feared, possibly dirty, sinful, disorderly, and neglectful, hiding under her feminine demeanor the potential of death. The mother, sister, or daughter, safely desexualized and under male dominance, posed no such threat. Beecher and Stowe advised that nuns, through their moral purity and selfless devotion to the sick, provided a model for the ideal nurse.[51] Close female kin were similarly believed to be virtuous, orderly, and devoted. By serving as nurses, women protected the boundaries of the family from the moral and physical pollution of strangers. Female kin thus provided a buffer from the dirt, disarray, disease, and evil of a world which was viewed as essentially threatening.

Both men and women feared being nursed by strangers. Electa Loomis wrote to her daughter Ann Gennette Loomis Preston that "it makes me sad to see you left alone if you should be sick and die no one too feel interested or know about your business but we must leave that to an all wise providence who will do wright."[52] Helen Elizabeth Miles, who went to New York City to nurse her uncle, expressed her fear that "he should die here in want, and alone, which will be the case if I leave him. Such friends as New York affords (most of them) will desert you when your money is gone."[53] When Lucy Parker's son was gravely ill with typhoid, she wrote her husband that, since the boy was living in California, he would "miss the nursing he has always had when he has been sick it makes my heart ache to think of him so sick among almost strangers with no Father Mother or Sister to care for him."[54] Another woman wrote of her anxiety for "poor Walter away off there where there is no one that cares for him and with no one but strangers to take care of him."[55] One young woman traveling in the West with her husband wrote of her impending childbirth, fearing that she "must stay, trusting in Providence that there may be somebody to care for me when I am sick in this land of strangers."[56]

Perhaps even more important than actual nursing care was the sense of security female kin provided. Indeed, the psychological attributes of the ideal nurse were those of the ideal mother. The nurse was to be a care-giver, providing an endless supply of affection and attention, enveloping the patient with an almost mystical healing power of love. Beecher and Stowe quote a description of the perfect nurse:

> O the pillowy, soothing softness of her touch, the neatness of her simple, unrustling dress, the music of her assured yet gentle voice and tread, the sense of security and rest inspired by her kind and hopeful face, the promptness and attention to every want, the repose that like an atmosphere encircles her, the evidence of heavenly goodness, and love that she diffuses![57]

The image invoked is that of a mother, creating a sense of security and love, a metaphor Beecher and Stowe make explicit in the comment that "whoever has the most maternal tenderness and warm sympathy with the sufferer is the best nurse."[58]

The psychological dynamics of nursing represent, in fact, an exaggeration of the woman's role as mother, the total interdependence of patient and nurse reflecting that of mother and child. While controlling the activities and environment of the patient, the nurse is at the mercy of the patient's demands. She responds to the needs of the patient, putting aside her own desires. This negation of self in the service of a helpless person creates between adults the relationship of mother and child. Beecher and Stowe write:

> God himself made and commissioned one set of nurses; and in doing this and adapting them to utter helplessness and weakness, . . . he made them to humor the caprices and regard both reasonable and unreasonable complainings. He made them to bend tenderly over the disturbed and irritated, and fold them to quiet assurance in arms made soft with love; in a word, he made *mothers!*[59]

Like the mother, the nurse was expected to sacrifice her own needs for those of another, believing that she was thus serving God as well as her patient. In this way the single woman, particularly liable to be called upon to serve as nurse, could simulate the womanly suffering of childbirth and child-rearing. How often, Beecher and Stowe write, have "the exhausted sister or mother or daughter . . . died prematurely or struggled through weary years with a broken constitution." They suggest that nursing, as represented by the Sisters of Charity, was "a work of self-abnegation, and of duty to God . . . . Is there any reason why every Protestant woman should not be trained for this self-denying office as *a duty owed to God?*"[60] Thus for every suffering invalid, there was a suffering nurse, sacrificing even her own health.

Women in Michigan in the nineteenth century clearly viewed nursing as a duty, accepted with varying degrees of satisfaction, resignation, and reluctance. When Abby Field's mother was terminally ill, a friend wrote Abby that "it is your duty as well as a ministration of love" to nurse her, requiring "all of your heart, time, and strength."[61] Helen Elizabeth Miles emphasized the sacrificial nature of nursing when she wrote to her parents and sisters of the trials of caring for her uncle, who needed to be "dressed, etc." She wrote that if she could "in any way contribute to his happiness or while away his lonely hours," she was "willing to do so if it is even by depriving myself of the society of my home friends which is quite a sacrifice to me who have never been from home so long before in my life."[62] In *Little Women*, Louisa May Alcott describes the moral lessons learned by Jo in nursing her sister Beth:

> . . . patience, . . . charity for all, the lovely spirit that can forgive and truly forget unkindness, the loyalty to duty that makes the hardest easy, and the sincere faith that fears nothing, but trusts undoubtingly.[63]

As illness was to test the moral character of the invalid, so nursing tested the moral character of the nurse, and single women like Abby Field, Helen Elizabeth Miles, and the fictional Jo March could prove their womanly fortitude and selflessness through nursing, if not through motherhood.

While most women at least overtly accepted the martyrdom of nursing, others rebelled. One young woman told her mother that she was tired of nursing her husband, who had been ill for four weeks, writing of her family:

> They are such a set of babies that they think they cannot spare me but I shall leave them if nothing more turns up to prevent. Louisa said when she was here that I made too great a slave of myself to my family, and sometimes I think so too, but perhaps it is all for the best . . . . I know this much that something is wearing me out, for at present I am not good for much.[64]

Throughout her life, Jessie Phelps expressed her ambivalent feelings towards her sister, writing in her diary shortly after her sister's death in the mid-twentieth century that she "exasperated me beyond endurance." Jessie wrote after the death of her sister that she "would not give up any of my experiences;—this last—seeing her so helpless and yeilding, yet going to sleep against her volition."[65] Jessie's satisfaction in seeing her sister "helpless and yeilding" in death expresses the ambivalent feelings of one woman about the covert power she held as a nurse.

While prisoner of the patient's needs, the nurse literally held the power of life and death. Only by her hands could the patient receive nourishment, be bathed, be given clean clothes and a clean chamberpot, the patient forced to ask assistance for even the most fundamental bodily processes. As a mother is both responsive to her child's needs and in control of the child's very life, so the nurse was both controller and controlled, an ambiguity that permeates the image of ideal womanhood in the nineteenth century. Presenting an image of total responsiveness and in fact largely responding to the needs of others, the woman simultaneously exercised a degree of hidden yet perceived control, epitomized in the image of the nurse.

In his rest cures, noted nineteenth-century physician Silas Weir Mitchell removed the woman from what he felt was the collusion of her female kin, preferring the less solicitous care of a professional nurse, the doctor rather than female relatives providing the personal authority and attention through which a medical cure could be achieved.[66] Mitchell thus suggests that the female invalid and nurse together acted out a relationship which enabled the invalid to play a role of dependency, both women enjoying the closeness of the bond between them. When female kin nursed one another in illness and in childbirth, then, males were excluded from the relationship. Women played the roles of both healer and healed.

Kathryn Sklar describes the intimacy which developed among women at a water cure. Sklar suggests that women's illnesses and the solicitous attitude they aroused in other women created a sense of female solidarity and an opportunity to express affection to other women.[67] Indeed, women used the concept of nursing metaphorically, as an expression of love analogous to that between husband and wife. For instance, Angelina Bingham wrote from Michigan to her newly-married sister:

> I wish I could be with you, so if you were sick I could watch over you, as I did a year ago last fall . . . . I loved to take care of you then, for you know how quick I would jump up, when you spoke. You have a good kind husband now, and I resign you into his hands.[68]

In *Little Women*, sisterly love is epitomized in the relationship of Jo and Beth, the healthy sister nursing the consumptive sister until her death, "all in all to each other." Jo "slept on a couch in the room, waking often to renew the fire, to feed, lift, or wait upon the patient creature . . . jealous of any other nurse."[69] Nursing thus provided an intimate bond among women, a channel through which feelings of affection could be expressed.

As medical care has moved from the home to the clinic, hospital, and nursing home by the mid-twentieth century, familial support networks for the care of the ill and elderly have in most cases weakened or even disappeared. As long as health care remained centered in the home, however, women provided a service which, given prevailing nineteenth-century attitudes towards health care and disease, was viewed as central to the functioning of the family unit, essential to the safety and comfort of its members. Perhaps even more important, nursing served as a metaphor for the role of women in the nineteenth-century family. While the female invalid represented an ideal of passive and frail femininity, the female nurse symbolized the self-abnegation and self-sacrifice believed to be the essence of feminine love. Through their selflessness, purity, and diligence, women were believed to hold in check forces of life and death, preserving the integrity of the family unit as well as the lives of its individual members. In nursing their kin, women manifested the paradox of the feminine domestic role in nineteenth-century America—powerful while powerless, controlling while controlled.

SIX

A Poor Dependent Being:
Women Without Husbands

In letters to their female kin, women expressed an awareness that husbands could not always provide their wives with lifetime support. A woman could be deserted by her husband or forced by his ill treatment to seek a divorce. And no matter how kind a husband was, his early death could leave his widow without means of support for herself and her children. Most important, women realized the likely possibility of being left, often in poverty, as elderly widows.

One study has shown that about 33% of white American women who reached the age of 60 in 1890 were widowed or divorced, as were almost 30% of 60-year-old white American women in 1910. Of all those women in Michigan who were over 15 years of age in 1900, 9.7% were widowed.[1]

In Michigan between 1890 and 1920, more than half of all women over 65 were widows. These figures represent only those who were divorcées or widows at the time of the census rather than the much larger number who had once been widowed or divorced but had since remarried.[2] While divorce was uncommon, widowhood was a real experience for a large percentage of women and appeared a realistic possibility to the rest of the female population, almost all of whom could have counted several widows among their friends and relatives.

For most women, the death of a husband was a financial as well as emotional disaster. Since for the past 130 years, the average family in the lower two-thirds of the population economically has held no savings, there was in many cases little for a wife to inherit.[3] Young widows were often left with debts to pay but without the ability to continue to operate the farms or businesses with which their husbands had intended to discharge the debts. Furthermore, widows with young children found it difficult to support and at the same time care for their children without assistance. Even the wife of an affluent husband had no guarantee of inheriting his estate in full. If her husband died without a will, a widow would be allowed only the lifetime use of his property. Regardless of the affluence of her husband, a woman could at any moment be left without means of support.

More frequently than men, women turned to relatives for assistance in their old age.[4] Indeed, the support of their kin networks was often all that stood between these elderly widows and starvation or the poorhouse. In nineteenth-century Michigan, alternatives to such familial help were few. While a man was able to support himself in case of widowhood or divorce, the lot of a divorced woman was similar to that of a widow; the plight of a separated or deserted wife was sometimes actually worse, since she received no financial settlement and was legally unable to conduct her own business affairs. There were no Social Security, no Aid to Dependent Children, no public assistance, no public housing, no food stamps, no Medicaid, and, indeed, very few substantial life insurance policies.[5] Since widows often were left without adequate financial support, women particularly felt the need to assure their future care, building lifelong networks of female kin to whom they could turn for assistance.

While men also expected and received such care, they expressed less anxiety about old age. Perhaps men had less reason for fear. In Michigan in 1890, the number of women who were widows was more than double the number of men who were widowers; for the nation as a whole, the ratio of widows to widowers was almost three to one. In 1900 and 1910 there were almost twice as many widows as widowers among the adult population of the state of Michigan. For the country as a whole, in 1910 almost twice as many women as men over the age of 65 were widowed. Because of greater ease of remarriage and a tendency to marry younger women, more men than women could expect to have a spouse to care for them in their old age.[6] Furthermore, men did not face the loss of their property or cessation of their income with widowhood.

Idealized images of the nineteenth-century extended family would lead us to believe that the helpless were welcomed into a family circle which was financially and emotionally able to absorb them without stress. The families examined in this study did feel and act upon a sense of obligation to aid helpless kin and, in most cases, help was willingly and lovingly given. But such assistance was accomplished only at great cost to all parties involved. Even among rural families and middle class urban families, neither money nor living space were boundless commodities. Furthermore, the loss of independence brought about by reliance on kin was keenly felt both by those who needed assistance and those who gave it. These problems were particularly acute in the case of the elderly, since most older relatives once dependent on their children or other kin would never again be able to care for themselves.

The popular image of the nineteenth-century extended family includes a grandmother surrounded by loving grandchildren and involved in family activities. In actuality, if living with her grandchildren, an elderly woman usually preferred to be elsewhere. In fact, living with a young family was often viewed as the last resort before the poorhouse. Both the elderly and the young perceived old age as a time of physical infirmity, financial insecurity, and loneliness, the elderly a burden on themselves and others. In his study of old age in nineteenth-century America, David Hackett Fischer notes that although until the middle of the nineteenth century elderly men were venerated, elderly widows often were neglected or abused.[7]

The period of life defined as old age came early for women, perhaps with menopause.[8] Henry Parker Smith wrote that his aunt was sick: "her system seems to be undergoing the change to old ladyhood and we fear she is in a critical situation." Another woman commented, "I am now in my forty-ninth year but a short time at longest I shall pass from time into eternity."[9] The elderly expected to be physically disabled.[10] One woman wrote that she was seventy-nine years old, "so I cannot expect to see or hear much longer."[11] But it was loneliness and depression that were the most common complaints of elderly women.

Sarah Regal's mother wrote to her daughter of "the greivous loneliness which has for more than two years overpowered mind."[12] Mary Cooley asked her son to write to his grandmother, who "talks of being old, and poor, and having nothing left to make life worth living."[13] Jane Howell, a Quaker from Philadelphia, wrote after her husband's death that "no place seems like home to me now . . . . Home, which I once dearly prized, has lost all its charms . . . so desolate . . . . I feel sometimes as if there was not a tie left." Five years later, she wrote:

Since my sister's removal, I feel so lonesome, so isolated, as if I
stood in the world alone, no one to care for, nor no one to care
for me, but I find it will not do to cherish such feelings, they would
prove inimical to my health if indulged in.[14]

Elderly women mourned the dispersal and deaths of their relatives,
the loss not only of husbands but of female kin as well.

Yet the elderly wanted to preserve their independence, choosing,
when possible, to remain in their own homes and provide their own
financial support. The opportunity to live alone was highly valued
by the elderly, the noise of children particularly bothersome. Electa
Loomis wrote to her daughter, Ann Gennette Loomis Preston, that
"it is a feast to be a lone some times."[15] Another woman wrote that
she had spent nine months in a household with young children and
could stand it no longer.[16] As an older woman, Jane Howell wrote
to her nephew that she had spent "an unpleasant winter, with close
confinement, and the noise of the children."[17] One woman expressed
a more fundamental reason for elderly parents to maintain a separate
residence. She had decided to share a house with her married children
but to keep her own independent living quarters within the house,
writing that it would be "easier for me our house is convenient to
do so and more pleasant for us all, you know young and old people
do not think alike."[18]

When Temperance Mack moved to the West with her daughter
and son-in-law, she tried to secure her financial independence, writing
to another son-in-law, "I want money by me as long as I live and
then if I am in want of anything I can get it."[19] Temperance's
children were concerned that she have her own room in the house
she shared with her daughter's family. Her son-in-law offered to
build a house in which she could have "a good room . . . where she
can be away from the noise of the children." Her children provided
the money for the house, to be repaid by the son-in-law with whom
she lived.[20]

Although they expected their sons to support them in their old
age, elderly women acutely felt their financial dependence and insecurity. Marilla Turrill and Myron Buck were left with the support
of their mother and their two young stepbrothers when their mother's
second husband deserted her. She fought for the right to keep their
homestead in spite of her husband's debts, telling her son that her
husband had sent her eight dollars and promised to send more:

> O how I wish we could take care of ourselves and not be so much
> trouble to you . . . . I hope he will [send more money] but I do
> not feel to put much dependence on him. So far so good. The first
> I have received from him in a year and a half.

Aware of the unavoidability of her dependence, she later told her
son that she would soon be forced to turn to him for assistance.
She wrote, "If I stay here I shall have to have help from some
quarters before long and if I go to you I shall be as dependent upon
some one so here I am a poor dependent being let it go which way
it will."[21] Delia Parker, an elderly widow, threatened that if she
received no financial assistance from her son she would have to "go
to the county house." "I would not call on you, if I could help it,"
she wrote, saying that he seemed "so backward about doing anything
but who have I got to depend on if I cannot depend on you."[22] These
women recognized and resented the dependence brought about by
their economic insecurity, and yet they had no choice but to rely
on their sons for financial support.

Parents and children alike viewed caring for an elderly parent
as a reciprocation of the nurturing received as a child. After several
nights of nursing his infant son, who was ill with the croup, Henry
Parker Smith wrote in his diary, "Will he live to take the like cares
and responsibilities in his turn as we slide down towards the grave?
Well—May God grant that our cares and anxiety may not go unre-
warded."[23] Edwin Phelps wrote to his wife about their young son,
"I am proud of Neds progress in learning & the interest he had in
writing me as I expect much of him when disease & old age unfits
me for business & should nothing befall him he can do me verry
much good even if young." About his daughters he wrote: "The time
may come when they will understand how much they owe their
parents & will do all they can to cheer our declining years."[24] Between
parents and children, reciprocation was delayed from the youth of
the children to the old age of the parents. But parents clearly expected
to receive, in their old age, a return on the investment they had
made in their children.

Edmund Hall, a Detroit attorney, was faced with the problem
of determining the extent of financial and emotional support he owed
his father. Edmund claimed that his father had been abusive and
alcoholic, financially and emotionally neglecting his family while
favoring a niece. Edmund's mother left his father when the boy was
young, taking the children to live with her kin. The niece, who cared

for Edmund's father in his old age, attempted to convince Edmund, by this time a successful attorney, to take over his father's care, or at least to support him financially, claiming this as his filial duty. Edmund refused to assume his father's care, citing his mistreatment as a child, but agreed to provide financial support because of the kinship ties and because his father had once given him financial help for his education. He thus repaid the financial assistance given him but refused to provide the type of nurturing he felt he had been denied as a child.[25]

The obligation to care for a parent persisted, however, even if the parent was unappreciative of the assistance. Marilla Turrill described her mother as "deranged," saying that "no doubt she would send her love if we were on speaking terms." Throughout the following years Marilla attempted to keep in contact with her mother, however, and when her mother was deserted by her husband, Marilla also assisted her financially.[26]

While elderly men and women expected their sons to provide financial support, they relied on their daughters for companionship and physical care. Edwin Phelps' son, as we have seen, was to assist him in business, his daughters to "cheer our declining years."[27] One woman who had five living sons wrote of her sorrow at having lost her only daughter in infancy. "Now, in my loneliness and poor health," she wrote, "what a treasure she might have been."[28] Another woman wrote that she was glad her sister had a "daughter to come and stay with you in your old age it must be a great comfort to you."[29] It was important to women to have not only the aid of female kin but specifically that of their own daughters. As an older woman wrote, "I often think when I am sick if I could have one of my own girls with me how glad I would be sons wives are not your own girls if they are ever so good, you do not feel as free with a Daughter in law as your owe child."[30]

Some young women were in fact reluctant to care for their husband's relatives. One woman wrote of the newly married woman who shared a home with two elderly women:

> sue has got a gud man but not a happy home with those old wimen
> I ham shure i could not live with them so i cannot blame her Naomi
> says she is goin to find her a man that has got a home of is hone.[31]

Another woman describing the same circumstances concurred that Sue "wishes she had a home to them selves she has gone to more plenty than I ever had but she said on sunday she would rather have less and live by themselves."[32] Another told of living with her husband's eighty-four-year-old father and mother and two maiden sisters. "I think many times we would enjoy life better were we living by our selves," she wrote.[33]

Some women expressed overt hostility to the elderly kin of their husbands or to step-kin. Marilla Turrill complained that her mother, whose second husband had left her, was forced to care for the husband's elderly father, supporting him with money provided by the sons of her first marriage. Marilla wrote to her brother, "It is a shame that she has that old drunken man to wait on, and then he lives on what you boys sent to her when he ought to be in the poor house."[34] Laura Gibbs told her cousin that her husband's father had left them one hundred dollars. "A good thing for us he died when he did," she wrote, noting that "if he had of lived any longer we would not got a cent."[35] Another woman wrote to her cousin about the cousin's sister's mother-in-law:

> his Mother come there not long ago she ren away from the county home and Orpha liked to have had a conniption, she stayed a few days, and Frank took her back, though the old lady begged of him not to, but I guess she will get along some way.[36]

Such attitudes, even if uncommon, would lead men and women to depend on their daughters rather than daughters-in-law to shelter them in their old age.

The reality of such care did not always meet expectations, however. One elderly divorced woman complained about the mistreatment she received at the hands of her son-in-law and criticized the daughter with whom she lived. Some of her complaints reflect only what she perceived as a lack of attention and concern; she complained of being left alone for an afternoon and of the house being kept too cold, for example. However, she also cited incidents of verbal abuse. Her son-in-law, she complained, "uses me worse than a humane man would a dog, calling me all the vile names the English language could produce."[37] This situation represents the only instance in the families studied in which a daughter, or any other female kin related by blood, was accused of condoning abuse or neglect, although, as discussed earlier, many women reproached their daughters for failing to write and visit as frequently as they desired.

When relatives were geographically dispersed, it was difficult to achieve an ideal balance of personal independence and familial companionship. Elderly women often were faced with a choice between leaving the communities in which they had always lived to become members of households which also included young children and the alternative of facing old age and death without the support and companionship of their kin. Yet while kin networks provided less than ideal solutions to the problems of the elderly, they did usually ensure at least a minimal level of physical comfort in old age.

Whether young or old, widows were often forced to turn to their relatives for support. While elderly widows usually required long-term assistance, younger widows often needed help only until they could become self-supporting or remarry. The Loomis family provides an example of the consequences of widowhood for a young woman. Ann Gennette Loomis Preston herself was widowed before the birth of her third son, and her sister Philamena was left a widow shortly thereafter. A third sister wrote to Ann describing the unfortunate situation of their recently widowed sister:

> She is left a *poor Widow*. God in his Providence has taken from her the support on which she has leaned he who labored to support her wants has been suddenly & with scarcely a moments warning smitten by the hand of death & she was left to pursue her journey in life alone compelled among strangers to depend upon herself & meet her own necessities—She had nothing to fall back upon in case of sickness of herself or child but the cold charities of a selfish world.[38]

Untrained to support herself, without any financial cushion, with a young child to feed and care for, she was left without shelter from the "cold charities of a selfish world," to face what she herself referred to as "the widow's desolate life."[39]

Initially, the unfortunate circumstances in which the young widow finds herself are attributed to an act of God rather than to her husband's lack of foresight. Yet as Philamena's sister proceeds to describe the deceased husband's financial affairs, the blame shifts from Providence to Mr. Brown:

> For her daily bread clothing & the various other things of which she stood in need she was to depend upon her own personal toil for a livelihood—These were found to be the startling & unexpected

facts after a week or two investigation by the administrator of his affairs which were left in a very bad state. Phila knew nothing about his affairs or troubled herself in the least she had enough of everything . . . When she was married she spent all she ever earned & all father could give her & she thought she never should want it more than now & never thought possible she could come to want.[40]

Trusting in her husband to protect her, she was left penniless and alone, her hopes "blighted and her prospects changed." She returned to the home of her parents, where her sisters contributed small amounts of money for her support. "Phila could not support herself now while Emma is so much trouble & besides there is so little that a woman can do," her sister wrote.[41] In a society where males were the family breadwinners and public assistance was virtually non-existent, female kin fulfilled an essential function in supporting those women who were without male protection.

As widows, women suddenly were forced to deal directly with the world outside the family. After trusting completely in their husbands to shelter them, many widows had to learn to become self-sufficient. As her sister noted, Philamena was "compelled among strangers to depend upon herself," an experience common to young

18.   Mary Hall Littlefield (b. 1818) (photo c. 1870)

widows. When Mary Littlefield's husband died, leaving her with three young sons, she moved to the farm her husband had owned. There she and her sons lived in a small cabin which, one son recalled in his autobiography, admitted snow through the shakes in the roof. With the help of her sons, she worked the farm until her youngest boy reached the age to attend college. She then sold the farm and moved to Ann Arbor, where she bought a house and boarded students so that her son could attend the University of Michigan.[42] Some women needed the help of friends or relatives to establish themselves in business. When Jane Howell was widowed, her cousin helped her open a store, assuring her that she could return all unsold goods to him if she decided to go out of business.[43] Jane wrote of one young widow with several children who had attempted to support her family with an illegal lottery operation. When that was uncovered, she tried to operate a tavern but was denied a license. The young widow would have been forced to leave Philadelphia had her neighbors not established her in a dry goods trade.[44]

Ann Gennette Loomis Preston, a widow with three young sons, rented property she owned, sold eggs and milk, took in boarders, and may have owned a tavern and roller-skating rink. Ann's sister, also widowed, wrote to her:

> Dear sister this is a cold selfish world—havent you found it so? you hav had enough business with people to know some thing about it & I think having to do with those we have to be suspicious of & to watch in business transactions has a tendency to blunt the finer feelings of our natures & to render us rather cold hearted & unsocial—but widows like you & me who are so far from their friends have to meet the rough storms of life alone.[45]

Without male protection, women were unable to preserve the traditional feminine modes of action and thought, "the finer feelings of our natures." Left for the first time without male protection, a widow realized her helplessness and vulnerability and felt the callousness of a society from which she had been sheltered. While kin could provide temporary assistance for the young widow, she was soon forced to decide whether to remarry if the opportunity was available, thus putting herself again under male control and protection, or earn her own support and that of her children.

While young widows were faced with the difficult task of supporting a family alone, elderly widows often were unable to support even themselves. Unless a husband specifically willed his property to his wife, his estate was divided among his wife and children, often leaving the widow with insufficient means. Since all property accumulated during the marriage belonged to the husband, with the exception of the wife's inheritance after 1844 and the wife's wages after 1911, a widow would find that she did not automatically inherit the farm, home, or business she may have helped to build.

All women were entitled by law to rights of dower, which could be claimed in lieu of the provisions of the husband's will. Dower rights entitled a widow to the use of a third of her husband's real property during her lifetime.[46] Widows also were allowed to claim homestead rights, and the property they claimed under these provisions was not subject to the claims of the deceased husbands' creditors. However, since many families owned little or no real estate, this provision assisted only some widows. And even when dower rights did apply, a widow held only the use of the property owned by her children. Thus a widow was placed in the position of occupying and using property which actually belonged to her children or stepchildren. She was required by law to preserve the property in good repair and was guaranteed occupancy of the family home only for the year following the death of her husband.[47] An older widow, formerly dependent on her husband, was dependent after his death upon her children. Until the passage of the Married Woman's Property Act gave women in Michigan control of inherited property in 1844, she was often dependent on her son-in-law.

From 1811 to 1846, the widow of a Michigan resident who died without a will inherited only a third of his personal property (or half if there were no children), and none of his real estate. If there were no children to inherit, the real estate passed to other blood kin, up to nieces and nephews, after which the estate reverted to the territory or state. Until 1846, therefore, a widow shared in any of her husband's real estate and in more than a third of his personal property only if he expressly granted her the privilege in his will. In 1846 the law was altered so that if there were no children to inherit, the estate passed to the widow for her use during her lifetime, after which it reverted to the husband's blood kin. Only if no blood kin were living at the time of the husband's death did his estate pass in full to his widow. Not until after 1909 was a widow guaranteed a share of her husband's estate if he died without a will. She received a third of his estate, his children two-thirds. If there were no children, the widow divided the estate evenly with her husband's parents.[48]

Thus until 1909 a widow held the legal right to inherit only a small portion of her husband's property. She was dependent on the provisions her husband made for her in his will, having little claim to the assets created during the marriage. A woman therefore could not depend on her husband for lifelong support unless he owned a sizable amount of property which was subject to dower. While laws concerning the right to dower ensured that some widows would receive some support from their husbands' estates, they placed the widow in a situation in which she could derive support from the property and enjoy its use but could not assume full control and ownership. The rights of dower, with their origin in common law, guaranteed a widow less financial autonomy than a married woman with inherited property was granted by the Married Woman's Property Act of 1855.

After the passage of the Married Woman's Property Act, the property a woman inherited or brought into the marriage was not included in her husband's estate but remained in her control after his death. A woman thus was forced to look not to her husband for her long-term financial security but to her blood relatives, from whom she would most likely receive an inheritance. A woman therefore would take care to maintain relationships with kin outside the household, with the reasonable expectation of the need of their assistance if she were to be widowed. Furthermore, since a woman could expect to inherit from her parents rather than her husband, her economic interests tied her to her blood kin and provided her in some cases with a bargaining tool within her marriage, a source of financial support which served to lessen her dependence on her husband. Thus laws concerning inheritance, combined with the Married Woman's Property Act, served to strengthen ties between a woman and her parents.

While many women were left alone through the deaths of their husbands, other marriages ended through desertion or divorce or were marked by periods of informal separation. In these instances also, women turned to their relatives for assistance. In divorce laws as well as laws involving inheritance, a woman was assumed to have no inherent right to assets accumulated during the marriage. Furthermore, she could forfeit, by her misconduct, the right to retain the property she had brought into the marriage. The division of property after a divorce was based on guilt, with the innocent party favored financially.

Husbands and wives were treated differently, however. Before 1812, divorces were granted only by act of the legislature. From 1819 until 1832, divorce was allowed only for adultery. If a wife was the complainant in a divorce suit, she was entitled to the possession of those assets which she had brought into the marriage or which she earned, inherited, or was given during the marriage, but she was not entitled to a share of her husband's property. She could also be awarded alimony or child support at the discretion of the court. If a husband was the complainant, however, he was entitled to retain possession of all his wife's property, and the wife in addition forfeited her dower rights.[49]

The allowable grounds for divorce were increased greatly during the nineteenth century. After 1832 impotence was also grounds for divorce, and the court was allowed to grant divorces at its discretion for extreme cruelty and for desertion for a period of five years or longer. The more liberal divorce laws of 1832 allowed the court to award a wife convicted of adultery some income for her subsistence from the personal and real estate which she had brought into the marriage and also granted an innocent wife some of her husband's property. By 1846 the admissible grounds for divorce were increased to include adultery, physical incompetence at the time of marriage, desertion for two years, habitual drunkenness, jail sentences of three years or more, and the award of a divorce to a spouse by another state. Either divorce or separation could be granted for desertion, extreme cruelty, or failure of a husband to support his wife. These laws remained in force into the twentieth century.[50]

The divorce laws of 1846, recognizing additional grounds for divorce, allowed a divorced woman the right to recover all of her own real estate, except in the case of her own adultery. The court maintained the right to order the return of property "come to the husband by reason of the marriage" and to require alimony, except when a husband obtained a divorce on the grounds of his wife's adultery. Furthermore, if a husband was found guilty of adultery, was imprisoned for three or more years, or was found guilty of habitual drunkenness or misconduct, his wife was entitled to dower rights as if he were dead.[51]

Unlike the divorce laws of some states and the English common law, a husband in Michigan could not divorce his wife more easily than she could divorce him. In fact, the contrary was true; while divorces were granted both men and women in the case of adultery, a wife also could divorce her husband on the grounds of his failure to support her. Furthermore, in the early years of the century wives but not husbands were protected from cruel treatment. Thus a woman could end her marriage if her husband failed to fulfill the basic responsibilities of providing financial support and protecting his wife's physical well-being.[52]

In practice, however, rules guiding the division of property after divorce, limited employment opportunities open to women, and social attitudes towards divorced women made divorce a desirable alternative only in cases of gross mistreatment or desertion.[53] Thus while divorce laws provided some protection to the wife, social conditions made divorce so obviously disadvantageous to women that it was used only in circumstances of extreme distress. Such a course of action was usually only feasible if a woman had the financial support of her relatives. Kin therefore could make it possible for a woman to divorce her husband if they believed she was being mistreated.

In Michigan between 1887 and 1907, most divorces were granted in the third and fourth years of marriage, with the likelihood of divorce declining steadily with length of marriage. Since most divorces were preceded by at least a year of separation, the greatest number of marriages actually were dissolved during the first year or two. Only about half of all divorces involved children. Thus a woman was most likely to divorce her husband when she had no children or few children and could more easily support herself or turn to her kin for assistance.[54]

Between 1887 and 1907, only 1200 divorces out of a total of 42,000 divorces in Michigan were granted on grounds of adultery, the only grounds for divorce used more frequently by husbands than by wives. Impotence was grounds for only 25 divorces during this period, while cruelty, desertion, and neglect account for the majority of divorces, with drunkenness also a common grounds for divorce. Women were granted divorces three times as often as were men.[55] Since the most frequent grounds for divorce were cruelty, desertion, and neglect, it is likely that a large number of these divorces were attempts by women to regain the legal rights they would hold as single women. While a husband could function legally after informally ending a marriage through desertion, a woman whose marriage was thus informally ended would be forced to sue for divorce in order to gain the legal and financial autonomy to support herself and protect her wages from her absent or neglecting husband. In practical terms, then, divorce provided a woman with the means of regaining her legal rights and her ability to support herself in the event of her husband's failure to support her.

While divorces were rare, marital separations of several months' duration were common and seldom were viewed as indicative of discord. Women made extended visits to kin while men traveled on business, established new homes for their wives and children, or went west to prospect for gold. Hannah Bingham, for instance, stayed with her mother while her husband became settled in a new mission.[56] Such temporary separations often were considered by both husband and wife to be an undesirable but necessary strategy to better the financial status of the family or avoid undue hardship for wives and children.

Men commonly traveled west alone, either preceding their families to establish a home or intending to return after a period of mining or farming. Harriet Matthews wrote to her mother, Harriet Whittemore, of several women whose husbands had gone west:

> Mrs. Bacon is breaking up housekeeping and going to board at Mr. Darrows. Her husband is going to Pikes Peak again. Mr. Frear starts for the Washoe Mines in June and he is going to bring his wife out here to stay with us part of the summer. Hattie Haworth is looking for her husband every day.[57]

One woman wrote that she had hoped to live her life near her relatives but her husband "prefers the western country." She complained that he had left her "the 12th of Aug. last & for more than nine months I have lived as *a widow* with a double portion of parental care and duty devolving upon me." She lived near her relatives in her husband's absence and was preparing to travel with her sister and her sister's children to join her husband.[58] Sarah Regal lived with her brother and parents when her husband rented their farm and went to Iowa, where he intended to stay for three years, bringing his family to join him after a year.[59] Kin networks thus enabled married couples to separate temporarily without extreme hardship for the wife. This aid also allowed family groups to migrate in sections, kin providing a place to live at either end of the migration. While individual households were temporarily separated, the extended family could be reunited in the West.

The West may have served in some cases as a safety valve for marriages, giving men an opportunity to leave their families behind and travel temporarily to new territory, alone or with male friends. Henry Parker Smith, husband of the former Harriet Johnson, wrote after an argument with his wife: "If I ever feel as I have this evening

19. Florence Pomeroy (lower left) and boarders on steps of Frances Pomeroy's Ann Arbor boarding house

again I will put out & leave the whole my relatives until I have drilled myself awhile upon the western prairies."[60] Frances Pomeroy traveled for months at a time selling books with her two daughters, her sister, and her sister's two daughters. Meanwhile, her husband traveled throughout the western territories, trading books in a less systematic fashion. Frances maintained until her death that she was devoted to her husband, yet her diary reveals the ambivalence of her feelings towards him, outwardly expressing dissatisfaction at having to earn her own support, although she may unconsciously have valued her independence. She wrote:

> I often think will the time ever come that I can live as other women live—freed from cares of business and harassing debts—which I am expected to bear the burden of and liquidate if ever done I

am the one to shoulder the burden sink or swin as I can by my individual effort.[61]

Thus some married women, like most widows, were forced to deal with a world of business from which they had expected their husbands to shelter them. Frances later ran a boarding house in Ann Arbor and bought her own house in Adrian. Her two daughters wrote after her death that although the "marriage of Henry Pomeroy and Frances Mills was incompatible . . . Mr. and Mrs. Pomeroy did not call themselves separated" but instead stated that "his work kept him away from home most of the time."[62] Sometimes these separations became semipermanent; some women heard nothing from their husbands for months or even years. Maria Bingham moved with her baby to her parents' home while her husband, a ship captain, was at sea. According to her parents, Maria's husband drank heavily and wrote infrequently.[63]

Most women could expect at some time during their lives to be separated from their husbands, through mutual or unilateral choice, or to be widowed. In any of these circumstances, women turned to their kin networks for financial and emotional support. Relatives provided assistance to women at the times in their lives when they were without husbands, a necessity in a society in which women found it extremely difficult to support a family or even themselves.

Conclusion

MOST adult women in nineteenth-century America included in their definition of the family their parents and siblings as well as husband and children. The roles of sister and daughter were not exchanged for those of wife and mother; the two sets of relationships existed simultaneously in the life of a married woman.

In nineteenth-century Michigan, kinship ties among mothers, daughters, and sisters were lifelong, continuing in spite of differences in education, social class, and wealth, differences marriage often made pronounced. Women visited and corresponded regularly in spite of geographic separation. Distance altered but failed to diminish ties among female kin. The lifelong responsibilities of mothers, daughters, and sisters remained unchanged. As Nancy Cott and Carroll Smith-Rosenberg have described, women in New England experienced similar bonds among sisters as well as among mothers and daughters.[1] And nineteenth-century female authors defined home, in the words of Nina Baym that we have already noted, as "not a space but a system of human relations."[2] They were relationships that reached beyond the limits of the nuclear family, networks of women that formed the backbone of the family in the nineteenth century. When women defined their place in society as the home and family, they referred not to the confines of the house or even to the household but also to networks of female kin.

Men and women perceived the world outside the family as threatening, a "land of strangers," offering only the "cold charities of a selfish world." No single household could guard against the possibility of death, illness, geographic separation, financial disaster. Indeed, in a society in which almost 20% of all children lost a parent before they reached the age of fifteen, in which almost 60% of women over 65 were widows, women and children constantly faced the possibility of losing what limited shelter even the most secure of nuclear families could offer.[3] Regardless of the affection a woman might feel toward her husband, she was forced to turn to relatives outside the household for long-term security for her children and herself.

While it is sometimes tempting to view these family networks with nostalgia, it is important to recognize the fear which sent women to their kin for assistance, the common sense of helplessness, the pervasive anxiety about the future. Kin networks are viable only as long as they maintain sufficient resources to share. While the networks examined here could cope with the isolated disasters that befell individual family members, what of economically marginal families who had no such resources to spare? What of those who left their kin behind to travel to a new continent? What of those who outlived the other members of their families? One study suggests that orphaned children and mothers without husbands were forced, in the absence of assistance from relatives, to turn to the poorhouse for sustenance.[4] Reliance on relatives was not merely desirable, it was often essential for survival.

In Michigan, as in many other states, married women did gain some legal autonomy during the nineteenth century, including the ability to control inherited property and to divorce their husbands for mistreatment. Women's letters and diaries indicate that they used their persuasive abilities as well as their legal rights to influence the behavior of their husbands. Yet while married women could often persuade successfully, while they could often garner assistance in an emergency, they remained essentially without power as individuals. The ability to persuade is a poor substitute for the authority to decide. It was, of course, the difficulty women experienced in supporting their families alone that made the aid of relatives so necessary. By joining with their female kin, women could create a tenuous web of security and to a very limited extent expand their autonomy in a society which left them essentially powerless.

In devoting herself to domestic duties, a woman was not subjecting herself to the total dominance of a husband, for the demands of parents and siblings could be balanced against those of husband and children, giving a woman, if not the right to assert her own needs and desires, at least some choice as to the priority of the demands others made on her time. Furthermore, the emotional and financial support a woman received from her kin enabled her to assert her independence from her husband. Kin provided a woman with an alternative source of support and could bring collective pressure to bear against a recalcitrant husband.

Paradoxically, it was only through affiliation with others that women were able to maintain a limited degree of autonomy within a marriage. For the woman, of course, these simultaneous relationships brought stress as well. Women sometimes felt torn by the conflicting needs of kin, forced to deny assistance to some, subject to guilt over their inability to serve all. And women's own needs and desires could be fulfilled, or even expressed, only covertly, under the guise of serving others.

Women viewed marriage as an institution distinct from the family, although marriages of course formed part of the family. Since the home and family were defined by prescriptive literature as the woman's domain, it is not surprising to find women perceiving the family as essentially female, composed primarily of women performing domestic duties. Thus while an increasing number of women during the nineteenth century, as Carl Degler notes, did reject marriage, often choosing instead to form households with other women,[5] this rejection of marriage was not by any means a rejection of the family. Female households were accepted into female kin networks and even served, in some cases, as units of child-rearing. Marriage constituted only a part, in fact a relatively unstable part, of the nineteenth-century family.

The domestic duties of a woman included not only rearing and educating her children, caring for her house, feeding and clothing her husband and children, and protecting the health of those in the household; she also cared for nieces, nephews, and grandchildren, nursed ill relatives, provided care for elderly kin, and exchanged goods and money with other households. Thus networks of female kin formed stable units in which to rear children, care for the ill and elderly, and provide emergency assistance to those temporarily unable to support themselves. Indeed, networks of female kin made possible the subsistence of separate nuclear families in a society which included neither extended patriarchal families nor governmental assistance to absorb the financial and emotional vicissitudes experienced by individual households.

Networks of female kin were thus compatible with marriage. Unless a husband was overtly cruel or neglectful, women supported one another in their roles as wives and mothers, providing assistance with domestic tasks, substituting for one another in case of illness or absence. Indeed, men knew that they might some day need to depend on their wife's female kin for child-rearing, care in illness, or financial aid. Hostility to the wife's kin was, in fact, seldom expressed. A woman's responsibilities as sister and daughter were accepted as an integral part of her domestic role, compatible with her responsibilities as wife and mother. Indeed, kin networks structured nineteenth-century families, providing a stability the nuclear family could not otherwise guarantee.

In spite of differences in wealth and social status, as well as geographic separation, female kin maintained lifelong bonds of obligation as well as emotion. Using correspondence and visits to maintain ties with distant relatives, women ensured support for themselves and their children in time of need. Sharing similar domestic roles as wives, mothers, sisters, and daughters, women exchanged with one another the services these roles entailed. Child-rearing, care of the ill and elderly, emergency financial assistance all occurred within the network of female kin. In nineteenth-century Michigan, the family was indeed the domain of women.

APPENDIX A

Demographic Analysis of Sample

THOSE households which appear in either the 1850 or 1880 census records can be compared to the sample included in a study of household composition in southern Michigan undertaken by Susan Bloomberg and others. The data for the Bloomberg study were drawn in clusters from rural, urban, and town/village locations, but the study does not control for ethnicity. Although the Bloomberg study is limited to the southern third of Michigan's Lower Peninsula, this region included 98.3% of the state's population in 1850 and 85.1% in 1880. A comparative analysis thus can place the group of families examined in this study of Michigan family letters in the context of virtually the total population of the state.[1]

To ensure that the specific families examined in this study are compared as closely as possible with the broader data presented by Bloomberg, the discussion in this appendix is limited to those households listed in either the 1850 or the 1880 Michigan manuscript census. Of the family units examined in this study, 25 households are listed in either the 1850 or the 1880 Michigan manuscript census. Thirteen of these households appear in the 1850 census and 12 in the 1880 census, representing eight different family groups in 1850 and nine in 1880. Four families appear in both the 1850 census and the 1880 census, although not the same households under the same household heads.[2]

With the exception of one household in the Upper Peninsula in 1850 and two related households in the northern portion of the Lower Peninsula in 1880, all the households examined here were living in the southern third of Michigan, the area included in the Bloomberg study. Bloomberg attempts to separate those who lived on farms from those who lived in towns and villages. The 1850 sample examined here follows closely the distribution of households in southern Michigan according to urban-rural location. While this delineation is subject to some errors, the 13 households included in this study were located as follows: two households (15.4%) were in Detroit, eight (61.5%) were rural, and three (23.1%) were living in towns and villages. The Bloomberg study found 62.2% of southern Michigan households in rural locations, a very close parallel. By 1880 the families examined in this study represent a disproportionate number of non-rural residents. While Bloomberg found 53.7% of the population of southern Michigan in non-rural locations, ten of the twelve households examined here (83.3%) were non-rural. Only two households (16.6%) were rural, compared to 46.3% of Bloomberg's sample.[3]

Excluding households headed by widows, in the present study slightly more than half of the heads of household examined for the year 1850 were farmers. Of the non-farmers, three were professionals (two ministers and one lawyer), making up 60% of the non-farm sample, and two were merchants. A disproportionate number of household heads were professionals. Bloomberg found only 20.8% of the southern Michigan village and town household heads in professions, along with 6.2% of Detroit household heads, a considerably smaller percentage of the population than found among the families studied here. The present sample also includes a higher than average percentage of proprietors, managers, and government officials, 40.0% among non-farm occupations, compared to 6.3% of the southern Michigan village and town population and 18.5% of Detroit's population as examined by Bloomberg. The present sample of Michigan non-farm households includes no skilled laborers, although this group comprised a large proportion of Bloomberg's sample: 39.6% in southern Michigan villages and towns and 37.1% in Detroit. Clerical and sales workers comprised less than 5% of Bloomberg's overall sample, as did unskilled, semi-skilled, and service workers in villages and towns in southern Michigan, although the latter category of laborer included 32.2% of the Detroit household heads. These occupational groups are unrepresented in the present study. The families examined here thus include, for 1850, a much larger percentage of household heads who were professionals, proprietors, or managers than was the average for the southern Michigan families examined by Bloomberg. (See Table 1.)

In 1880, again excluding households headed by widows, only two of the ten household heads in the present study were farmers. Of the remaining eight families, five household heads (more than 71% of the non-farm sample) were professionals (two attorneys, two judges, and a college professor), one was a merchant, one was a miller, and one was a surveyor. The Bloomberg study found only 5% of village and town household heads and 1% of those in Detroit in professions in 1880, a notably smaller percentage than in the sample examined here. While the percentage of proprietors and managers in this study (25%) was only slightly higher than Bloomberg's average, the sample here includes only one laborer or tradesman, groups which comprise more than half of the Bloomberg sample. (See Table 1.)

TABLE 1

Percentage Distribution of Occupations of Non-Farming Household Heads, Michigan, 1850 and 1880

Occupation	Southern Michigan Census Sample		Family Document Sample
	Town/Village	Detroit	
	1850		N = 5
Unskilled, semi-skilled, service workers	4.2	32.3	0
All other skilled workers	39.6	37.1	0
Clerical and sales workers	2.1	3.1	0
Proprietors, managers, government officials	6.3	18.5	40.0
Professionals	20.8	6.2	60.0
Other	27.0	2.8	0
Total	100.0	100.0	100.0
	1880		N = 8
Unskilled, semi-skilled, service workers	32.4	32.4	0
All other skilled workers	24.6	25.5	12.5
Clerical and sales workers	5.0	6.9	0
Proprietors, managers, government officials	13.1	20.6	25.0
Professionals	5.0	1.0	62.5
Other	19.9	13.6	0
Total	100.0	100.0	100.0

NOTE: The town/village and Detroit statistics are from Bloomberg et al., p. 41. No sample size is given.

These differences in distribution of occupation can be attributed to two factors. First, this study is limited to white, native-born Americans, who would account for a disproportionate percentage of the professional population and a relatively small percentage of laborers. In this respect, the families examined here may be representative of their ethnic group, although not of the population as a whole. Second, the professions over-represented in this study, those of minister, attorney, and teacher, are verbally oriented and therefore likely to value and preserve, and possibly also to produce, correspondence.

Although Bloomberg does not provide data on average real property ownership in southern Michigan and information on property ownership was not included in the 1880 census, a general idea of the wealth in real estate of the families examined in 1850 can be determined. Of the six farm families examined here, one household head possessed less than $1000 in real estate and was probably a tenant, while the other five household heads owned moderate land holdings ranging from $2000 to $4000 in value. Of the seven non-farm households examined, two were headed by ministers who owned no real estate.[4] Two household heads, one a widow, owned between $100 and $500 of real estate, while another widow owned $3000 of real property. The other two household heads were prosperous merchants owning $8000 and $9000 of real property.[5] The families studied here thus represent a wide economic range, including five households with less than $1000 of real estate, six with $2000 to $4000, and two with at least $8000.[6] (See Table 2.)

For the census year 1850, the average size of the households examined here was 5.5, identical to the average Michigan household size as determined by the Census Bureau (See Table 3.) Of the 13

TABLE 2
Household Distribution of Wealth in Real Estate Among Sample from Family Documents, Michigan, 1850

Occupation of Household Head	Value of Real Estate (in thousands)										
	<$1	$1	$2	$3	$4	$5	$6	$7	$8	$9	$10+
Farm	1	0	1	2	2	0	0	0	0	0	0
Non-farm	3	0	0	0	0	0	0	0	1	1	0
Widow	1	0	0	1	0	0	0	0	0	0	0
Total	5	0	1	3	2	0	0	0	1	1	0

households studied here for the year 1850, six had fewer than five members while seven had more than five members. In 1880, according to the Census Bureau, the average size of the Michigan household had fallen to 4.9. The 12 households examined here then had an average size of 5.6, higher than that of the population as a whole. The distribution of household size among the families examined reveals that this figure represents not a large number of slightly larger families but rather the effects of a few unusually large households. (See Table 4.) Of the households examined, two were composed of five members, six consisted of fewer than five members, and four had more than five members. The households examined included slightly fewer than the average number of children in 1850 and slightly more than the average in 1880. In both census years, the households cluster closely around the average number of children per household found by Bloomberg. (See Table 5.)

The 1850 census did not list the relationship of those living in the household to the household head. Therefore, statistics on the number of kin other than minor children and on the numbers of

TABLE 3

Average Household Size, Michigan, 1850 and 1880

Region	1850	1880
United States	5.6	5.0
Michigan	5.5	4.9
Southern Michigan Census Sample		
Rural	5.4	4.8
Village/Town	5.0	4.4
Detroit	5.2	5.0
Michigan Family Correspondence Sample	5.5	5.6

NOTE: Southern Michigan figures are from Bloomberg et al., p. 30. Data on United States and Michigan is from the *U.S. Eleventh Census: 1890: Population,* I, Part one, clxxcii, pp. 914, 938, cited by Bloomberg et al., p. 30.

TABLE 4

Distribution of Household Size among Sample from Family Documents, Michigan, 1850 and 1880

Census Year	Number in Household 1	2	3	4	5	6	7	8	9	10	11	12+	Total Households
1850	0	1	2	3	0	1	3	3	0	0	0	0	13
1880	0	0	2	4	2	0	1	1	1	0	1	0	12

boarders and servants in the average household are unavailable. For the families studied here, however, information on family genealogy establishes that none of the households included a parent of the head of household or of his wife. Seven of the 13 households included adults who were either boarders or servants, although it is impossible to determine which of the two they were. Each of the households including boarders or servants contained either two or three such individuals, some of whom were related to household members. The average number of children in the 13 households studied is slightly smaller than the average found by Bloomberg (see Table 5), while the total household size is equal to the average for the state and larger than the average household size of the Bloomberg sample. (See Table 3.) We can assume, therefore, that the households represented in this study included a slightly larger than average aggregate number of boarders and servants, although it is impossible to determine how close to average the number of households may have been that included at least one boarder or servant.[7]

For 1880, statistics on the average number of southern Michigan households including a parent of the household head or of his spouse, a boarder, or a servant are presented by Bloomberg. The small number of households with a parent of a household head or of his spouse in the sample examined here is well within the range of the Bloomberg

TABLE 5
Average Number of Children per Household, Michigan, 1850 and 1880

Census Year	Southern Michigan Census Sample			Family Documents Sample
	Rural	Village/Town	Detroit	
1850	3.1	2.4	2.5	2.2
1880	2.3	2.0	2.4	3.1

NOTE: Southern Michigan figures are from Bloomberg et al., p. 33. No sample size is given.

TABLE 6
Distribution of Number of Children per Household Among Family Documents Sample, Michigan, 1850 and 1880

Census Year	Number of Children per Household											Total Households
	0	1	2	3	4	5	6	7	8	9	10+	
1850	2	2	3	3	3	0	0	0	0	0	0	13
1880	0	3	4	1	1	2	0	0	0	1	0	12

data. (See Table 7.) Of the 12 households studied, one (8.3%) included a parent of the household head, compared to the Bloomberg findings of 6.6% in Detroit, 9.0% in villages and towns, and 7.1% in rural areas. One of the 12 households (8.3%) included a boarder, compared to Bloomberg's statistics of 15.7% in Detroit, 8.5% in villages and towns, and 5.7% in rural areas. The percentage of families with servants in the present study is larger than the Bloomberg average, however. One third of the 12 households examined here included at least one servant, and three of these four households included two servants each. The Bloomberg study found servants in only 11.8% of Detroit households, 9.3% of village and town households, and 15.7% of rural households. This disparity accounts in part for the larger average size of the 12 households examined (see Table 3), although the households included a larger than average number of children as well (see Table 5). These figures may indicate that the sample includes a greater than average number of families able to afford servants and choosing to hire them, although most of the families studied do not fall into this category. This assessment correlates with the larger than average number of professionals and the relatively few laborers in 1880 among the group examined here. (See Table 1.)

The boarders in the Bloomberg study include kin of household members. It is impossible to determine from census data alone which boarders were related to other household members, since relatives may have been, and were in the instances examined here, listed as "boarder" rather than as "sister-in-law" or by other kinship term. Census data used in combination with genealogical information reveals that of the 13 households studied for the year 1850, four included kin of the household head or his wife other than their children. One

TABLE 7
Percentage of Households with Parents of the Household Head or of Spouse, Boarders, or Servants, Michigan, 1880

| Household Member | Southern Michigan Census Sample | | | Family Documents Sample (N = 12) |
	Rural (N = 401)	Village/Town (N = 365)	Detroit (N = 102)	
Parent	7.1	9.0	6.6	8.3
Boarder	5.7	8.5	15.7	8.3
Servant	15.7	9.3	11.8	33.3

NOTE: Southern Michigan figures are from Bloomberg et al., p. 34.

included the husband's brother, another the husband's widowed brother and his two young children, another the wife's sister's son (a young physician who was simultaneously listed as a member of his parents' household), and the fourth a 14-year-old female relative of the wife of the household head. Another household included a married daughter. In 1880, one of the households examined included the widowed mother of the male household head and another included the unmarried sister of a widowed female household head.

The percentage distribution of age of household head in both 1850 and 1880 is similar to that found in the Bloomberg study. For 1880 the distribution is close; for 1850 the sample includes a larger percentage of household heads older than 45 and fewer of age 35 to 44 than was found by Bloomberg. (See Table 8.)

TABLE 8
Percentage Distribution of Age of Household Head, Michigan, 1850 and 1880

Age Group	Southern Michigan Census Sample			Family Documents Sample
	Rural	Village/Town	Detroit	
		1850		(N = 13)
15–24	4.0	1.6	8.5	0
25–34	25.2	32.1	27.3	30.8
35–44	37.0	26.4	38.5	15.4
45–54	17.8	22.6	21.4	30.8
55–64	8.4	12.1	2.8	15.4
65+	—	5.7	1.4	7.7
Total	92.4	100.5	99.9	100.1
		1880		(N = 12)
15–24	3.2	4.1	7.8	0
25–34	21.9	21.9	20.7	25.0
35–44	22.2	26.4	21.7	25.0
45–54	24.4	24.9	30.4	33.0
55–64	18.5	14.6	12.9	17.0
65+	9.7	8.0	7.0	0
Total	99.9	99.9	100.5	100.0

NOTE: Figures for southern Michigan are derived from Bloomberg, p. 35. The missing figure cannot be supplied due to missing data in the article. No sample size is given. No explanation is provided for discrepancy in totals. Total of 100.1 for family documents sample is due to rounding.

Although the Bloomberg study did not examine the range of age differences between husband and wife, such figures can be derived for the sample group, using genealogical information to determine which women were the wives of household heads in 1850. In 1850, three of the 13 household heads were unmarried, including one widow, one widower, and one mother of five children who had never married. One head of household was married to a woman 24 years his junior. The remaining nine households were approximately evenly divided between those in which the head of household was married to a woman less than five years younger than himself and those in which the age difference was five to nine years. (See Table 9.)

The families examined in 1880 reveal a larger age difference between husband and wife. Of the nine households in which the household head was married, none had less than a five-year age difference between husband and wife. Two thirds of the men were married to a woman five to nine years their junior, one man to a woman 10 to 14 years younger, and two men to women 15 to 24 years younger than themselves. This difference over three decades in the relative age of husband and wife cannot be attributed to a change in the ages of the household heads, since the 1880 household heads show a similar age distribution to those of 1850. However, the Bloomberg study reveals an increase between 1850 and 1880 in the percentage of household heads over 44 years of age, suggesting a demographic climate with a shortage of young marriageable men, a

TABLE 9

Distribution of Age Differences Between Household Head and Spouse among Family Documents Sample, Michigan, 1850 and 1880

Age Difference in Years	Number of Households	
	1850	1880
<5	5	0
5–9	4	6
10–14	0	1
15–19	0	1
20–24	1	1
25+	0	0
Total	10	9

NOTE: In all the households examined, the husband was the same age as or older than his wife. The sample of households examined also included three households in each census year headed by unmarried persons.

situation which could create a pattern of greater age difference in marriage than was usual in 1850. (See Table 9.)

The households examined here include a large percentage with oldest children age six to 10 in 1850 and under six in 1880, and a small percentage with oldest children age 15 to 20. The percentage of households with oldest children over 21 years of age was 27.3% in 1850 and 25% in 1880, slightly higher than the Bloomberg figures for 1850, slightly lower than those for 1880.

In the 1850 sample, among households whose head was between the ages of 15 and 44, none had more than a 9-year age range among their children, and none of the families with household heads older than 44 years of age had an age range of 15 years or more among their children, a smaller range of ages than was found among the

TABLE 10
Percentage Distribution of Age of Oldest Child in Household, Michigan, 1850 and 1880

Age of Oldest Child	Southern Michigan Census Sample			Family Documents Sample
	Rural	Village/Town	Detroit	
	1850			
	(N = 176)	(N = 47)	(N = 56)	(N = 11)
<6	12.0	21.3	26.9	9.1
6–10	15.8	17.0	21.4	36.4
11–14	26.2	21.3	19.6	18.2
15–20	26.1	14.9	23.2	9.1
21+	19.9	25.5	8.9	27.3
Total	100.0	100.0	100.0	100.1
	1880			
	(N = 324)	(N = 280)	(N = 85)	(N = 12)
<6	15.7	15.4	20.0	41.7
6–10	15.7	15.0	20.0	8.3
11–14	18.8	18.6	17.6	16.7
15–20	20.5	23.6	12.9	8.3
21+	29.9	27.4	29.5	25.0
Total	100.8	100.0	100.0	100.0

NOTE: Figures for southern Michigan are derived from Bloomberg et al., p. 37. Bloomberg's figures include only households in which a spouse of the household head is present (which is not possible to determine with certainty for the 1850 census). Rural 1880 total of 100.8% is due to apparent error in Bloomberg's figures. (Total for children of household head age 15–44 equals 111.7% in Bloomberg's table.) Total of 100.1% for family documents sample is due to rounding.

TABLE 11
Percentage Distribution of Age Differences between Youngest and Oldest Child, Michigan,
1850 and 1880

Age Difference	Southern Michigan Census Sample			Family Documents Sample
	Rural	Village/Town	Detroit	
	1850			
	Household Head Aged 15-44			
	(N = 93)	(N = 21)	(N = 29)	(N = 4)
<5	37.6	42.8	48.3	50.0
5-9	30.1	28.6	24.1	50.0
10-14	23.7	28.6	24.1	0
15-19	5.4	0	0	0
20+	3.2	0	3.5	0
Total	100.0	100.0	100.0	100.0
	Household Head Aged 45-65			
	(N = 52)	(N = 13)	(N = 11)	(N = 6)
<5	28.9	7.7	9.1	0
5-9	19.2	15.4	27.3	66.7
10-14	25.0	23.1	54.5	33.3
15-19	19.2	46.1	9.1	0
20+	7.7	7.7	0	0
Total	100.0	100.0	100.0	100.0
	1880			
	Household Head Aged 15-44			
	(N = 117)	(N = 108)	(N = 25)	(N = 4)
<5	41.0	39.8	48.0	75.0
5-9	41.0	37.1	40.0	25.0
10-14	17.1	19.4	12.0	0
15-19	0.9	3.7	0	0
20+	0	0	0	0
Total	100.0	100.0	100.0	100.0
	Household Head Aged 45-65			
	(N = 117)	(N = 87)	(N = 33)	(N = 5)
<5	28.2	18.4	21.2	20.0
5-9	24.8	31.0	39.4	0
10-14	27.4	32.2	30.3	20.0
15-19	13.7	17.2	6.1	60.0
20+	6.0	0.2	3.0	0
Total	100.1	99.0	100.0	100.0

NOTE: Southern Michigan figures are from Bloomberg et al., p. 38. No explanation is given for discrepancy in totals for age 45-65 rural and village/town 1880 figures.

families examined by Bloomberg. The same small age range is found in the sample group for the year 1880 among those households whose head was under 45 years of age. Among households with heads over 45, however, a larger percentage than average had a 15-to-19-year age range among their children.[8] (See Table 11.)

The families examined in this study are representative of the total population of the state in family size and age of household head. Furthermore, the sample is characterized by a wide range of wealth in real estate. Yet the percentage of household heads who were members of professional occupations is considerably greater than for the population as a whole, while relatively few household heads were skilled or unskilled laborers. The sample also includes a larger than average number of servants. While diverging from the average for the population of Michigan in these factors, the families in this study may still be representative of the white, Protestant, native-born population of the state.

APPENDIX B

History of Michigan to 1920

ALTHOUGH Michigan was not open to agricultural settlement until the 1820s, the history of European exploration of the region dates back to the early seventeenth century, when French explorers from the Quebec region of Canada traveled up the St. Lawrence River and across the Great Lakes to Michigan. Fur traders and French Catholic missionaries to the Native Americans soon followed. The fur traders dispersed into the wilderness while the priests established missions at Sault Ste. Marie and St. Ignace, in what is now Michigan's Upper Peninsula, and at Niles, on the shore of Lake Michigan. Detroit was founded in 1701, primarily as a military outpost guarding access to the Great Lakes. In the early years of the eighteenth century, about a thousand French Canadian men, women, and children farmed in Detroit in an essentially feudal pattern under the control of a "seigneur" who held title to the land.[1]

Although the British army assumed control of Detroit in 1760, the settlement remained predominantly French Canadian. The Proclamation of 1763 established the region that is now Michigan as part of a territory to be inhabited only by Native Americans, with settlement by colonists forbidden. The proclamation failed to stipulate, however, what was to be done with settlements already in existence. In the absence of other provisions for its government, Detroit remained under military rule, governed in accordance with French Canadian law. Detroit remained *de facto* in the hands of the British after the Revolutionary War, with settlement outside the city still forbidden. Popular government was instituted in 1788 and four years later British law replaced the laws of French Canada. In 1796 the Americans finally assumed control of Detroit under the terms of Jay's Treaty and in 1805 Michigan was established as a separate territory.

At this time the only towns outside Detroit were the old frontier outposts of Sault Ste. Marie and Mackinac in the Upper Peninsula and Monroe, a town south of Detroit. Although most of the Native American population had been forced westward, the land of the Michigan territory was still largely under their ownership. The only white settlers of the interior were squatters with no legal claims to their land. In 1807 Native Americans ceded to the government the quarter of the Lower Peninsula to the north, south, and west of Detroit. This land, however, was not surveyed and ready for public sale until 1818.

The War of 1812 interrupted the development of the region. When Detroit was occupied by the British for a year, the loyalties of the citizens, who had been under American rule for only sixteen years, were sharply divided. After the Americans recaptured Detroit in 1813, many residents joined those who had moved across the river to the section of the settlement which had become the Canadian city of Windsor when the Americans first took control of Detroit in 1796. By 1814, with the region still under military rule and suffering from famine, some military officials considered abandoning the area as unfit for human habitation. A report on the feasibility of agricultural settlement in 1815 described Michigan as an immense and impassable swamp, further discouraging settlement.[2]

In addition to these political, geographic, and climatic disadvantages, Michigan was difficult to reach from both the east and the south. The western region of the state had no roads, and the section of Ohio to the south of Detroit and along the southern shore of Lake Erie was a huge swamp, slow and hazardous to cross. Approach to Detroit by water was the only feasible route, but transportation to the embarkation point at Buffalo was itself arduous and the trip across Lake Erie slow and uncomfortable as well as expensive. The difficulty of transportation not only discouraged settlers from reaching Michigan but also raised the cost of all consumer goods brought into the settlement, making the export of all but very valuable products such as furs unprofitable. Even as late as 1817 goods shipped from New York City were carried by wagon caravan to Buffalo, a journey of four to six weeks, before being sent by packet across Lake Erie to Detroit.[3]

In 1818 the steamship "Walk-in-the-Water" made its first trip from Buffalo to Detroit, completing what had been a 10-day trip in two or three days, and in 1819 the route was extended north to Mackinac.[4] The completion of the Erie Canal in 1825 simplified the trip from New England to Buffalo, making travel to Michigan quicker and more comfortable. Now the journey to Michigan was feasible for families.

Cessions by Native Americans in 1819 and 1812 opened to settlement the lower half of Michigan, an area comprising the major agricultural portion of the state in the late nineteenth century.[5] Families from New York and New England traveled to the territory in large numbers, most settling in the frontier regions of southern Michigan. By the 1820s several roads were completed from Detroit into the interior of the state.[6] Although these were unfinished trails, barely cleared of tree stumps, they provided the first access into the wilderness. The early settlers found that while the region immediately surrounding Detroit was swampy, the land farther west was excellent for farming. Some of the land consisted of broad expanses of grass-covered prairie requiring little labor to cultivate, while other desirable regions, known as "oak openings," were only sparsely covered by trees. The population of the territory increased from 9000 people in 1820 to 17,000 in 1827, and 32,000 in 1830.[7]

The large amounts of land suddenly made available, the advent of rapid and convenient transportation to Michigan, and the discovery that the land of Michigan was, contrary to earlier reports, excellent for agriculture, led to a deluge of settlers in the 1830s, especially after the end of the Black Hawk War and the cholera epidemic that had marked the first half of the decade. One contemporary account reports that 2000 settlers per day disembarked in Detroit in 1836.[8] While this perhaps was an exaggeration, the population of Michigan did increase almost 600% during the decade, reaching 212,000 in 1840. Most of this increase in population was concentrated in the agricultural regions of Michigan, although the population of Detroit rose from 1400 in 1820 to 2200 in 1830, and 9000 in 1840.[9] Most settlers came in family groups to farm the newly available land.

The rapid increase in population that Michigan experienced in the 1830s led to the improvement of transportation within the territory, a factor which in turn encouraged further immigration. In 1834 six roads led from Detroit into the interior, one crossing the state to Chicago. By the end of the decade, these roads were served by daily stagecoaches from Detroit to Toledo, Chicago, St. Joseph,

Flint, and Fort Gratiot.[10] By 1840 rails reached west to Ann Arbor and Adrian and then south to Toledo. The railroad from Albany to Buffalo, completed in 1842, further facilitated the transport of goods as well as settlers to Michigan.[11]

Although Michigan grew rapidly during the 1830s, it was still a frontier territory. Travel was tedious and access to markets difficult. A round trip from Ann Arbor to Detroit by way of Plymouth, a distance of seventy miles, required a week.[12] Throughout the decade, poor roads made access to markets difficult and limited the importation of goods into the back country. Poor drainage led to the malaria which plagued Michigan's settlers in the 1830s. Families living on Michigan's frontier were isolated from their kin in eastern states, with mail service slow and infrequent and transportation difficult.[13] Indeed, poor roads and harsh winters isolated families from even their closest neighbors.

By the time Michigan was admitted to statehood in 1837, most of the land which was accessible and available for sale had been distributed and the rapid rate of migration was beginning to decline. By the 1840s Michigan could no longer be characterized as a frontier. Railroads and roads connected most settlements to the city of Detroit, which had developed from a frontier outpost to a small city with industrial and cultural activities. Settled towns developed throughout the lower third of the state, breaking the isolation suffered by farmers in the previous decade. The University of Michigan's Ann Arbor campus was founded in 1837 and soon a state agricultural college, a normal school, and several academies were in operation in Michigan.

Advances in transportation provided access to New York and New England as well as to the cities and towns of Michigan. In 1852 a railroad from Detroit to Chicago was completed. The improvement in roads and rails during the middle years of the century made access to agricultural markets more feasible for farmers, encouraging a shift from subsistence to market agriculture. The availability of consumer goods from the East was increased by the completion of a railroad through Canada to Niagara Falls in 1854, Buffalo having been linked to New York City in 1842, providing the first year-round access to New England and New York for both commercial trade and travelers. By 1857 steamers ran three times a day from Detroit to Buffalo in only 15 hours,[14] enabling families in Michigan to visit conveniently their relatives in the East and to exchange household goods. Improvements in postal service made correspondence rapid and dependable.

The 1860s and 1870s were years of industrial growth for the state, the number of manufacturing concerns tripling between 1860 and 1870. Manufacturing establishments were located in small cities such as Grand Rapids, as well as in Detroit.[15] By the 1860s Detroit was a major city, its population increasing from 9000 in 1840 to 46,000 in 1860.[16] Now the city was served by systems of waterworks and street lights while many houses had such amenities as bathtubs, sewing machines, and ice boxes.[17] By this time the small towns of Michigan were similar to towns in Midwestern states settled decades earlier.

Under the Homestead Act of 1862, land in the upper half of the Lower Peninsula was made available for agriculture, although most farming was concentrated in the southern portion of the state.[18] By 1880 Michigan boasted the highest yield of wheat per acre of any state in the nation and was also important for fruit growing and sheep raising. By the end of the century, however, the opening of the western prairies provided competition for Michigan's wheat, cattle, and sheep. While it was argued that Michigan's proximity to New England would keep the transportation costs of its farm products lower, its farmers were unable to cultivate the larger expanses of land available to farmers in the prairie states. Many farmers turned to dairy farming, while others diversified into crops such as mint and celery that were suited to Michigan's marshy terrain.[19] By the early years of the twentieth century, Michigan's farmers had ready access to markets, with the mileage of rails in the state increasing from 350 miles in 1850 to 9000 miles in 1918.[20]

The institution of rural free delivery of mail in the last decade of the nineteenth century further lessened the isolation of the farm family. The first rural free delivery route was begun in 1896, and by 1920, 1800 rural free delivery routes were in existence, providing convenient access to newspapers and mail order catalogs as well as rapid and secure delivery of personal letters. In 1910 parcel post was instituted, replacing the nineteenth-century method of transporting packages by boat or rail or in the hands of travelers.[21]

Although telephones were in use in Detroit business establishments as early as 1870, only by the early years of the twentieth century were they found in small towns and on farms. By 1920, however, half of the farms in Michigan were served by telephone. And in 1920 the first commercial radio broadcast in the state began. By this time the automobile was widely used by farmers. The 200,000 farms then in the state accounted for the ownership of 80,000 automobiles and the same number of trucks.[22]

In spite of these rapid gains in communication and transportation, however, work on the farm was not yet mechanized. In 1920 less than 3% of all farmers owned tractors and only about 8% of all farms were served by either gas or electric power.[23] Electric light, gas stoves and furnaces, and electrically-powered home appliances were still unavailable to the farm family, and the daily work of women on the farm remained basically unchanged from the middle years of the nineteenth century.

In Detroit, the industrial developments occurring in the early years of the twentieth century altered drastically the development not only of Michigan but of the country as a whole. Automobiles were produced in Detroit before the turn of the century and by 1915 Henry Ford had instituted an assembly line producing a million automobiles a year.[24] As other industries grew to feed the automobile factories, Detroit rapidly became a major industrial city. By 1920 the population of Detroit was five times larger than it had been just 30 years earlier, numbering nearly a million inhabitants. In 1890, 35% of the state's population was found in towns and cities, with 65% living on farms and in villages. By 1920 these figures were nearly reversed: 61% of the population now found in towns and cities, 39% in villages and on farms.[25]

Between 1820 and 1920 Michigan developed from an almost inaccessible frontier territory into a state that included a major industrial city as well as farms and small towns. The rapid settlement of the state and the subsequent development of transportation and communication networks enabled the residents of Michigan to maintain contact with relatives living in the Far West as well as those in the East.

Notes

INTRODUCTION

1. Vital Statistics Folder, Taylor Family Collection, Michigan Historical Collections, Bentley Historical Library, University of Michigan (hereafter MHC). All quotations are in original spelling, without notation of errors.

2. Nina Baym, *Woman's Fiction: A Guide to Novels by and about Women in America, 1820-1870* (Ithaca, N.Y.: Cornell University Press, 1978), p. 49.

3. Christopher Lasch, *Haven in a Heartless World: The Family Besieged* (New York: Basic Books, 1977).

4. Catharine E. Beecher and Harriet Beecher Stowe, *The American Woman's Home* (1869; reprint, Hartford, Conn.: Stowe-Day Foundation, 1975).

5. Harriet Beecher Stowe [Christopher Crowfield], *House and Home Papers* (Boston: Ticknor and Fields, 1865), p. 77.

6. Genevieve, "Woman's Duties," *Godey's Ladies Book*, February 1873, p. 166.

7. Carl Degler, *At Odds: Women and the Family in America from the Revolution to the Present* (New York: Oxford University Press, 1980); see especially pp. vi-vii and 3-9.

8. Degler, pp. 109-110.

9. Elizabeth B. Bott, *Family and Social Network: Roles, Norms, and External Relationships in Ordinary Urban Families* (London: Tavistock, 1957); Eugene Litwack, "Geographic Mobility and Extended Family Cohesion," *American Sociological Review*, 25 (1960), pp. 385-394; Paul J. Reiss, "The Extended Kinship System: Correlatives of and Attitudes on Frequency of Interaction," *Marriage and Family Living*, 24 (1962), pp. 333-339; Lee N. Robins and Miroda Tomanec, "Closeness to Blood Relatives outside the Immediate Family," *Marriage and Family Living*, 24 (1962), pp. 340-346.

10. Tamara K. Hareven, "Family Time and Historical Time," *Daedalus*, 106 (1977), pp. 63–66.

11. Nancy F. Cott, *The Bonds of Womanhood: 'Woman's Sphere' in New England, 1780-1835* (New Haven, Conn.: Yale University Press, 1977), pp. 176–177; Carroll Smith-Rosenberg, "The Female World of Love and Ritual: Relations between Women in Nineteenth-Century America," *Signs*, 1 (1975), pp. 1–29.

12. Carol B. Stack, *All Our Kin: Strategies for Survival in a Black Community* (New York: Harper and Row, 1974).

13. In 1850, over 87% of all white women in the United States over 30 years of age could read and write. One study of Northern farm families found that 88% of the wives could read and write in 1860. In 1870, only 11.5% of the white population was illiterate, a percentage that dropped steadily to 4% in 1920. Rates of literacy in Michigan were even higher. In 1880 only 4.8% of white persons in Michigan over nine years of age were illiterate. By 1890 the figure was 5.92%. Between 1900 and 1920, the percentage of adult females who were illiterate ranged from 5.4% to 3.8%. For native-born white women with native-born parents the illiteracy rate was less than 2% during this time period. Degler, p. 308. R.A. Easterlin, G. Alters and G.A. Condran, "Farms and Farm Families in Old and New Areas: The Northern States in 1860," in *Family and Population in Nineteenth-Century America*, ed. Tamara K. Hareven and Maris A. Vinovskis (Princeton, N.J.: Princeton University Press, 1978), p. 35. U.S., Dept. of Interior, *A Compendium of the Ninth Census: 1870*, Francis A. Walker (Wash. D.C.: Government Printing Office, 1872), pp. 456–459, Tables XXIV–XXVI; U.S., Dept. of Interior, *Tenth Census of the United States: 1880*, I: Statistics of the Population (Wash. D.C.: Government Printing Office, 1883), p. 920, Table VIII; U.S., Dept. of Interior, *Eleventh Census of the United States: 1890*, I: Population, Part II (Wash. D.C.: Government Printing Office, 1897), p. xxxiii; U.S., Dept. of Interior, *Twelfth Census of the United States: 1900*, II: Population (Wash. D.C.: Government Printing Office, 1902), p. 413, Table 56; U.S., Dept. of Commerce: Census Bureau, *Thirteenth Census of the United States: 1910*, I: Population (Wash. D.C.: Government Printing Office, 1913), p. 1220, Table 27; *Fourteenth Census of the United States: 1920*, II: Population (Wash. D.C.: Government Printing Office, 1920), p. 1157, Table 8, p. 1150.

14. In 1850, 86% of Michigan's population was American-born. This group was barely a majority in Detroit. Almon Ernest Parkins, *The Historical Geography of Detroit* (Lansing, Mich.: The Michigan Historical Commission, 1918), pp. 188, 194.

15. The "cult of domesticity" was defined by Barbara Welter in "The Cult of True Womanhood, 1820-1860," *American Quarterly*, 18 (1966), pp. 151–174, and has been discussed by many historians, notably Ann Douglas, *The Feminization of American Culture* (New York: Alfred A. Knopf, 1977), and Cott.

16. Bloomberg et. al., "A Census Probe into Nineteenth-Century Family History: Southern Michigan, 1850–1880," *Journal of Social History*, 5 (1971), pp. 26–45. The sample used by Bloomberg et al. includes 326 households in 1850 and 868 households in 1880, drawn in clusters from rural, town and village, and Detroit locations. Because of the relatively small sample size and the sampling method, the figures derived may not be completely representative of the population as a whole. They do, however, represent a significantly larger number of households than those examined here and can provide a frame of reference with which to look at this smaller sample of families. The Bloomberg study does not control for ethnicity or any other variables and is limited to the southern third of Michigan, the location of 98.3% of the state's population in 1850 and 85.1% of the state's population in 1880 (see Bloomberg et al., p. 29). For more detailed comparison, see Appendix A.

17. Bloomberg et al., p. 29.

18. Bloomberg et al., p. 36.

19. Parkins, p. 196.

20. Bloomberg et al., p. 30.

21. Bloomberg et al., p. 34.

22. From the Gernsey Manuscript in *Ballads and Songs of Southern Michigan*, collected and edited by Emelyn Elizabeth Gardner and Geraldine Jencks Chickering (Ann Arbor, Mich.: The University of Michigan Press, 1939), pp. 4–5.

23. For a more detailed discussion of the early history of Michigan, see Appendix B.

24. Lew Allen Chase, *Rural Michigan* (New York: Macmillan, 1922), p. 256.

ONE: INTO THE GULF OF MATRIMONY

1. Emma Regal to Eli Regal, November 29, 1868, Regal Family Collection, MHC.

2. Elizabeth Gurney, diary, April 12, 1863, July 22, August 5, August 12, 1866. Taylor Family Collection, MHC.

3. Harriet Johnson, diary, June 25–26, 1853, Henry Parker Smith Collection, MHC.

4. Harriet Johnson, diary, June 20, 1853, Henry Parker Smith Collection, MHC.

5. Harriet Johnson, diary, June 26, 1853, Henry Parker Smith Collection, MHC.

6. Harriet Johnson, diary, May 5, 1853, Henry Parker Smith Collection, MHC.

7. Harriet Johnson, diary, June 4, 1853, Henry Parker Smith Collection, MHC.

8. Harriet Johnson, diary, June 6, 1853, Henry Parker Smith Collection, MHC.

9. Harriet Johnson, diary, July 3, October, 27, 1853, Henry Parker Smith Collection, MHC.

10. Harriet Johnson, diary, October 21, 1853, Henry Parker Smith Collection, MHC.

11. Harriet Johnson, diary, July 10, 1853, Henry Parker Smith Collection, MHC.

12. Harriet Johnson, diary, July 2, 1853, Henry Parker Smith Collection, MHC.

13. Degler, p. 154. On similar feelings among eighteenth-century women, see Mary Beth Norton, *Liberty's Daughters: The Revolutionary Experience of American Women, 1750-1800* (Boston: Little, Brown, 1980), p. 41.

14. Degler, p. 153. See also Norton, pp. 41-42, 240-242, for eighteenth-century women.

Relatively few women, however, remained single. Between 10% and 11% of all women born in the United States between 1860 and 1880 never married. The 1920 census of Michigan, when those born in 1860 would have been 60 years old and those born in 1880 would have been 40, shows that 8.9% of white women of native-born parents between the ages of 35 and 44 were single, as were 5.7% of those between the ages of 55 and 64. Presumably some of these women remained single by choice. Since males outnumbered females in Michigan in most young marriageable age groups in most census years between 1820 and 1920, women should have faced favorable marriage opportunities. Nonetheless a woman who refused a proposal of marriage would realize that she might remain part of the substantial minority of permanently unmarried women. Degler, p. 152. U.S., Dept. of Commerce: Census Bureau, *Fourteenth Census of the United States: 1920*, II, p. 430, Table 11.

15. Jennie Peckens to Ella, April 14, 1878, Peckens Family Collection, MHC.

16. Flora to Abby Field, January 21, 1872, Field Family Collection, MHC.

17. Mary Emerson to Harriet Hatch [1820], Whittemore Family Collection, MHC.

18. Naomi to Ellen Wilson, December 30, 1870, Whitehead Family Collection, MHC.

19. Orpha to Nellie Whitehead, January 4, 1880, Whitehead Family Collection, MHC.

20. Mary Raynale to Mollie Irish, August 4, 1856, Jessie Phelps Collection, MHC.

Norton notes a similar fear of marriage, called a "dark leep" by one woman in the eighteenth century. Norton, pp. 42-43. Nancy Cott discusses marriage anxiety among New England women in the early years of the nineteenth century in "Young Women in the Second Great Awakening in New England," *Feminist Studies*, 3 (Fall 1975), pp. 15-29.

21. Unsigned to Harriet Hatch, October 17, 1818, Whittemore Family Collection, MHC.

22. Mary Raynale to Mollie Irish, December 12, 1856, Jessie Phelps Collection, MHC.

23. Mary Raynale to Mollie Irish, December 12, 1856, Jessie Phelps Collection, MHC. For the Far West, see Julie Roy Jeffrey, *Frontier Women: The Trans-Mississippi West, 1840-1880* (New York: Hill and Wang, 1979), p. 76.

24. C.S. Barker to Mrs. Orson Swift, December 29, 1850, Swift Family Collection, MHC.

25. Degler discusses the acceptance of such relationships in the nineteenth century. Degler, pp. 156-157, 163-165.

26. Unsigned to Carrie, January 18 [no year], Whittemore Family Collection, MHC.

27. Mary Lee to Weltha Field, November 11, 1893, Field Family Collection, MHC.

28. Eleanor Cresswell to Abby Field, January 14, 1889, Field Family Collection, MHC; Susan Field Buck to Abby Field, February 14 [1889], Field Family Collection, MHC, Jessie Phelps, diary, June 15 [1915], Jessie Phelps Collection, MHC.

29. Eleanor Cresswell to Abby Field, January 14, 1889; Field Family Collection, MHC; Susan Field Buck to Abby Field, February 14 [1889], Field Family Collection, MHC.

30. Jessie Phelps, diary, June 15 [1915], Jessie Phelps Collection, MHC.

31. Abba Carr to [aunt], December 19, 1869, Peckens Family Collection, MHC.

32. Stephen Mack to Lovicy and Harriet Mack, September 9, 1818, Whittemore Family Collection, MHC.

33. Jane Riddall to Harriet Mack, August 16, 1818, Whittemore Family Collection, MHC.

34. Harriet Johnson, diary, June 19, 1853, Henry Parker Smith Collection, MHC.

35. Autograph book, Minnie C. Fay Collection, MHC. The poem is "To Anna," by Susanna Rowson. Dorothy Weil, *In Defense of Women: Susanna Rowson (1762-1824)* (University Park, Penn.: Pennsylvania State University Press, 1976), p. 43.

36. Henry Parker Smith, diary, May 6, 1853, Henry Parker Smith Collection, MHC.

37. Judson Bingham to Maria Bingham Seymour, December 11, 1846, January 20, 1847, Hannah Bingham Collection, MHC.

38. Judson Bingham to Maria Bingham Seymour, January 20, 1847, Hannah Bingham Collection, MHC. For the eighteenth century, see Norton, p. 43. Unmarried men sometimes joked with one another about their search for wives. Chas. to Myron Buck, August 1, 1856, Field Family Collection, MHC; Martin Sterling to Myron Buck, July 10 [1856], Field Family Collection, MHC.

39. Frances Hall to Josiah Littlefield, September 9, 1872, June 16, 1873, Littlefield Family Collection, MHC.

40. Jennie M. Blaherly to Edwin Phelps, September 29, 1867, Jessie Phelps Collection, MHC.

41. *The Compiled Laws of the State of Michigan: 1915*, Edmund C. Shields, Cyrenius P. Black, and Archibald Broomfield (Lansing, Mich.: Wyncoop, Hallenbeck Crawford, 1916), pp. 4077-4078.

42. *The Compiled Laws of the State of Michigan: 1915*, Title XV, Chapter 259, Section 1, Compiler's Number 15462, p. 5346.

43. *The Compiled Laws of the State of Michigan: 1915*, Title VII, Chapter 147, Section 1, Compiler's Number 7774, pp. 2791-2792; Section 1, Compiler's Number 7789, p. 2796; Section 2, Compiler's Number 7775, pp. 2792-2793.

44. Michigan was one of the first states to pass such legislation. Mississippi enacted the first Married Woman's Property Act, essentially similar to Michigan's law, in 1839. During the 1840s, most states passed similar legislation altering the former common law status of the wife as merged both legally and financially into the person of her husband.

45. *Laws of the Territory of Michigan*, III (Lansing, Mich.: W.S. George, 1874), pp. 931-932; *Laws of the Territory of Michigan*, II (Lansing, Mich.: W.S. George, 1871), pp. 533-534.

46. *The Compiled Laws of the State of Michigan: 1915*, Title IX, Chapter 218, Section 25, Compiler's Number 11475, pp. 4072-4073.

47. *The Compiled Laws of the State of Michigan: 1915*, Title IX, Chapter 218, Section 1, Compiler's Number 11485, p. 4077.

48. When partible inheritance became not only customary but required by law, it was necessary to protect the inheritance of women who had needed no such protection under the English common law system of impartible inheritance. (The Territory of Michigan as early as 1818 effectively disallowed impartible inheritance by allowing any child not given an inheritance under the terms of a parent's will to claim under the laws governing intestate estates. The law did not require that the portions be equal in value, however.) The loosening of restrictions on divorce, and probably the existence of a western frontier into which deserting husbands could effectively disappear, created further urgent need for a married woman to maintain control of her inheritance if it was to pass to her children. Previously, as in English common law until the early part of the nineteenth century, any real estate which came to the husband by right of the wife's inheritance was his under the provision of "tenancy by the curtesy" if his wife died after producing a

live child in the marriage. Under tenancy by the curtesy, the husband held a lifetime use of his deceased wife's property. After his death, the property would pass to her heirs, thus remaining in her family. All other property owned by the woman before her marriage came into the direct possession of her husband. Tenancy by the curtesy was abrogated by the Married Woman's Property Act of 1855, which gave a married woman the right to dispose of her inherited property as she chose. Thus after 1855 a married woman could will her inherited property to her children, parents, or siblings if she so desired. Obviously, these provisions were of benefit only to those women who owned inherited property. Although the act also covered money earned by a woman prior to her marriage, the level of wages available to women would have precluded most women from accumulating substantial savings from such earnings. *Laws of the Territory of Michigan*, I, (Lansing, Mich.: W.S. George, 1871) p. 347; *The Compiled Laws of the State of Michigan: 1915*, Title IX, Chapter 218, Section 27, Compiler's Number 11477, p. 4073.

49. *The Compiled Laws of the State of Michigan: 1915*, Title IX, Chapter 218, Section 1, Compiler's Number 11485, pp. 4077–4079; Section 1, Compiler's Number 11478, p. 4073.

50. *The Compiled Laws of the State of Michigan: 1915*, Title IX, Chapter 218, Section 1, Compiler's Number 11485, pp. 4077–4079.

51. *The Compiled Laws of the State of Michigan: 1915*, Title IX, Chapter 218, Section 25, Compiler's Number 11475, p. 4073. One side effect, however, of the Married Woman's Property Act was that a married woman could legally retain a "nest egg" accumulated before marriage for her own use and security during the marriage. In discussing the Married Woman's Property Act of 1844, the compiler concluded in 1915 that:

> The main purpose of the statutory provisions which protected her in the title, would seem to have been to preserve the property for the benefit of the family, against its being squandered by the husband or seized by his creditors. But the Constitution of 1851 went further and added to a provision, in substance the same as the act of 1844, the words "and may be devised or bequeathed by her as if she were unmarried."

This change in the law gave the married woman control as well as ownership of her inherited property.

52. Sarah Regal to Eli Regal, October 8, 1854, Regal Family Collection, MHC.

53. E. B. Hutchins to Edmund Hall, August 19, 1857, Littlefield Family Collection, MHC.

54. Elsie Cooley to Charles Horton Cooley, December 2, December 3, December 12, 1890, Charles Horton Cooley Collection, MHC.

55. Sarah Regal to Eli Regal, October 6, 1858, Regal Family Collection, MHC.

56. Eliza Granger to Sarah Regal, March 17, 1851, Regal Family Collection, MHC.

57. Lucy Parker to Franklin Parker, 1866–1876, e.g., February 18, 1866, Franklin Parker Collection, MHC.

58. Harriet Whittemore to James Whittemore, January 28, 1859, Whittemore Family Collection, MHC.

59. Harriet Whittemore to G. O. Whittemore, February 10, 1859, Whittemore Family Collection, MHC.

60. L. C. Francis to Olive and Eliza Rogers, March 11, 1866, Peckens Family Collection, MHC.

61. Josiah Littlefield, autobiography, pp. 4–6, Littlefield Family Collection, MHC.

62. Lovicy Cooper to Harriet Whittemore, April 19, 1852, Whittemore Family Collection, MHC.

63. Mary Lee to Weltha Field, February 26, 1886, April 21, 1887, June 6, 1889, Field Family Collection, MHC.

64. C. A. Kinsley to Edmund Hall, August 13, 1855, Edmund Hall to C. A. Kinsley, October 2, 1855, Martha Hitchcock to Edmund Hall, October 20, 1855, Littlefield Family Collection, MHC.

65. Marilla Turrill to Myron Buck, April 28, 1863, Field Family Collection, MHC.

66. Marilla Turrill to Myron Buck, August 7, 1866, Field Family Collection, MHC.

67. Olive to Josie Smith, April 29 [1896], Josie Smith Collection, MHC.

68. Olive to Josie Smith, February 7, 1896, Josie Smith Collection, MHC.

69. Will to Josie Smith, February 13, 1896, Josie Smith Collection, MHC.

70. Marie to Josie Smith, March 26, 1896, Olive to Josie Smith, April 29, 1896, Josie Smith Collection, MHC.

71. Marie to Josie Smith, April 25, 1896, Josie Smith Collection, MHC.

72. Olive to Josie Smith, April 29, 1896, Josie Smith Collection, MHC.

73. Martha Cole, diary, 1901, Martha Cole Collection, MHC.

74. Elizabeth Pleck, "Wifebeating in Nineteenth-Century America," *Victimology*, 4 (1979), pp. 60–74.

75. Nellie Hart to Josiah Littlefield, March 5, 1874, Littlefield Family Collection, MHC.

76. Josiah Littlefield to Nellie Littlefield, January 17, 1875, Littlefield Family Collection, MHC.

77. A. B. Matthews to James Whittemore, December 19, 1866, Whittemore Family Collection, MHC.

78. Ellen Whitehead to brother and sister, October 28 [no year], Whitehead Family Collection, MHC. See also A. B. Matthews to James Whittemore, December 19, 1866, Whittemore Family Collection, MHC.

79. Eli Regal to Sarah Regal, February 21, 1859, Regal Family Collection, MHC.

80. Letters exchanged between Charles Horton Cooley and Elsie Cooley, 1888-1914, Charles Horton Cooley Collection, MHC. These letters cannot be quoted in print.

81. Jack Goody, *Comparative Studies in Kinship* (London: Routledge and Kegan Paul, 1969), pp. 184-215, discusses the relationship of women and children to the maternal kin group in unilineal (patrilineal) and bilineal descent groups in Northern Ghana. He finds that women in tribes with bilineal descent maintain a lifelong relationship with their family of origin, returning to their kin for long visits and in old age, and sharing child-rearing with their kin. Those women in tribes with unilineal descent groups sever ties with their kin upon marriage, entering fully into the husband's kin group.

82. George L. Haskins, "The Beginnings of Partible Inheritance in the American Colonies," in *Essays in the History of Early American Law*, edited by David Flaherty (Chapel Hill, N. C.: University of North Carolina Press, 1969), pp. 204-244.

83. *Laws of the Territory of Michigan*, I, p. 347.

84. *The Compiled Laws of the State of Michigan: 1915*, Title IX, Chapter 218, Section 1, Compiler's Number 11485, pp. 4077-4079; Section 1, Compiler's Number 11478, p. 4073.

85. Richard Emerson, "Power-Dependence Relationships," *American Sociological Review*, 27 (1962), pp. 31-41.

Two: A Sister's Privilege—Perhaps her Duty

1. Horatio Turrill to Myron Buck, July 21, 1855, Field Family Collection, MHC.

2. In the families examined here, four women were members of family networks including their aunts and cousins, two maintained contact with no kin outside the family of procreation, and 16 maintained contact with most of their family of procreation and family of origin, as well as their husband's family of origin. Of the four women in networks which included aunts and cousins, two were unmarried while two were married but childless.

3. Sister to Olive Rogers, January 31 [1872], Peckens Family Collection, MHC; Abby Field to Abram Field, September 17, 1871, Field Family Collection, MHC; A. M. Whittemore to James Whittemore, July 30, 1863, Whittemore Family Collection, MHC.

4. Mary Cooley correspondence, Thomas McIntyre Cooley Collection, MHC; Nellie Whitehead correspondence, Whitehead Family Collection, MHC.

5. R. A. Field to Weltha, March 31, 1890, Field Family Collection, MHC.

6. Lucy Sexton to sister, June 12, 1887, Field Family Collection, MHC.

7. Rhoda Buckland to Harriet Mack, February 19, 1817, Whittemore Family Collection, MHC.

8. D. D. Spencer to brother, February 21, 1851, Spencer Family Collection, MHC. See also R. D. Parker to Franklin and Lucy Parker, July 3, 1888, Franklin Parker Collection, MHC, and D. Whitehead to friends, February 4 [no year], Whitehead Family Collection, MHC, as well as Jeffrey, p. 75.

9. Mary Cooley to Thomas McIntyre Cooley, February 4, 1888, in Thomas McIntyre Cooley, diary, February 4, 1888, Thomas McIntyre Cooley Collection, MHC.

10. Mother to Ann Gennette Loomis Preston, September 26, 1864, Preston Family Collection, MHC.

11. Hannah Slayton and Caroline Bullis to son and brother [undated], Julia Bird Martin Collection, MHC. See also Lewis O. Saum, "Death in the Popular Mind of Pre-Civil War America," *American Quarterly*, 26 (December 1974), pp. 477–495.

12. D. D. Spencer to brother, February 12, 1851, Spencer Family Collection, MHC.

13. Henry Parker Smith, diary, December 7, 1862, Henry Parker Smith Collection, MHC.

14. Elnathan Phelps to Edwin Phelps, August 24, 1857, Jessie Phelps Collection, MHC.

15. Almeda to mother, June 23, 1847, Lucy Wyman Smith Collection, MHC.

16. Smith-Rosenberg, "Female World," pp. 23–24.

17. Florence Pomeroy Raab, September 28, 1904, Raab Family Collection, MHC.

18. Elizabeth Stuart (Phelps) Ward, *The Gates Ajar* (Boston: Fields, Osgood, 1870).

19. Harriet Johnson, diary, July 4, 1852, Henry Parker Smith Collection, MHC.

20. Harriet Beecher Stowe, *Uncle Tom's Cabin; or, Life Among the Lowly* (1852; reprint Garden City, N.Y.: Dolphin Books, 1960), pp. 367–368.

21. See Ann Douglas, "Heaven Our Home: Consolation Literature in the Northern United States, 1830–1880, *American Quarterly*, 26 (December 1974), pp. 496–515.

22. Stanley French writes about the fencing of family plots in "The Cemetery as Cultural Institution: The Establishment of Mount Auburn and the 'Rural Cemetery' Movement," *American Quarterly*, 26 (March 1974), pp. 37–59.

23. Kate Cooley to Mary Cooley [undated], Thomas McIntrye Cooley Collection, MHC. See also Franklin Parker to Will Loomis, June 29, 1888, and Franklin Parker to Lucy Parker, July 1, 1888, Franklin Parker Collection, MHC; Mary Littlefield to Martha Hall, February 25, 1865, Littlefield Family

Collection, MHC; unsigned to brother, January 23, 1890, Twichell Family Collection, MHC.

One man took his wife's body from Michigan to Ohio so she could be buried "among her friends." Lucy and Morton Smith to Mr. and Mrs. O. M. Smith, March 16, 1846, Lucy Wyman Smith Collection, MHC.

24. Hannah Slayton and Caroline Bullis to brother and son [undated], Julia Bird Martin Collection, MHC.

25. Juliana Caster to Harriet Whittemore, May 18, 1847, Whittemore Family Collection, MHC. Women in the Far West also lamented leaving the graves of children and parents. See Jeffrey, pp. 3-31.

26. Marilla Turrill to Myron Buck, November 1, 1857, Field Family Collection, MHC.

27. Marilla Turrill to Myron Buck, March 31, 1856, Field Family Collection, MHC.

28. C. P. Peckens to George and family, January 3, 1892, Peckens Family Collection, MHC.

29. *Laws of the Territory of Michigan*, I, pp. 531-532, 90-91.

30. *Laws of the Territory of Michigan*, II, pp. 287-288.

31. *Laws of the Territory of Michigan*, II, p. 599.

32. *The Compiled Laws of the State of Michigan: 1857*, Thomas McIntyre Cooley (Detroit, Mich.: Raymond and Selleck, 1857), Title XIII, Chapter XXXIX, Section 1, Compiler's Number 1418, pp. 451-454.

33. Mary Littlefield to Josiah Littlefield, May 11, 1872, Littlefield Family Collection, MHC; Newton Buck to Myron Buck, January 3, 1867, August 17, 1869, Field Family Collection, MHC; Fanny Angell to Thomas Cooley, January 9, 1885, Thomas McIntyre Cooley Collection, MHC; Jennie to Edwin Phelps, September 29, 1867, Jessie Phelps Collection, MHC; Marilla Turrill to Myron Buck, August 29, 1863, Field Family Collection, MHC; brother and sister to Thomas Cooley, February 10, 1881, Thomas Cooley to Mary Cooley, September 12, 1878, Thomas McIntyre Cooley Collection, MHC; Mary to Edwin Phelps, February 11, 1878, Jessie Phelps Collection, MHC.

34. Thomas McIntyre Cooley, diary, November 29, 1884, Thomas McIntyre Cooley Collection, MHC.

35. Thomas Cooley to Eugene Cooley, July 25, 1882, Thomas McIntyre Cooley Collection, MHC.

36. Mary Louise Miles to Mary Cushman Miles, November 9, 1839, Parker Family Collection, MHC.

37. Marie to Josie Smith, March 26, April 25, 1896, Olive to Josie Smith, April 29, 1896, Josie Smith Collection, MHC.

38. Abby Field to Susan Field Buck, February 16, 1866, Field Family Collection, MHC.

39. Hannah Bingham to Maria Bingham, April 2, 1846, Bingham Family Collection, MHC.

40. Almyra to Ann Gennette Loomis Preston, November 22, 1860, Preston Family Collection, MHC.

41. Abby Field to Susan Field Buck, August 9, 1870, Field Family Collection, MHC; Fanny Cooley to Kate Cooley, January 4, 1885, Thomas McIntyre Cooley Collection, MHC; Ellen Regal to Sarah Regal, October 24, 1870, Regal Family Collection, MHC; Sarah to Alice Peckens, September 11, 1872, Peckens Family Collection, MHC; Mollie to Nellie Whitehead, January 22, 1874, Whitehead Family Collection, MHC; Ellen Regal to Emma Regal, November 3 [no year], Regal Family Collection, MHC.

42. Marilla Buck to Myron Buck, March 4, 1856, Field Family Collection, MHC.

43. Thomas Cooley to Mary Cooley, September 12, 1878, June 18, 1879, Thomas McIntyre Cooley Collection, MHC.

44. Betsy Phelps to Harriet Whittemore, February 5, 1859, Whittemore Family Collection, MHC.

45. Martha Hall to Mary Littlefield, April 18 [no year], Littlefield Family Collection, MHC.

46. Ann Gennette Loomis Preston to Fowler Preston, March 23, 1863, January 26, 1864, Preston Family Collection, MHC.

47. Thomas and Elizabeth Chandler to William Chandler, 2nd month, 3rd, 1833, Elizabeth Chandler Collection, MHC.

48. Stephen Mack to Harriet Whittemore, February 6, 1846, Whittemore Family Collection, MHC.

49. Mary Louise Miles to Mary Cushman Miles, September 21, 1839, Parker Family Collection, MHC.

50. Jane Howell to Elizabeth Chandler, 6th month, 3rd, 1832, Elizabeth Chandler Collection, MHC.

51. Hannah Bingham, diary, August 8, 1832, Bingham Family Collection, MHC.

52. See Norton, pp. 56–58, on eighteenth-century women asking parental advice on choice of marriage partner.

53. Martha Hall to Mary Littlefield, April 18 [no year], Littlefield Family Collection; Henry Parker Smith, diary, July 18, 1853, Henry Parker Smith Collection, MHC.

54. Harriet Whittemore to James Whittemore, March 17, 1855, Whittemore Family Collection, MHC.

55. Jane Howell to Thomas Chandler, 10th month, 12th, 1837, Elizabeth Chandler Collection, MHC.

56. Judson Bingham to Maria Bingham Seymour, November 30, 1836, Hannah Bingham Collection, MHC.

57. Frances Hall to Josiah Littlefield, September 9, 1872, June 16, 1873, Littlefield Family Collection, MHC.

58. Mary Cooley to Kate Cooley, January 30, 1875, Thomas McIntyre Cooley Collection, MHC.

59. Mary Cooley to Eugene Cooley, September 20, 1876, Thomas McIntyre Cooley Collection, MHC.

60. Eugene Cooley to Mary Cooley, September 8, 1870, Thomas McIntyre Cooley Collection, MHC.

61. Harriet Johnson, diary, June 19, 1852, Henry Parker Smith Collection, MHC.

62. Fanny Angell to Mary Cooley, February 14, 1890, Thomas McIntyre Cooley Collection, MHC.

63. Gussie Rouse to Abby Field, March 21, 1869, Field Family Collection, MHC.

64. Many women in the eighteenth century also felt that they could express their true feelings only to other women. Norton, pp. 14–15. Norton also describes the intimate friendships that developed between women and their adult daughters. Norton, pp. 102–105. A similar pattern appears in the Far West in the nineteenth century, where one woman wrote of her husband, "I have been very blue for I cannot make a friend like mother out of Henry." Jeffrey, pp. 55–56.

65. Abby Field, diary, April 20, May 7, 1863, Field Family Collection, MHC.

66. Harriet Johnson Smith, diary, June 22, 1862, Henry Parker Smith Collection, MHC. See Jeffrey, p. 75, on female friendship in the Far West.

67. A. C. Covington to Mary Cooley, April 14, 1890, Thomas McIntyre Cooley Collection, MHC. Jeffrey quotes one woman in the Far West who wrote: "'Tis true we may have friends among strangers; but, ah, they are not parents, brothers nor sisters." Jeffrey, p. 75.

68. Bert N. Adams, "Interaction Theory and the Social Network," *Sociometry*, 30 (1967), pp. 64–78, suggests that kinship relationships, which are long-term and based on confluence of interests, needs, and obligations, are more conducive to the exchange of advice, confidences, and other intimate communication than are relationships between friends, which are short-term and based on consensus of values and interests. He finds that obligation rather than affection leads to long-term relationships as well as to greater intimacy. Jane Hubert, "Kinship and Geographical Mobility in a Sample from a London Middle-Class Area" and Helgi Osterreich, "Geographical Mobility and Kinship: A Canadian Example," both in *International Journal of Comparative Sociology*, 6 (1965), pp. 61–80, 131–144, suggest that among contemporary families geographic mobility does not preclude close kinship ties, a finding Osterreich attributes to the potential for assistance from kin and the sense of belonging fostered by a kinship network.

69. Abby Field, diary, January 30, 1872, Field Family Collection, MHC.

70. Harriet Johnson, diary, March 19, 1853, Henry Parker Smith Collection, MHC.

71. Sarah Regal to Eliza Granger, December 6, 1857, Regal Family Collection, MHC; Electa Loomis to Ann Gennette Loomis Preston, March 11,

1863, Preston Family Collection, MHC; Jane Howell to Thomas Chandler, 5th month, 7th, 1839, Elizabeth Chandler Collection, MHC; Lucy Smith to Mrs. O. M. Smith, February 14 [1840], Lucy Wyman Smith Collection, MHC; Florence Pomeroy to Frances Pomeroy, March 14, 1894, Raab Family Collection, MHC.

72. Elizabeth Chandler to Jane Howell, 3rd month, 9th, 1834, Elizabeth Chandler Collection, MHC.

73. Jane Howell to Ruth Evans, 10th month, 15th, 1831, 3rd month, 23rd, 1833, Elizabeth Chandler Collection, MHC.

Three: A Letter Traced by a Friendly Hand

1. John Mack Faragher, *Women and Men on the Overland Trail* (New Haven, Conn.: Yale University Press, 1979), pp. 130-138.

2. Priscilla Leonard, "The Laws of Letter Writing," *Harper's Bazar*, November 1904, pp. 1125-1127.

3. Lois A. White to Abby Field, October 5, 1895, Field Family Collection, MHC.

4. Newton Buck to Myron and Susan Buck, June 18, 1862, Field Family Collection, MHC.

5. Edwin Phelps to Helen and Mary Phelps, May 31, 1871, Jessie Phelps Collection, MHC. For examples of correspondence between unmarried men, see Chas. to Myron Buck, August 1, 1856, and Martin Sterling to Myron Buck, July 10 [1856], Field Family Collection, MHC.

6. Edith Schel, "Women as Letter-Writers," *Littell's Living Age*, February 25, 1899, p. 523.

7. Mary E. Sterling to Myron Buck, August 19, 1857, Field Family Collection, MHC.

8. Irving to Mary, February 1, 1877, Lucy Ann Wyman Smith Collection, MHC.

9. See Horatio Turrill to Myron Buck, July 21, 1885, Field Family Collection, MHC.

10. Judson Bingham to Maria Bingham, November 31, 1836, Hannah Bingham Collection, MHC.

11. Charles Horton Cooley to Elsie Jones, January 4, 1888, Charles Horton Cooley Collection, MHC. Abby Field, diary, March 28, 1863, Field Family Collection, MHC..

12. Harriet Johnson, diary, September 17, 1853, Henry Parker Smith Collection, MHC; Mary Emerson to Harriet Hatch, October 17, 1818, Whittemore Family Collection, MHC; Angelina Bingham to Maria Bingham Seymour, March 14, 1847, Hannah Bingham Collection, MHC.

13. Fanny Cooley to Eugene Cooley, February 19, 1875, Thomas McIntyre Cooley Collection, MHC.

14. Electa Phelps to Mollie Phelps, November 2, 1858, Jessie Phelps Collection, MHC.

15. Charles Horton Cooley to Mary Cooley, June 9, 1883, Charles Horton Cooley Collection, MHC.

16. Lucy Smith to Mrs. O. M. Smith and Jane Smith, February 18, 1843, Lucy Wyman Smith Collection, MHC. See also Jeffrey, p. 127.

17. Lucy and Morton Smith to Mr. and Mrs. O. M. Smith, August 5, 1845, Lucy Wyman Smith Collection, MHC. For another example of a letter exchanged between male kin, see E. L. Peckens to G. S. Peckens, February 7, 1872, Peckens Family Collection, MHC.

18. Jane Howell to Ruth Evans, 5th month, 15th, 1834, Jane Howell to Thomas Chandler, 5th month, 29th, 1838, Jane Howell to Ruth Evans, 1st month, 20th, 1834, Elizabeth Chandler Collection, MHC.

19. Lucy and Morton Smith to Mr. and Mrs. O. M. Smith, March 16, 1846, Lucy Wyman Smith Collection, MHC.

20. Mary Lee to Weltha Field, June 6, 1889, Field Family Collection, MHC.

21. Sarah to Mollie Phelps, December 1, 1856, Jessie Phelps Collection, MHC; Elizabeth Chandler to Jane Howell, 3rd month, 9th, 1834, Elizabeth Chandler Collection, MHC.

22. Lucy Smith to Mrs. O. M. Smith, February 18, 1843, Lucy Wyman Smith Collection, MHC.

23. Schel, p. 513; Andrew Lang, "Telephones and Letter-Writing, *Critic*, June 1906, p. 508. Charles Knight, "Half Hours with the Best Letter Writers," *Eclectic Magazine*, February 1869, p. 203.

24. "Female Letter-Writers," *Tait's Edinburgh Magazine*, May 1832, pp. 197–198; Schel, p. 523; "Letter-Writing," *Littell's Living Age*, August 20, 1870, pp. 451–452; "Letter-Writing and Letter-Writers," *Littell's Living Age*, January 24, 1857, p. 200.

25. Schel, p. 523; Herbert W. Horwill, "Literature: The Art of Letter-Writing," *Forum*, July 1904, p. 72; "Letter-Writing," p. 452.

26. Anne H. Wharton, "A Lost Art," *Lippincott's Magazine*, March 1891, pp. 369–375; Horwill, pp. 70–84; "Survival of Letter-Writing," *Nation*, January 4, 1900, pp. 5–6; Richard Gee, "Letters and Letter-Writers," *Eclectic Magazine*, June 1897, pp. 850–855; "Letters and Letter-Writing," *Littell's Living Age*, November 25, 1871, pp. 477–489; "English Letter-Writers of the Eighteenth Century," *Littell's Living Age*, January 20, 1855, pp. 183–192; "The Lost Art of Letter-Writing," *Nation*, November 11, 1857, pp. 370–371.

27. See Degler, pp. 308–315. Degler notes that after 1870 female high school graduates outnumbered males. One study of Northern farm communities found males only slightly more likely than females to be attending school. In 1860 81% of girls between the ages of 10 and 14 attended school, the study found. In Michigan, between 1850 and 1900, the ratio of males to females attending school was close to the ratio of males to females in

the school-age population. Indeed, after 1900, the percentage of females in the school population was slightly higher than that in the total population. Easterlin et al., p. 34; U.S., Dept. of Interior, *A Compendium of the Ninth Census: 1870*, pp. 452–455, Tables XXI-XXIII; U.S., Dept. of Interior, *Tenth Census of the United States: 1880*, I, p. 918, Table VII; U.S., Dept. of Interior *Compendium of the Eleventh Census of the United States: 1890*, II, p. 214; U.S., Dept. of Interior, *Twelfth Census of the United States: 1900*, II, p. 361, Table 42; U.S., Dept of Commerce: Census Bureau, *Thirteenth Census of the United States: 1910*, I, pp. 1110–1120, Tables 18, 25; U.S., Dept. of Commerce: Census Bureau, *School Attendance in 1920*, Census Monograph V (Fourteenth Census), Frank Alexander Ross (Wash. D.C.: Government Printing Office, 1924), p. 232, Table 1.

28. "Letter-Writing and Letter-Writers," p. 200.

29. Robin Lakoff, in *Language and Woman's Place* (New York: Harper and Row, 1975), pp. 55–56, 73–78, finds similar patterns in the speech of contemporary American women. Eugene Genovese, in *Roll, Jordan, Roll* (New York: Random House, 1974), pp. 431–441, describes the use of indirect language among American slaves. In *Toward A New Psychology of Women* (Boston: Beacon, 1976), pp. 9–10, Jean Baker Miller analyzes the psychological basis for indirect modes of action among subordinate groups, while Baym, pp. 37–40, discusses the attempt of fictional heroines to integrate outward submission with inward independence. Susan Harding, in "Women and Words in a Spanish Village," in *Toward an Anthropology of Women*, ed. Rayna R. Reiter (New York: Monthly Review Press, 1975), pp. 283–308, finds that women in the village studied maintain a limited degree of power within a patriarchal society through their use of gossip. She finds, however, that gossip serves to preserve social norms among women, thus strengthening patriarchal authority.

30. Sarah Regal to sister [undated], Regal Family Collection, MHC.

31. Sarah Regal to Eli Regal, October 8, 1854, September 10, 1858, December 5, 1866, Regal Family Collection, MHC.

32. Eli Regal to Sarah Regal, July 19, 1858, Regal Family Collection, MHC.

33. Sarah Regal to Eli Regal, July 26, 1858, Regal Family Collection, MHC.

34. Hannah Bingham to Angelina Bingham, December 24, 1846, Hannah Bingham Collection, MHC.

35. Weltha Field to Abby Field [April 1878], Field Family Collection, MHC.

36. Lottie to Nellie Whitehead, March 28 [no year], Whitehead Family Collection, MHC.

37. Electa Loomis to Ann Gennette Loomis Preston, January 8, 1865, Preston Family Collection, MHC.

38. Ellen Whitehead Gascoyne to Edward Whitehead, August 2, 1878, Whitehead Family Collection, MHC.

166   TRUE SISTERHOOD

39. Jane Howell to Thomas Chandler, 6th month, 20th, 1841, Elizabeth Chandler Collection, MHC.

40. See for example Florence Pomeroy to Frances Pomeroy, April 13, 1891, Raab Family Collection, MHC; Mary Louise Miles to Mary Cushman Miles, November 9, 1839, Mary Cushman Miles to Mary Louise Miles, August 26, 1855, Parker Family Collection, MHC.

41. Abel Sabin to Eli Regal, October 30, 1841, Regal Family Collection, MHC.

42. Jane Sabin to Sarah Regal, October 30, 1841, Regal Family Collection, MHC; Jane Howell to Ruth Evans, December 30, 1830, 6th month, 28th, 1831, Elizabeth Chandler Collection, MHC; Mary Littlefield to Josiah Littlefield, September 24, 1871, Littlefield Family Collection, MHC; Mary Cooley to Charles Horton Cooley, November 20, 1870, Thomas McIntyre Cooley Collection, MHC; Frances Pomeroy to Florence Pomeroy, March 7, 1892, Raab Family Collection, MHC.
Lucy Smith wrote to her mother, "I have never yet wanted patience to read a long letter in fact I never had one yet half long enough." Lucy Smith to Mrs. O. M. Smith, February 18, 1843, Lucy Wyman Smith Collection, MHC. One woman Jeffrey discusses writes that she would give "particulars" because she was "'a woman and a sister' and [was] writing to women and sisters." Jeffrey, pp. 74, 127.

43. Mary Louise Miles to Mary Cushman Miles, September 21, 1839, Parker Family Collection, MHC.

44. Jane Howell to Ruth Evans, 7th month, 25th, 1832, Elizabeth Chandler Collection, MHC.

45. Abby Field to Susan Field Buck, December 24 [1861], Field Family Collection, MHC; Lucy to Nellie Littlefield, April 25, 1875, Littlefield Family Collection, MHC. See also Jeffrey, p. 74.

46. Temperance Mack to children, July 30, 1847, Whittemore Family Collection, MHC.

47. Jane Howell to Elizabeth Chandler, 6th month, 3rd, 1832, Elizabeth Chandler to Jane Howell, 10th month, 28th, 1833, Jane Howell to Ruth Evans, 1st month, 20th, 1834, Elizabeth Chandler Collection, MHC.

48. Hannah Bingham to Angelina Bingham, February 5, 1847, Hannah Bingham Collection, MHC.

49. Lucy Smith to Mrs. O. M. Smith, December 14, 1845, Lucy Wyman Smith Collection, MHC; Jane Howell to Ruth Evans, 1st month, 14th, 1836, Elizabeth Chandler Collection, MHC. See also Jeffrey, p. 74.

50. Lucy and Morton Smith to Mr. and Mrs. O. M. Smith, August 5, 1845, Lucy Wyman Smith Collection, MHC.

51. Jane Howell to Elizabeth Chandler, 7th month, 1st, 1834, 1st month, 20th, 1834, Elizabeth Chandler Collection, MHC.

52. Nellie Hart to Josiah Littlefield, October 4, 1874, Littlefield Family Collection, MHC.

53. Jane Sabin to Sarah Regal, August 18, 1863, Regal Family Collection, MHC; Abby Field, diary, January 8, July 13, 1863, Field Family Collection, MHC; Electa Loomis to Ann Gennette Loomis Preston, April 8, August 31, 1862, March 11, 1863, Preston Family Collection, MHC; Philamena to Ann Preston, January 3, 1862, Preston Family Collection, MHC; Martha Hall to Mary Littlefield, August 22 [no year], Littlefield Family Collection, MHC.

54. Smith-Rosenberg, "Female World," pp. 1–29.

55. Ellen Regal to Emma Regal, three undated letters and August 16, 1882, Regal Family Collection, MHC.

56. Angelina Bingham to Maria Bingham Seymour, February 4, 1847, Hannah Bingham Collection, MHC.

57. Marilla Buck to Myron Buck, December 7, 1855, Field Family Collection, MHC; Judson Bingham to Angelina Bingham, November 17, 1846, Hannah Bingham Collection, MHC.

For a New England woman's attachment to her brothers, see Mary Kelly, "A Woman Alone: Catharine Maria Sedgwick's Spinsterhood in Nineteenth-Century America," *The New England Quarterly*, LI (June 1978), pp. 209–225.

58. "Female Letter-Writers," p. 198.

59. Basil Bernstein, *Class, Codes and Control*, 2nd rev. ed., I (London: Routledge and Kegan Paul, 1974).

60. Faragher, pp. 130–138.

61. Julia Slayton, diary, April 14, 1883, William C. Slayton, diary, April 14, 1883, MHC.

62. For discussions of metaphoric and metonymic modes, see Terence Hawkes, *Structuralism and Semiotics* (Berkeley and Los Angeles: University of California Press, 1977), pp. 76–82, and Roland Barthes, *Elements of Semiology*, trans. Annette Lavers and Colin Smith (New York: Hill and Wang, 1967), pp. 60–61.

63. Jane Sabin to Sarah Regal [undated], Regal Family Collection, MHC.

64. Smith-Rosenberg, "Female World" pp. 1–29.

65. Faragher, pp. 133–143.

FOUR: THE VALLEY OF THE SHADOW OF DEATH

1. C. A. Kinsley to Edmund Hall, August 13, 1855, Edmund Hall to C. A. Kinsley, October 2, 1855, Littlefield Family Collection, MHC.

2. William Boyd to Mr. Bliss, March 30, 1898, Josie Smith Collection, MHC.

3. Florence Pomeroy to Frances Pomeroy, March 14, 1894, Raab Family Collection, MHC.

4. Almyra to Ann Gennette Loomis Preston, November 22, 1860, Preston Family Collection, MHC.

5. Stack, pp. 33-44; see also Donal E. Muir and Eugene A. Weinstein, "The Social Debt: An Investigation of Lower-Class and Middle-Class Norms of Social Obligation," *American Sociological Review*, 27 (1962), pp. 532-539. Muir and Weinstein find among lower class women a tendency to exchange favors with family members with little obligation to return specific favors, while middle class women were involved in immediately completed exchanges with friends. While Muir and Weinstein believe such patterns reflect class differences, they fail to examine the extent to which direct versus indirect exchanges and degree of delay accepted in repayment may be due to kin versus non-kin relationships, with kinship allowing for a greater delay in repayment and greater flexibility in nature of favor returned. The authors find that women "administer" social exchanges for the nuclear family unit. The patterns found by Muir and Weinstein, along with Stack's data, suggest that among those in tenuous economic circumstances, exchanges among kin, mediated by women, serve an important economic function. Alvin Gouldner, in "The Norm of Reciprocity: A Preliminary Statement," *American Sociological Review*, 25 (1960), p. 175, suggests that some people choose to keep others in a state of social indebtedness and that the difficulty in equating the value of social exchanges allows for flexibility in calculating degrees of social indebtedness.

6. Peter Uhlenberg, "Changing Configurations of the Life Course," in *Transitions: The Family and Life Course in Historical Perspective*, ed. Tamara K. Hareven (New York: Academic Press, 1978), pp. 79, 84. Peter Uhlenberg, "A Study of Cohort Life Cycles: Cohorts of Native Born Massachusetts Women, 1830-1920," *Population Studies*, 23 (November 1969), p. 414.

7. According to the United States census reports, 74 women in Michigan died in 1850 during childbirth, of puerperal fever, or of complications of pregnancy. By 1890, the number had risen to 398. From 1850 to 1900, less than one maternal death relating to childbirth is reported for every 100 children in the state under the age of one year. Although some of these children were born out of the state, others born in Michigan would have died before the census data was collected. As a very rough estimate, it thus appears that less than 1% of births resulted in a maternal death. However, even a small statistical likelihood of death could cause great anxiety for those who faced the risk. U.S., Dept. of Interior, *Mortality Statistics of the Seventh Census of the United States: 1850*, J. D. B. DeBow (Wash. D.C.: A. O. P. Nicholson, printer, 1855), pp. 136-139; U.S., Dept. of Interior, *Eighth Census of the United States: 1860*, IV: Statistics of the United States (including mortality, property, &c.) in 1860 (Wash. D.C.: Government Printing Office, 1866), p. 12, Table III; U.S., Dept. of Interior, *Ninth Census of the United States: 1870*, II: The Vital Statistics of the United States, Francis A. Walker (Wash. D.C.: Government Printing Office, 1872), pp. 101-103, Table V; U.S., Dept. of Interior, *Tenth Census of the United States: 1880*, XI: Report on the Mortality and Vital Statistics of the United States (Part

I), John S. Billings (Wash. D.C.: Government Printing Office, 1885), pp. 238-245, Table VII; U.S., Dept. of Interior, *Eleventh Census of the United States: 1890*, IV: Report on Vital and Social Statistics (Part III: Statistics of Deaths), John S. Billings (Wash. D.C.: Government Printing Office, 1894), pp. 194-201, Table V; U.S., Dept. of Interior, *Twelfth Census of the United States: 1900*, Vol. IV: Vital Statistics (Part II: Statistics of Deaths) (Wash. D.C.: Government Printing Office, 1902), pp. 372-379, Table 8.

8. Betsey Phelps to Harriet Whittemore, July 22, 1851, Whittemore Family Collection, MHC.

9. Degler, p. 108.

10. Frances Pomeroy, diary, March 27, 1881, Raab Family Collection, MHC.

11. Robert Grant, *Law and the Family* (New York: Scribner's, 1919), pp. 185-187.

12. Philamena to Ann Gennette Loomis Preston, January 3, 1862, Preston Family Collection, MHC.

13. "The Palmer Letters," ed. Louisa Fidelia Palmer, 1963, pp. 7-8, 51-52, manuscript in David Wheeler Palmer Collection, MHC.

14. Almeda Smith to Mrs. O. M. Smith, June 23, 1847, Abba Smith to Mrs. O. M. Smith, July 4, 1847, Emily Pope to Mrs. O. M. Smith, August 2, 1847, Lucy Wyman Smith Collection, MHC. This situation is unusual since Lucy Smith's mother, as a widow, had married Lucy's husband's father.

15. John Dort to Harriet Whittemore, September 4, 1865, March 19, 1865, Mary L. Hutchins to Harriet Whittemore, Monday 31, 1865 [sic], March 10, May 22, 1866, Whittemore Family Collection, MHC.

16. Mary Cooley to Elsie Jones, November 23, 1888, Thomas McIntyre Cooley Collection, MHC; Josiah Littlefield, autobiography, p. 19, Littlefield Family Collection, MHC.

17. Lucy Wyman Smith to Mr. & Mrs. O. M. Smith, December 29, 1839, Lucy Wyman Smith Collection, MHC.

18. Unsigned to brother and sister, April 29 [1865], Field Family Collection, MHC.

19. Kate Cooley to Mary Cooley, September 8, November 5, 1889, Thomas McIntyre Cooley Collection, MHC.

20. Mary Ann to Harriet Whittemore, February 28, 1864, April 19, December 10, 1863, Whittemore Family Collection, MHC.

21. Thomas McIntyre Cooley, diary, November 29, 1884, Thomas McIntyre Cooley Collection, MHC.

22. Charles Horton Cooley to Elsie Cooley, November 3, 1892, Charles Horton Cooley Collection, MHC.

23. Nellie Littlefield to Jessie Hart Williams, September 12, 1875, Littlefield Family Collection, MHC.

24. Martha Slayton to Mrs. Slayton and Gussie Slayton, July 31, 1917, Slayton Family Collection, MHC.

25. Mrs. Raab to Florence Pomeroy Raab [December 1907] Raab Family Collection, MHC.

26. Ellen Whitehead to Nellie Whitehead, January 28, 1877, Whitehead Family Collection, MHC.

27. Mary Cooley to Kate Cooley, April 10, 1875, Thomas McIntyre Cooley Collection, MHC.

28. Ellen Regal to Isaac Demmon, May 13, 1872, Regal Family Collection, MHC.

29. Jennie Bates to Nellie Whitehead, December 7, 1880, Whitehead Family Collection, MHC.

30. Nellie Littlefield to Josiah Littlefield, January 11, January 15, 1875, Littlefield Family Collection, MHC.

31. Ellen Regal to Isaac Demmon, June 16, 1872, Regal Family Collection, MHC. Norton notes a similar anxiety over childbirth in the eighteenth century. Norton, pp. 73-78.

32. Louise Smith to Jennie Keal, December 10, 1871, Lucy Wyman Smith Collection, MHC.

33. Nellie Littlefield to Josiah Littlefield, June 28, 1875, Littlefield Family Collection, MHC.

34. Abby Field to Flora, May 25, 1864, Field Family Collection, MHC. On similar assistance in the eighteenth century, see Norton, pp. 78-79.

35. Hannah Bingham to Maria Bingham Seymour, April 10, 1844, Bingham Family Collection, MHC.

36. Ellen Regal to Isaac Demmon, May 13, 1872, Regal Family Collection, MHC.

37. Erva Slayton to Mrs. Slayton, January 1, 1919, Slayton Family Collection, MHC. See also Catherine Scholten, "On the Importance of the Obstetrick Art: Changing Customs of Childbirth in America, 1760-1825," *William and Mary Quarterly*, 3rd Series, XXXIV (1977), p. 429.

38. Scholten, p. 434.

39. Electa White to Edwin Phelps [undated], 1870, Jessie Phelps Collection, MHC.

40. Nellie Littlefield to Josiah Littlefield, January 11, January 15, 1875, Littlefield Family Collection, MHC.

41. "The Palmer Letters," p. 8, David Wheeler Palmer Collection, MHC.

42. Harriet Whittemore to Abby Whittemore, October 8, 1858, Whittemore Family Collection, MHC.

43. Emma Hart to Josiah Littlefield, July 5, 1876, Margrit Hart to Josiah Littlefield, July 11, 1876, May 21, 1877, Littlefield Family Collection, MHC. The prevalence of aunts rather than grandmothers as foster mothers can be partially explained by the old age or deaths of some of the older women.

44. David Woodruff to Mary A. Woodruff, May 7, 1849, David Woodruff to Mrs. Woodruff, May 15, 1851, David Woodruff to Mrs. Woodruff and

Mary A. Woodruff, July 7, 1851, David Woodruff to Mary A. Woodruff, October 22, 1851, David Woodruff Collection, MHC.

45. Harriet Seymour to Maria Bingham Seymour, May 14 [1844], Bingham Family Collection, MHC.

46. Lucy Wyman Smith to Mrs. O. M. Smith, March 15, 1843, Lucy Wyman Smith Collection, MHC.

47. Abba Carr to Olive, December 22, 1872, Peckens Family Collection, MHC.

48. Lucy Smith to Mrs. O. M. Smith, July 21, 1839, Lucy Wyman Smith Collection, MHC.

49. Abby Field, diary, January 3, 1863, Field Family Collection, MHC.

50. Ellen Cresswell to Abby Field, May 5, 1893, Field Family Collection, MHC.

51. Mary Littlefield to Edmund Hall, December 12, 1839, Littlefield Family Collection, MHC.

52. Thomas McIntyre Cooley, diary, November 29, 1884, Thomas McIntyre Cooley Collection, MHC.

53. James Whittemore to Harriet and G. O. Whittemore, April 22, 1852, Betsey Phelps to Harriet Whittemore, December 28, 1861, Mary Ann to Harriet Whittemore, April 19, 1863, Whittemore Family Collection, MHC.

54. *Laws of the Territory of Michigan*, IV (Lansing, Mich.: 1884), p. 59. This law is similar to those found in Plymouth Colony in the seventeenth century. Thorp L. Wolford, "The Laws and Liberties of 1648," in *Essays in The History of Early American Law*, ed. David Flaherty (Chapel Hill, N.C.: University of North Carolina Press, 1969), p. 179.

55. *Laws of the Territory of Michigan*, III, p. 1139; I, p. 189.

56. *The Compiled Laws of the State of Michigan: 1871*, James S. Dewey (Lansing, Mich.: W. S. George, 1872), Title XXXIX, Chapter CCXLIV, Section 31, Compiler's Number 7540, p. 2075.

57. *The Compiled Laws of the State of Michigan: 1915*, Title VII, Chapter 134, Compiler's Number 7222-7236, pp. 2626-2633.

58. *The Compiled Laws of the State of Michigan: 1915*, Title XV, Chapter 256, Section 1, Compiler's Number 15230, pp. 5280-5281.

59. The character of the wicked stepmother is readily identifiable in many fairy tales popular in nineteenth-century America. While the character of the wicked stepmother has been interpreted as a projection of unacceptable hostility toward the biological mother, this theory assumes a cultural acceptance of distrust of a stepmother. Bruno Bettelheim, *The Uses of Enchantment* (New York: Vintage Books, 1977), pp. 66-70. The stepmother character may more directly represent a real anxiety about the potential rivalry between a stepmother and her stepdaugher, as Louise Bernikov suggests. She discusses the prevalent nineteenth-century fear of stepmothers, suggesting that stepmothers did perhaps often resent the daughters of their predecessors, seeing in them reminders of a husband's former wife and

competition for the affection and resources of the husband/father. Louise
Bernikov, *Among Women* (New York: Harper and Row, 1980), pp. 18–38.

In a poem reprinted in the nineteenth century, seventeenth-century poet
Anne Bradstreet addressed her husband before the birth of their child, asking
him in the event of her death to:

> Look to my little babes, my dear remains.
> And if thou loves thyself, or loved'st me,
> These protect from step-dame's injury.

Anne Bradstreet, "Before the Birth of One of Her Children," in *America's
Families: A Documentary History*, ed. Donald M. Scott and Bernard Wishy
(New York: Harper and Row, 1982), p. 128.

One male director of a home for girls used the term "step-mother" metaphorically, writing that one of his charges "has come to rest awhile upon
the heart of the State-as-a-mother. I trust it will not prove a *step*-mother
to her." Barbara Brenzel, "Lancaster Industrial School for Girls: A Social
Portrait of a Nineteenth-Century Reform School for Girls," *Feminist Studies*,
3 (Fall 1975), p. 45.

The cruel stepmother is a prevalent theme in folktales in many cultures.
See Stith Thompson, *Motif-Index of Folk-literature*, V (Bloomington, Ind.:
Indiana University Press, 1957), 300 (Type S31). In *Woman's Fiction: A
Guide to Novels by and about Women in America, 1820–1870*, pp. 37–38,
Nina Baym discusses the prevalence of abused orphans as heroines in
nineteenth-century women's fiction. Baym finds, however, that fictional aunts
as well as stepmothers mistreated the orphans left in their care.

60. Frances Pomeroy, diary, March 27, 1881, Raab Family Collection,
MHC.

61. Mary L. Hutchins to Harriet Whittemore, Monday 31, 1865 [sic],
Whittemore Family Collection, MHC.

62. Cf. Stack, on twentieth-century urban black kinship systems.

FIVE: WOMAN AND NURSE

1. Catharine E. Beecher, "Statistics of Female Health," in *The Oven Birds:
American Women on Womanhood, 1820–1920*, ed. Gail Parker (New York:
Anchor, 1972), pp. 165–178; Barbara Ehrenreich and Deirdre English, *For
Her Own Good: 150 Years of the Experts' Advice to Women* (Garden City,
N.Y.: Anchor, 1979), pp. 101–140. See also G. J. Barker-Benfield, *The Horrors
of the Half-Known Life: Male Attitudes Toward Women and Sexuality in
Nineteenth-Century America* (New York: Harper and Row, 1976); Carroll
Smith-Rosenberg, "The Hysterical Woman: Sex Roles and Role Conflict in
Nineteenth-Century America," *Social Research*, 39 (1972), pp. 652–678; Ann

Douglas Wood, "The Fashionable Diseases: Women's Complaints and Their Treatment in Nineteenth-Century America," in *Clio's Consciousness Raised: New Perspectives on the History of Women*, ed. Mary S. Hartman and Lois Banner (New York: Harper and Row, 1974), pp. 2-3.

2. Charles E. Rosenberg, "Florence Nightingale on Contagion: The Hospital as Moral Universe," *Healing and History*, ed. Charles E. Rosenberg (New York: Dawson, 1979), pp. 116-136.

3. Joseph B. and Laura E. Lyman, *The Philosophy of Housekeeping*, 10th ed. (Hartford, Conn.: Betts, 1869), p. 359.

4. Lucy Parker to Franklin Parker, June 28, 1888, Franklin Parker Collection, MHC.

5. Abby Field to Flora, February 18, 1871, Field Family Collection, MHC.

6. Electa White to Edwin Phelps [undated], 1870, Jessie Phelps Collection, MHC.

7. Helen Elizabeth Miles to Mary Cushman Miles, April 6, 1847, Parker Family Collection, MHC.

8. Jessie Phelps, diary, May 7-June 21, 1844, Jessie Phelps Collection, MHC; Marie Boyd to Jennie, August 17, 1898, William Boyd to Mr. Bliss, March 30, 1898, Josie Smith Collection, MHC.

9. Frances Pomeroy, diary, November 24, 1878, Raab Family Collection, MHC.

10. Nellie Littlefield to Josiah Littlefield, January 11, 1875, January 15, 1875, Littlefield Family Collection, MHC.

11. Weltha Field to Abby Field [April 1878], Field Family Collection, MHC.

12. Abel Regal, diary, November 22, 1854-December 24, 1854, Regal Family Collection, MHC.

13. Sarah Chandler to Ruth Evans, 11th month, 8th, 1835, Elizabeth Chandler Collection, MHC. On the importance of women in health care see Degler, p. 108. See Jeffrey, pp. 41-42, on health care by women on wagon trains to the Far West.

14. Frances Pomeroy, diary, November 24, 1878, Raab Family Collection, MHC.

15. Josiah Littlefield to Mary Littlefield, January 24, 1874, Littlefield Family Collection, MHC.

16. Henry Parker Smith, diary, March 24, 1852, Henry Parker Smith Collection, MHC.

17. Richard W. Wertz & Dorothy C. Wertz, *Lying-In: A History of Childbirth in America* (New York: Schocken, 1979), pp. 29-76; Barker-Benfield, pp. 61-71.

18. Unsigned to Abby Field [1887], Field Family Collection, MHC.

19. Lucy Wyman Smith to Mrs. O. M. Smith, December 14, 1845, Lucy Wyman Smith Collection, MHC.

20. R. A. Field to aunt, March 31, 1890, Field Family Collection, MHC.

21. Wertz, pp. 2-6.

22. Laura Gibbs to Nellie Whitehead, August 25, 1872, Whitehead Family Collection, MHC.

23. Ehrenreich and English, pp. 33-41; Josiah Littlefield, autobiography, p. 9, Littlefield Family Collection, MHC.

24. Lydia Maria Child, *The American Frugal Housewife* (1829; reprint New York: Harper and Row, 1972), pp. 24-26.

25. Mary L. Edgeworth, *The Southern Gardener and Receipt Book*, 3rd ed. (Philadelphia: Lippincott, 1860), pp. 281-324.

26. Mary Cooley to Kate Cooley, December 16, 1875, Thomas McIntyre Cooley Collection, MHC.

27. Orpha White to Nellie Whitehead, Monday 12, 1872 [sic], Whitehead Family Collection, MHC.

28. Mary A. Watson, diary, 1905, Schlesinger Library, Radcliffe College, Cambridge, Mass.

29. Ellen Whitehead Gascoyne to Nellie Whitehead, January 28, 1877, Whitehead Family Collection, MHC.

30. Ellen Whitehead Gascoyne to Edward Whitehead, May 4, 1876, Whitehead Family Collection, MHC.

31. Helen Elizabeth Miles to brother, October 29, 1848, Parker Family Collection, MHC.

32. James Harvey Young, *The Toadstool Millionaires: A Social History of Patent Medicines in America Before Federal Regulation* (Princeton, N.J.: Princeton University Press, 1961), pp. 68-69.

33. In Sarah Stage, *Female Complaints: Lydia Pinkham and the Business of Women's Medicine* (New York: Norton, 1979), Sarah Stage discusses the connection between the marketing of patent medicine and traditional women's health care, pp. 129-131, 247-257.

34. Wertz, p. 60.

35. Wertz, pp. 52-55.

36. Abby Field to Abram Field, September 17, 1871, Field Family Collection, MHC.

37. Smith-Rosenberg, "Hysterical Woman," pp. 652-678.

38. Jane Howell to Thomas Chandler, 3rd month, 12th, 1836, Elizabeth Chandler Collection, MHC.

39. Elizabeth Parker Robinson, journal [February 1897], Parker Family Collection, MHC.

40. See Kathryn Kish Sklar, *Catharine Beecher: A Study in American Domesticity* (New Haven, Conn.: Yale University Press, 1973).

41. Catharine E. Beecher, *Housekeeper and Healthkeeper* (New York: Harper, 1873), pp. 235, 130, 390-394.

42. Beecher and Stowe, pp. 43-65, 150; Beecher, pp. 130, 390-394.

43. Lyman, pp. 341, 359.

44. Rosenberg, pp. 118-119.

45. Lyman, p. 347.

46. Beecher, *Housekeeper and Healthkeeper*, pp. 322, 458.

47. Helen E. Marshall, *Dorothea Dix: Forgotten Samaritan* (New York: Russell and Russell, 1937), p. 206.

48. Mary Douglas, *Purity and Danger: An Analysis of Concepts of Pollution and Taboo* (London: Routledge and Kegan Paul, 1966).

49. Ehrenreich and English, pp. 33–39; Wertz, pp. 6–7.

50. Louisa May Alcott, *Life, Letters and Journals*, ed. Ednah D. Cheney (Boston: Roberts, 1890), p. 147.

51. Beecher and Stowe, p. 346.

52. Electa Loomis to Ann Gennette Loomis Preston, August 31, 1862, Preston Family Collection, MHC.

53. Helen Elizabeth Miles to Mary Cushman Miles, April 16, 1847, Parker Family Collection, MHC.

54. Lucy Parker to Franklin Parker, June 28, 1888, Franklin Parker Collection, MHC.

55. Unsigned letter, February 4, 1884, Julia Bird Martin Collection, MHC.

56. Mary Bird to Cora, January 21, 1878, Julia Bird Martin Collection, MHC.

57. Beecher and Stowe, pp. 342, 346.

58. Beecher and Stowe, p. 343.

59. Beecher and Stowe, pp. 342–343.

60. Beecher and Stowe, pp. 345–346.

61. Lois White to Abby Field, August 30, 1898, Field Family Collection, MHC.

62. Helen Elizabeth Miles to Mary Cushman Miles, April 16, 1847, Parker Family Collection, MHC.

63. Louisa May Alcott, *Little Women* (1869; reprint, New York, Grossett and Dunlap, 1947), p. 542.

64. Harriet Whittemore Matthews to Harriet Whittemore, August 17, 1857, Whittemore Family Collection, MHC.

65. Jessie Phelps, diary, June 27, 1944, Jessie Phelps Collection, MHC.

66. Barker-Benfield, p. 130; Ehrenreich and English, p. 136; Regina Morantz, "The Lady and her Physician," in *Clio's Consciousness Raised*, ed. Hartman and Banner, p. 42.

67. Sklar, p. 214.

68. Angelina Bingham to Maria Bingham Seymour, April 21, 1847, Bingham Family Collection, MHC.

69. Alcott, *Little Women*, pp. 541–542.

SIX: A POOR DEPENDENT BEING

1. Uhlenberg, "Changing Configurations of the Life Course," p. 89.

2. U.S., Dept. of Interior, *Compendium of the Eleventh Census: 1890*, Part III (Wash. D. C.: Government Printing Office, 1897), p. 150, Table 20; U.S., Dept. of Interior, *Twelfth Census of the United States: 1900*, II, pp. xc, lxxxiv, Tables XLIX, XLVII; U.S., Dept. of Commerce: Census Bureau, *Thirteenth Census of the United States: 1910*, I, p. 558, Table 32; U.S. Dept. of Commerce: Census Bureau, *Fourteenth Census of the United States: 1920*, II, p. 430, Table 11.

3. David Hackett Fischer, *Growing Old in America: The Bland-Lee Lectures Delivered at Clark University* (New York: Oxford University Press, 1977) pp. 62-63, 93, 163. On widowhood, see also W. Andrew Achenbaum, *Old Age in the New Land: The American Experience Since 1790* (Baltimore: The Johns Hopkins University Press, 1978), p. 29.

4. Achenbaum, pp. 75-86. Howard P. Chudacoff and Tamara K. Hareven, "Family Transitions into Old Age," in *Transitions: The Family and the Life Course in Historical Perspective*, ed. Tamara K. Hareven (New York: Academic Press, 1978), pp. 217-243.

5. Fischer, pp. 164-168.

6. *Eleventh Census of the United States: 1890*, Compendium, pp. 115, 150, Table 20; *Twelfth Census of the United States: 1900*, II, p. lxxxii, Table XLV, p. lxxxiii, Table XLVI; *Thirteenth Census of the United States: 1910*, I, p. 558, Table 32, p. 517, Table 14.

7. Achenbaum, pp. 28-31; Fischer, pp. 62-63, 93.

8. Maris Vinovskis discusses the frequency with which both men and women in their fourth and fifth decades expected imminent death, citing the example of a man who, having reached the age of 50, felt he might "justly be classed among the old." Maris Vinovskis, "Angels' Heads and Weeping Willows: Death in Early America," in *Themes in the History of the Family*, ed. Tamara Hareven (Worcester, Mass.: American Antiquarian Society, 1978), pp. 40-44.

9. Henry Parker Smith, diary, September 25, 1856, Henry Parker Smith Collection, MHC; Mrs. Bailey to Myron Buck, March 2, 1858, Field Family Collection, MHC.

10. Achenbaum, pp. 28-29.

11. Jane Sabin to Sarah Regal, August 18, 1863, Regal Family Collection, MHC.

12. Jane Sabin to Sarah Regal, October 30, 1841, Regal Family Collection, MHC.

13. Mary Cooley to Eugene Cooley, March 12, 1871, Thomas McIntyre Cooley Collection, MHC.

14. Jane Howell to Thomas Chandler, 8th month, 22nd, 1837, 2nd month, 13th, 1842, Elizabeth Chandler Collection, MHC.

15. Electa Loomis to Ann Gennette Loomis Preston, March 11, 1863, Preston Family Collection, MHC.

16. Mother to Isaac Demmon, April 30, 1882, Regal Family Collection, MHC.

17. Jane Howell to Thomas Chandler, 5th month, 7th, 1839, Elizabeth Chandler Collection, MHC.

18. Sister to Olive Rogers, January 31, [1872], Peckens Family Collection, MHC.

19. Temperance Mack to children, July 30, 1847, Whittemore Family Collection, MHC.

20. Almira Covey to Almira Mack, February 24, 1842, Whittemore Family Collection, MHC.

21. Mrs. Bailey to Myron Buck, October 15, 1861, [undated, 1864], Field Family Collection, MHC.

22. Delia Parker to Franklin Parker, January 21 [1853], February 7, 1853, Franklin Parker Collection, MHC.

23. Henry Parker Smith, diary, February 15, 1861, Henry Parker Smith Collection, MHC.

24. Edwin Phelps to Delia Phelps, August 13, 1889, Jessie Phelps Collection, MHC.

25. C. A. Kinsley to Edmund Hall, August 13, 1885, Edmund Hall to C. A. Kinsley, October 2, 1855, Littlefield Family Collection, MHC.

26. Marilla Turrill to Myron Buck, November 1, 1857, Field Family Collection, MHC.

27. Edwin Phelps to Delia Phelps, August 13, 1889, Jessie Phelps Collection, MHC.

28. Unsigned to James Whittemore, December 29, 1858, Whittemore Family Collection, MHC.

29. Lucy Sexton to sister, June 12, 1887, Field Family Collection, MHC.

30. R. A. Field to aunt, March 31, 1890, Field Family Collection, MHC.

31. Aunt Susan to Nellie Whitehead, July 14 [no year], Whitehead Family Collection, MHC.

32. Mollie Baker to Nellie Whitehead, December 8, 1872, Whitehead Family Collection, MHC.

33. Abba Carr to aunt, October 8, 1872, Peckens Family Collection, MHC.

34. Marilla Turrill to Myron Buck, April 28, 1863, Field Family Collection, MHC.

35. Laura Gibbs to Nellie Whitehead, September 10, 1871, Whitehead Family Collection, MHC.

36. Jennie Bates to Nellie and Edward Whitehead, December 7, 1880, Whitehead Family Collection, MHC.

37. Martha Cole, diary, January 5, January 16, January 25, March 31, June 21, July 5, July 24, 1901, Martha Cole Collection, MHC.

38. Almyra to Ann Gennette Loomis Preston, November 22, 1860, Preston Family Collection, MHC.

39. Philamena Loomis Brown to Ann Gennette Loomis Preston, January 3, 1862, Preston Family Collection, MHC.

40. Almyra to Ann Gennette Loomis Preston, November 22, 1860, Preston Family Collection, MHC.

41. Almyra to Ann Gennette Loomis Preston, November 22, 1860, Preston Family Collection, MHC.

42. Josiah Littlefield, autobiography, pp. 5-24, Littlefield Family Collection, MHC.

43. Jane Howell to Thomas Chandler, 2nd month, 21st, 1840, 5th month, 31st, 1840, Elizabeth Chandler Collection, MHC.

44. Jane Howell to Ruth Evans, 1st month, 14th, 1836, Elizabeth Chandler Collection, MHC.

45. Mary to Ann Gennette Loomis Preston, January 25, 1864, and biographical data, Preston Family Collection, MHC. Widows in the Far West expressed a similar perception of their sudden immersion in the business world. One woman wrote of her loneliness in dealing with "courser minds who cannot understand" a woman's more sensitive nature. Jeffrey, pp. 64-65.

46. *Laws of the Territory of Michigan*, I, p. 347, and II, pp. 35-36, 534; *The Compiled Laws of the State of Michigan: 1915*, Title IX, Chapter 218, Section 25, Compiler's Number 11475, pp. 4070-4072; Section 1, Compiler's Number 11485, p. 4077; Title X, Chapter 223, Section 1, Compiler's Number 11654, pp. 4120-4122; Section 22, 23, Compiler's Number 11671-11672, p. 4126.

47. *Laws of the Territory of Michigan*, II, p. 738; *The Compiled Laws of the State of Michigan: 1915*, Title X, Chapter 223, Sections 22, 23, Compiler's Number 11671-11672, p. 4126.

48. *Laws of the Territory of Michigan*, I, pp. 160-161; *The Compiled Laws of the State of Michigan: 1857*, Title XXII, Chapter XCI, Section 1, pp. 858-860; *The Compiled Laws of the State of Michigan:* 1915, Title X, Chapter 225, Section 1, Compiler's Number 11795, pp. 4178-4181.

49. *Laws of the Territory of Michigan*, I, pp. 496-499; II, pp. 363-366.

50. *Laws of the Territory of Michigan*, III, pp. 931-932. The law allowed for some property of a woman found guilty of adultery to revert eventually to her kin. In such instances, a husband held his wife's personal property forever but held her real estate only during his life if there were children of the marriage and during her life only, if there were no children of the marriage. *The Compiled Laws of the State of Michigan: 1857*, Title XXVII, Chapter CVIII, Section 25, Compiler's Number 3246, p. 957; *The Compiled Laws of the State of Michigan: 1915*, Title IX, Chapter 217, Sections 6, 7, 8, Compiler's Number 11397-11399, p. 4049. Limits were imposed on divorce on the grounds of adultery. No divorce was allowed if there was connivance, if the parties cohabited after knowledge of the adultery, or if more than five years had passed since obtaining this knowledge. Thus adultery was not an absolute grounds for divorce but was allowed only when it appeared to have

disrupted the marriage relationship. *Compiled Laws of the State of Michigan1857,* Title XXVII, Chapter CVIII, Section 41, p. 960.

51. *The Compiled Laws of the State of Michigan: 1857,* Title XXVII, Chapter CVIII, Compiler's Number 3239–3249, pp. 956–958.

52. *The Compiled Laws of the State of Michigan: 1915,* Title IX, Chapter 217, Section 7, Compiler's Number 11398, pp. 4051–4053.

53. One woman wrote that a friend of hers, who had refused to join her husband after he moved west, "seems crushed with the disgrace, more than the loss of Shaw." Mary Lee to Weltha Field, June 6, 1889, Field Family Collection, MHC.

54. U.S., Dept. of Interior, *Special Report of the Census Office: Marriage and Divorce 1867–1906* (Washington, D.C.: U.S. Government Printing Office, 1908), II, pp. 580–581, 630.

55. U.S., Dept. of Interior, *Special Report of the Census Office,* II, pp. 33–35.

56. Hannah Bingham, diary, September 9, 1828, December 8, 1828, Bingham Family Collection, MHC.

57. Harriet Mathews to Harriet Whittemore, April 9, 1863, Whittemore Family Collection, MHC.

58. Juliana Caster to Harriet Whittemore, May 18, 1847, Whittemore Family Collection, MHC.

59. Sarah Regal to Eliza Granger, December 6, 1857, Regal Family Collection, MHC.

60. Henry Parker Smith, diary, March 16, 1857, Henry Parker Smith Collection, MHC.

61. Frances Pomeroy, diary, March 27, 1884, Raab Family Collection, MHC.

62. Margaret Pomeroy, Florence Raab, and Irving Raab, undated manuscript, Raab Family Collection, MHC.

63. Hannah and Abel Bingham to Angelina Bingham, August 20, 1847, Bingham Family Collection, MHC.

CONCLUSION

1. Cott, *The Bonds of Womanhood;* Smith-Rosenberg, "The Female World of Love and Ritual", pp. 1–29.

2. Baym, p. 49.

3. Uhlenberg, "Changing Configurations of the Life Course," p. 79.

4. Elizabeth Gaspar Brown, "Poor Relief in a Wisconsin County, 1846–1866: Administration and Recipients," *American Journal of Legal History,* 20 (April 1976), pp. 79–117. Brown finds that from 1858 to 1866, 37.7% of those admitted to the county poorhouse she examined were women with children, but without husbands, while 15.2% were children without parents.

5. Degler, pp. 151–165.

APPENDIX A

1. Susan Bloomberg et al., pp. 26–45. They examine 326 households in 1850 and 868 households in 1880, drawn in clusters from rural, town and village, and Detroit locations.

2. The sample examined here of course indicates nothing about general demographic trends; the figures are presented solely to determine the extent to which the families examined in this study are representative of Michigan families in the nineteenth century. The households in the sample have been located on the 1850 and 1880 United States census report by means of indexes listing the names of household heads. Some of the households examined were living outside Michigan at the time of the census, and the lifetimes of a generation in some households fell between the two census years used here. Some households have probably been missed due to indexing errors or omission from the census records; most households not found on the census, however, are known to have been living outside Michigan in the census years or to have fallen between the two years.

I have used genealogical data and evidence from family correspondence to determine which households were members of the same extended families. Information available through these sources is compared with the names of family members, their ages, occupations, and location as listed on the census. In cases of uncertainty as to the identity of the household listed on the census, I have omitted the household from the study. One unmarried woman was located as a boarder in an apparently unrelated household; this household was not included in the study.

In correlating information from family letters with census data, it becomes apparent that the census information is sometimes misleading. For example, one apparent boarder with a different surname was actually a married daughter; in another instance, several children with the same surname as the household head were actually nieces and nephews rather than sons and daughters of the household head. In another family, one individual appears twice in the census, as a member of two households. For purposes of comparison with the Bloomberg study, I have used the census information without correction, since such discrepancies would also occur in a larger sample.

3. Bloomberg et al., p. 36.

4. The ministers' lack of real estate is not indicative of low social status, however.

5. In the household of one of these merchants, half of the real estate was listed under the wife's name. I have included the wife's wealth as if it

belonged to the head of the household for comparative purposes. In the other households examined, only the household head owned real estate.

6. Because of the small number of families examined here, a single household can significantly alter statistical patterns. Since this skewing effect is more apparent, and thus more easily accounted for, in looking at distributions of figures rather than average figures, I have attempted to use the former method of analysis whenever possible. Because of the small sample size, minor differences from the larger sample are not signficant; large statistical differences, however, can point to unique characteristics of the sample group.

7. Since occupation of adult males is listed by the census, it is possible to assess from the occupation listed whether the non-related individual worked outside the household. Since occupation was not listed for women on the 1850 census, it is impossible to determine which adult women were servants and which were boarders. Because of the differences in surnames, it is not possible to determine which adult women living in the same household were related to one another. Compared to the Bloomberg figures for percentages of rural households without a spouse of the household head, the percentage of such households was higher than average in the sample examined here. This factor therefore cannot account for the larger household size relative to the smaller number of children. (Since the Bloomberg data is only for rural households, a more systematic comparison of the number of households without a spouse of the head present is not possible. Because relationships are not listed in the 1850 census, women who would appear to be wives of household heads may actually have been sisters or daughters of the household heads.)

8. Since these figures cover only those households with more than one child, and are further broken down by age of household head, only general patterns can be determined, due to the small size of the sample. The difference in range of age among children may not be representative of completed family size. Since a large percentage of the households in the sample included oldest children under six years of age in 1880, these data may represent a greater frequency of delayed childbearing rather than tighter spacing of children, since a larger than average number of households headed by those over 45 years of age in the sample group had at least a 15-year age span among their children.

APPENDIX B

1. Accounts of the early exploration and settlement of Michigan can be found in F. Clever Bald, *Michigan in Four Centuries* (New York: Harper and Row, 1961), and Willis Frederick Dunbar, *Michigan: A History of the Wolverine State* (Grand Rapids, Mich.: Eerdmans, 1970).

2. Bald, pp. 144–146.

3. Parkins, pp. 244-245.

4. Parkins, pp. 216-218.

5. The remaining land in the northern Lower Peninsula was ceded by the Native Americans in 1836 but was mainly a lumbering rather than a farming region.

6. Parkins, p. 257.

7. Milton M. Quaife and Sidney Glazer, *Michigan: From Primitive Wilderness to Industrial Commonwealth* (New York: Prentice-Hall, 1948), p. 150.

8. Bald, p. 156.

9. Parkins, p. 170.

10. Parkins, pp. 259-261.

11. Parkins, pp. 262-264.

12. Parkins, p. 260.

13. Ralph R. Tingley, "Postal Service in Michigan Territory," *Michigan History*, 35 (1951), pp. 447-460.

14. Parkins, pp. 265-266, 226.

15. Frederick Morley, *Michigan and Its Resources* (Lansing, Mich.: State Printers and Binders, 1881), pp. 12, 15-32.

16. Parkins, p. 170.

17. Dunbar, pp. 434-435.

18. After 1841, land was sold by the government under a system similar to the later homestead provision. The land, however, was sold for prices ranging from $1.25 to $2.50 per acre, while under the Homestead Act land was provided free of charge, except for small fees, to anyone who lived on the homestead for a minimum of five years. Under both systems, the maximum amount of land distributed to any one person was 160 acres. During the 1860s and 1870s, about 10% of Michigan's land was settled as homesteads. Harriette M. Dilla, *The Politics of Michigan, 1865-1878* (New York: Columbia University Press, 1912), pp. 241-242.

19. Morley, pp. 33-51; Dunbar, pp. 615-616.

20. Chase, p. 250.

21. Dunbar, p. 612; Chase, p. 255.

22. Chase, pp. 256, 459; Bald, p. 388.

23. Chase, p. 459; Dunbar, p. 614.

24. Siegfried Giedion, *Mechanization Takes Command* (New York: Norton, 1969), p. 162.

25. Bald, pp. 370-371.

Bibliography

Published Primary Sources

Alcott, Louisa May. *Life, Letters, and Journals.* Ed. Ednah D. Cheney. Boston: Roberts, 1890.

———. *Little Women.* 1869; reprint, New York: Grosset and Dunlap, 1947.

Beecher, Catharine E. *Housekeeper and Healthkeeper.* New York: Harper, 1873.

———. "Statistics of Female Health." In *The Oven Birds: American Women on Womanhood, 1820-1920.* Ed. Gail Parker. New York: Anchor, 1972, pp. 165-178.

Beecher, Catharine E., and Harriet Beecher Stowe. *The American Woman's Home.* 1869; reprint, Hartford, Conn.: Stowe-Day Foundation, 1975.

Child, Lydia Marie. *The American Frugal Housewife.* 1829; reprint, New York: Harper and Row, 1972.

Edgeworth, Mary L. *The Southern Gardener and Receipt Book.* 3rd ed. Philadelphia: Lippincott, 1860.

"English Letter-Writers of the Eighteenth Century." *Littell's Living Age,* January 20, 1855, 183-192.

"Female Letter-Writers." *Tait's Edinburgh Magazine,* May 1832, 197-207.

Gee, Richard. "Letters and Letter-writers." *Eclectic Magazine,* June 1897, 850-855.

[Genevieve]. "Women's Duties." *Godey's Lady's Book and Magazine,* February 1873, 166-167.

"Half Hours with the Best Letter Writers." *Eclectic Magazine,* February 1869, 199-203.

Horwill, Herbert W. "Literature: The Art of Letter-Writing." *Forum,* July 1904, 70-84.

Lang, Andrew. "Telephones and Letter-Writing." *Critic*, June 1906, 507–508.

Leonard, Priscilla. "The Laws of Letter Writing." *Harper's Bazar*, November 1904, 1125–1127.

"Letter-Writing." *Littell's Living Age*, August 20, 1870, 451–462.

"Letter-Writing and Letter-Writers." *Littell's Living Age*, January 24, 1857, 193–204.

"Letters and Letter-Writing." *Littell's Living Age*, November 25, 1871, 477–489.

"The Lost Art of Letter-Writing." *Nation*, 65 November 11, 1897, 370–371.

Lyman, Joseph B. and Laura E. *The Philosophy of Housekeeping*. 10th ed. Hartford, Conn.: Betts, 1869.

Michigan. *Laws of the Territory*. I–IV. Lansing, Mich.: W. S. George, 1871.

Michigan. *The Compiled Laws of the State of Michigan: 1857*. Thomas McIntyre Cooley. Detroit, Mich.: Raymond and Selleck, 1857.

Michigan. *The Compiled Laws of the State of Michigan: 1871*. James S. Dewey. Lansing, Mich.: W. S. George, 1872.

Michigan. *The Compiled Laws of the State of Michigan: 1915*. Edmund Shields, Cyrenius P. Black, Archibald Broomfield. Lansing, Mich.: Wynkoop Hallenbeck Crawford, 1916.

Schel, Edith. "Women as Letter-Writers." *Littell's Living Age*, February 25, 1899, 513–523.

Stowe, Harriet Beecher [Christopher Crowfield]. *House and Home Papers*. Boston: Ticknor and Fields, 1865.

———. *Uncle Tom's Cabin; or, Life Among the Lowly*. 1852; reprint, Garden City, N.Y.: Dolphin, 1960.

"Survival of Letter-Writing." *Nation*, January 4, 1900, 5–6.

Ward, Elizabeth Stuart (Phelps). *The Gates Ajar*. Boston: Fields, Osgood, 1870.

Wharton, Anne H. "A Lost Art." *Lippincott's Magazine*, March 1891, 369–375.

U.S., Department of Interior, *Special Report of the Census Office: Marriage and Divorce 1867–1906*. Wash. D.C.: U.S. Government Printing Office, 1908.

U.S., Department of Interior. *Mortality Statistics of the Seventh Census of the United States: 1850*. J. D. B. Debow. Wash. D.C.: A. O. P. Nicholson, printer, 1855.

———. *Eighth Census of the United States: 1860*. IV: Statistics of the United States (including mortality, property, &c.) in 1860. Wash. D.C.: Government Printing Office, 1866.

———. *Ninth Census of the United States: 1870*. II: The Vital Statistics of the United States. Francis A. Walker. Wash. D.C.: Government Printing Office, 1872.

———. *A Compendium of the Ninth Census: 1870*. Francis A. Walker. Wash. D.C.: Government Printing Office, 1872.

———. *Tenth Census of the United States: 1880*. I: Statistics of the Population. Wash. D.C.: Government Printing Office, 1883.

————. *Tenth Census of the United States: 1880*. XI: Report on the Mortality and Vital Statistics of the United States. John S. Billings. Wash. D.C.: Government Printing Office, 1885.

————. *Eleventh Census of the United States: 1890*. I: Report on the Population. Wash. D.C.: Government Printing Office, 1897.

————. *Eleventh Census of the United States: 1890*. IV: Report on Vital and Social Statistics. Part III: Statistics of Deaths. John S. Billings. Wash. D.C.: Government Printing Office, 1894.

————. *Compendium of the Eleventh Census: 1890*. Part III. Wash. D.C.: Government Printing Office, 1897.

————. *Twelfth Census of the United States: 1900*. II: Population. Wash. D.C.: Government Printing Office, 1902.

————. *Twelfth Census of the United States: 1900*. IV: Vital Statistics. Part II. Statistics of Deaths. Wash. D.C.: Government Printing Office, 1902.

U.S., Department of Commerce: Census Bureau. *Thirteenth Census of the United States: 1910*. I: Population. Wash. D.C.: Government Printing Office, 1913.

————. *Fourteenth Census of the United States: 1920*. II: Population. Wash. D.C.: Government Printing Office, 1920.

————. *School Attendance in 1920*. Fourteenth Census: Monograph IV. Frank Alexander Ross. Wash. D.C.: Government Printing Office, 1924.

SECONDARY SOURCES

Abrahams, Roger. "Negotiating Respect: Patterns of Presentation Among Black Women." In *Women and Folklore*. Ed. Claire R. Farrar. Austin, Texas: University of Texas Press, 1975, pp. 58-80.

Achenbaum, W. Andrew. *Old Age in the New Land: The American Experience Since 1790*. Baltimore: The Johns Hopkins University Press, 1978.

Adams, Bert N. "Interaction Theory and the Social Network." *Sociometry*, 30 (1967), 64-78.

Aldous, Joan, and Murray A. Strauss. "Social Networks and Conjugal Roles: A Test of Bott's Hypothesis." *Social Forces*, 44 (1966), 576-580.

Anderson, Michael. *Family Structure in Nineteenth-Century Lancashire*. Cambridge: Cambridge University Press, 1971.

Ayoub, Millicent R. "The Child's Control of His Kindred in View of Geographic Mobility and Its Effects." *International Journal of Comparative Sociology*, 6 (1965), 1-6.

Bald, F. Clever. *Michigan in Four Centuries*. New York: Harper and Row, 1961.

Barker-Benfield, G. J. *The Horrors of the Half-Known Life: Male Attitudes Toward Women and Sexuality in Nineteenth-Century America*. New York: Harper and Row, 1976.

Barnes, J. A. "Graph Theory and Social Networks: A Technical Comment on Connectedness and Connectivity." *Sociology*, 3 (1969), 215-232.

Barron, Nancy. "Sex-Typed Language: The Production of Grammatical Cases." *Acta Sociologica*, 14 (1971), 24-42.

Barthes, Roland. *Elements of Semiology*. Trans. Annette Lavers and Colin Smith. New York: Hill and Wang, 1967.

Basch, Francoise. *Relative Creatures: Victorian Women in Society and the Novel*. Trans. Anthony Rudolf. New York: Schocken, 1974.

Basso, Keith H. "The Ethnography of Writing." In *Explorations in the Ethnography of Speaking*. Ed. Richard Bauman and Joel Scherzer. Cambridge: Cambridge University Press, 1974, pp. 425-432.

Baym, Nina. *Woman's Fiction: A Guide to Novels by and about Women in America, 1820-1870*. Ithaca, N.Y.: Cornell University Press, 1978.

Bernikov, Louise. *Among Women*. New York: Harper, 1980.

Bernstein, Basil. *Class, Codes and Control*, I. 2nd rev. ed. London: Routledge and Kegan Paul, 1974.

Bettelheim, Bruno. *The Uses of Enchantment*. New York: Vintage Books, 1977.

Bloomberg, Susan, Mary Fox, Robert M. Warner, and Sam Bass Warner, Jr. "A Census Probe into Nineteenth-Century Family History: Southern Michigan, 1850-1880." *Journal of Social History*, 5 (1971), 26-45.

Blumin, Stuart M. "Rip Van Winkle's Grandchildren: Family and Household in the Hudson Valley, 1800-1860." *Journal of Urban History*, 1 (1975), 293-315.

Bott, Elizabeth B. *Family and Social Network: Roles, Norms, and External Relationships in Ordinary Urban Families*. London: Tavistock, 1957.

Brenzel, Barbara. "Lancaster Industrial School for Girls: A Social Portrait of a Nineteenth-Century Reform School for Girls." *Feminist Studies*, 3 (Fall 1975), 40-53.

Brown, Elizabeth Gaspar. "Poor Relief in a Wisconsin County, 1846-1866: Administration and Recipients." *American Journal of Legal History*, 20 (April 1976), 79-117.

Chase, Lew Allen. *Rural Michigan*. New York: Macmillan, 1922.

Chekki, Danesh A. *Modernization and Kin Network*. Leiden: Brill, 1974.

Chodorow, Nancy. *The Reproduction of Mothering: Psychoanalysis and the Sociology of Gender*. Berkeley and Los Angeles: University of California Press, 1978.

Chudacoff, Howard P. "Newlyweds and Family Extension: The First Stage of the Family Cycle in Providence, Rhode Island, 1864-1865 and 1879-1880." In *Family and Population in Nineteenth-Century America*. Ed. Tamara K. Hareven and Maris A. Vinovskis. Princeton, N.J.: Princeton University Press, 1978, pp. 179-205.

Chudacoff, Howard P., and Tamara K. Hareven. "Family Transitions into Old Age." In *Transitions: The Family and the Life Course in Historical*

Perspective. Ed. Tamara K. Hareven. New York: Academic Press, 1978, pp. 217-243.

Conklin, Nancy Faires. "Toward a Feminist Analysis of Linguistic Behavior." *The University of Michigan Papers in Women's Studies,* 1 (1974), 51-73.

Cott, Nancy F. *The Bonds of Womanhood: 'Woman's Sphere' in New England, 1780-1835.* New Haven, Conn.: Yale University Press, 1977.

————. "Eighteenth-Century Family and Social Life Revealed in Massachusetts Divorce Records." *Journal of Social History,* 10 (1976), 20-43.

————. "Young Women in the Second Great Awakening in New England." *Feminist Studies,* 3 (Fall 1975), 15-29.

Degler, Carl. *At Odds: Women and the Family in America from the Revolution to the Present.* New York: Oxford University Press, 1980.

Demos, John. "Old Age in Early New England." In *Turning Points: Historical and Sociological Essays on the Family.* Ed. John Demos and Sarane Spence Boocock. Chicago: The University of Chicago Press, 1978, pp. 248-287.

Dilla, Harriette M. *The Politics of Michigan, 1865-1878.* New York: Columbia University Press, 1912.

Douglas, Ann. *The Feminization of American Culture.* New York: Knopf, 1977.

————. "Heaven Our Home: Consolation Literature in the Northern United States, 1830-1880." *American Quarterly,* 26 (December 1974), 496-515.

Douglas, Mary. *Purity and Danger: An Analysis of Concepts of Pollution and Taboo.* London: Routledge and Kegan Paul, 1966.

Dunbar, Willis Frederick. *Michigan: A History of the Wolverine State.* Grand Rapids, Mich.: Eerdmans, 1970.

Easterlin, Richard A., G. Alters, and G. A. Condran. "Farms and Farm Families in Old and New Areas: The Northern States in 1860." In *Family and Population in Nineteenth-Century America.* Ed. Tamara K. Hareven and Maris A. Vinovskis. Princeton, N.J.: Princeton University Press, 1978, pp. 22-73.

Ehrenreich, Barbara, and Deirdre English. *For Her Own Good: 150 Years of the Experts' Advice to Women.* Garden City, N.Y.: Anchor, 1979.

Emerson, Richard. "Power-Dependence Relationships." *American Sociological Review,* 27 (1962), 31-41.

Faragher, John Mack, *Women and Men on the Overland Trail.* New Haven, Conn.: Yale University Press, 1979.

Farber, Bernard, ed. *Kinship and Family Organization.* New York: Wiley, 1966.

Fischer, David Hackett. *Growing Old in America: The Bland-Lee Lectures Delivered at Clark University.* New York: Oxford University Press, 1977.

Freedman, Estelle B. "Their Sisters' Keepers: An Historical Perspective on Female Correctional Institutions in the United States: 1870-1900." *Feminist Studies*, 2 (1974), 77-95.

French, Stanley. "The Cemetery as Cultural Institution: The Establishment of Mount Auburn and the 'Rural Cemetery' Movement." *American Quarterly*, 26 (March 1974), 37-59.

Gardner, Emelyn Elizabeth, and Geraldine Jencks Chickering, eds. *Ballads and Songs of Southern Michigan*. Ann Arbor, Mich.: The University of Michigan Press, 1939.

Genovese, Eugene D. *Roll, Jordan, Roll*. New York: Random House, 1974.

Giedion, Siegfried. *Mechanization Takes Command*. New York: Norton, 1969.

Gluckman, Max. "Gossip and Scandal." *Current Anthropology*, 4 (1963), 307-316.

Goody, Jack. *Comparative Studies in Kinship*. London: Routledge and Kegan Paul, 1969.

Gordon, Linda. *Woman's Body, Woman's Right: A Social History of Birth Control in America*. New York: Penguin, 1977.

Gordon, Michael, ed. *The American Family in Social-Historical Perspective*. New York: St. Martin's, 1973.

Gouldner, Alvin. "The Norm of Reciprocity: A Preliminary Statement." *American Sociological Review*, 25 (1960), 161-178.

Grant, Robert. *Law and the Family*. New York: Scribner's, 1919.

Greven, Philip J. *Four Generations: Population, Land, and Family in Colonial Andover, Massachusetts*. Ithaca, N.Y.: Cornell University Press, 1970.

Gutman, Herbert G. *The Black Family in Slavery and Freedom, 1750-1925*. New York: Pantheon, 1976.

Harding, Susan. "Women and Words in a Spanish Village." In *Toward an Anthropology of Women*. Ed. Rayna R. Reiter. New York: Monthly Review Press, 1975, pp. 283-308.

Hareven, Tamara. "The Dynamics of Kin in an Industrial Community." In *Turning Points: Historical and Sociological Essays on the Family*. Ed. John Demos and Sarane Spence Boocock. Chicago: The University of Chicago Press, 1978, pp. 151-182.

―――. "Family Time and Historical Time." *Daedalus*, 106 (1977), 57-70.

―――. "The Historical Study of the Family in Urban Society." *Journal of Urban History*, 1 (1975), 259-267.

―――. "Modernization and Family History: Perspectives on Social Change." *Signs*, 2 (1976), 190-206.

Haskins, George L. "The Beginnings of Partible Inheritance in the American Colonies." In *Essays in the History of Early American Law*. Ed. David Flaherty. Chapel Hill, N.C.: University of North Carolina Press, 1969, pp. 204-244.

Hawkes, Terence. *Structuralism and Semiotics*. Berkeley and Los Angeles: University of California Press, 1977.

Hubert, Jane. "Kinship and Geographical Mobility in a Sample from a London Middle-Class Area." *International Journal of Comparative Sociology*, 6 (1965), 61–80.

Janeway, Elizabeth. *Powers of the Weak*. New York: Knopf, 1980.

Jeffrey, Julie Roy. *Frontier Women: The Trans-Mississippi West, 1840–1880*. New York: Hill and Wang, 1979.

Juhasz, Suzanne. "'Some Deep Old Desk or Capacious Hold-All': Form and Women's Autobiography." *College English*, 39 (1978), 663–668.

Keenan, Elinor. "Norm-makers, Norm-breakers: Uses of Speech by Men and Women in a Malagasy Community." In *Explorations in the Ethnography of Speaking*. Ed. Richard Bauman and Joel Sherzer. Cambridge: Cambridge University Press, 1974, pp. 125–143.

Kelly, Mary. "A Woman Alone: Catherine Maria Sedgwick's Spinsterhood in Nineteenth-Century America." *The New England Quarterly*, LI (June 1978), 209–225.

Key, Mary Ritchie. *Male/Female Language*. Metuchen, N.J.: Scarecrow Press, 1975.

Kohl, Seena, and John W. Bennett. "Kinship, Succession, and the Migration of Young People in a Canadian Agricultural Community." *International Journal of Comparative Sociology*, 6 (1965), 95–116.

Komarovsky, Mirra. *Blue-Collar Marriage*. New York: Random House, 1964.

Lakoff, Robin. *Language and Woman's Place*. New York: Harper and Row, 1975.

Lamphere, Louise. "Strategies, Cooperation, and Conflict among Women in Domestic Groups." In *Woman, Culture, and Society*. Ed. Michelle Zimbalist Rosaldo and Louise Lamphere. Stanford, Calif.: Stanford University Press, 1974, pp. 97–112.

Lasch, Christopher. *Haven in a Heartless World: The Family Besieged*. New York: Basic Books, 1977.

Lasch, Christopher, and William R. Taylor. "Two 'Kindred Spirits': Sorority and Family in New England, 1839–1846." *New England Quarterly*, 36 (1963), 23–41.

Lawton, Denis. "Social Class Differences in Language Development: A Study of Some Examples of Written Work." *Language and Speech*, 6 (1963), 120–143.

Lerner, Gerda. "The Lady and the Mill Girl: Changes in the Status of Women in the Age of Jackson, 1800–1840." In *A Heritage of Her Own: Toward a New Social History of American Women*. Ed. Nancy F. Cott and Elizabeth H. Pleck. New York: Simon and Schuster, 1979, pp. 182–196.

Levy, Helen Fiddyment. "No Hiding Place on Earth: The Female Self in Eight Modern American Women Authors." Diss. The University of Michigan. 1982.

Litwack, Eugene. "Geographic Mobility and Extended Family Cohesion." *American Sociological Review*, 25 (1960), 385-394.

—————. "Occupational Mobility and Extended Family Cohesion." *American Sociological Review*, 25 (1960), 9-21.

Marshall, Helen E. *Dorothea Dix: Forgotten Samaritan*. New York: Russell and Russell, 1937.

Mauss, Marcel I. *The Gift: Forms and Functions of Exchange in Archaic Societies*. Trans. Ian Cunnison. London: Cohen and West, 1954.

Miller, Jean Baker. *Toward a New Psychology of Women*. Boston: Beacon, 1976.

Mitchell, J. Clyde. *Social Networks in Urban Situations: Analyses of Personal Relationships in Central African Towns*. Manchester: Manchester University Press, 1969.

Morantz, Regina. "The Lady and Her Physician." In *Clio's Consciousness Raised: New Perspectives on the History of Women*. Ed. Mary S. Hartman and Lois Banner. New York: Harper and Row, 1974, pp. 38-53.

Morley, Frederick. *Michigan and Its Resources*. Lansing, Mich.: State Printers and Binders, 1881.

Muir, Donald E., and Eugene A. Weinstein. "The Social Debt: An Investigation of Lower Class and Middle Class Norms of Social Obligation." *American Sociological Review*, 27 (1962), 532-539.

Nelson, Joel I. "Clique Contacts and Family Orientations." *American Sociological Review*, 31 (1966), 663-672.

Norton, Mary Beth. *Liberty's Daughters: The Revolutionary Experience of American Women, 1750-1800*. Boston: Little, Brown, 1980.

O'Neill, William. *Divorce in the Progressive Era*. New Haven, Conn.: Yale University Press, 1967.

Osterreich, Helgi. "Geographical Mobility and Kinship: A Canadian Example." *International Journal of Comparative Sociology*, 6 (1965), 131-144.

Paine, Robert. "What is Gossip About? An Alternative Hypothesis." *Man*, 2 (1967), 278-285.

Parkins, Almon Ernest. *The Historical Geography of Detroit*. Lansing, Mich.: The Michigan Historical Commission, 1918.

Piddington, Ralph. "The Kinship Network among French Canadians." *International Journal of Comparative Sociology*, 6 (1965), 145-165.

Platt, Jennifer. "Some Problems in Measuring the Jointness of Conjugal Role-Relationships." *Sociology*, 3 (1969), 287-297.

Pleck, Elizabeth. "Wifebeating in Nineteenth-Century America." *Victimology*, 4 (1979), 60-74.

Quaife, Milo M., and Sidney Glazer. *Michigan: From Primitive Wilderness to Industrial Commonwealth*. New York: Prentice-Hall, 1948.

Reiss, Paul J. "The Extended Kinship System: Correlates of and Attitudes on Frequency of Interaction." *Marriage and Family Living*, 24 (1962), 333–339.

Robins, Lee N., and Miroda Tomanec. "Closeness to Blood Relatives Outside the Immediate Family." *Marriage and Family Living*, 24 (1962), 340–346.

Rosenberg, Charles E. "Florence Nightingale on Contagion: The Hospital as Moral Universe." In *Healing and History*. Ed. Charles E. Rosenberg. New York: Dawson, 1979, pp. 116–136.

Rubin, Lillian B. *Worlds of Pain: Life in the Working-Class Family*. New York: Basic Books, 1976.

Saum, Lewis O. "Death in the Popular Mind of Pre-Civil War America." *American Quarterly*, 26 (December 1974), 477–495.

Schlossman, Stephen. *Love and the American Delinquent*. Chicago: University of Chicago Press, 1977.

Scholten, Catherine. "On the Importance of the Obstetrick Art: Changing Customs of Childbirth in America, 1760–1825." *William and Mary Quarterly*, 3rd Series, XXXIV (1977), 426–445.

Scott, Donald M., and Bernard Wishy, eds. *America's Families: A Documentary History*. New York: Harper and Row, 1982.

Shanas, Ethel, and Gordon F. Streib, eds. *Social Structure and the Family: Generational Relations*. Englewood Cliffs, N.J.: Prentice-Hall, 1965.

Sklar, Kathryn Kish. *Catharine Beecher: A Study in American Domesticity*. New Haven, Conn.: Yale University Press, 1973.

Smith, Daniel Scott. "Family Limitation, Sexual Control, and Domestic Feminism in Victorian America." *Feminist Studies*, 1 (1973), 40–57.

Smith, Judith E. "Our Own Kind: Family and Community Networks in Providence." In *A Heritage of Her Own: Toward a New Social History of American Women*. Ed. Nancy F. Cott and Elizabeth H. Pleck. New York: Simon and Schuster, 1979, pp. 393–411.

Smith, Raymond T. "The Matrifocal Family." In *The Character of Kinship*. Ed. Jack Goody. Cambridge: Cambridge University Press, 1973, pp. 121–144.

Smith-Rosenberg, Carroll. "The Female World of Love and Ritual: Relations between Women in Nineteenth-Century America." *Signs*, 1 (1975), 1–29.

———. "The Hysterical Woman: Sex Roles and Role Conflict in Nineteenth-Century America." *Social Research*, 39 (1972), 652–678.

Stack, Carol B. *All Our Kin: Strategies for Survival in a Black Community*. New York: Harper and Row, 1974.

Stage, Sarah. *Female Complaints: Lydia Pinkham and the Business of Women's Medicine*. New York: Norton, 1979.

Stannard, David E., ed. *Death in America*. Philadelphia: University of Pennsylvania Press, 1975.

――――. *The Puritan Way of Death; A Study in Religion, Culture, and Social Change.* New Haven, Conn.: Yale University Press, 1975.

Thorne, Barrie, and Nancy Henley, eds. *Language and Sex: Difference and Dominance.* Rowley, Mass.: Newbury House, 1975.

Tingley, Ralph R. "Postal Service in Michigan Territory." *Michigan History,* 35 (1951), 447–460.

Tucker, Susie I. *Protean Shape: A Study in Eighteenth-Century Vocabulary and Usage.* London: Athlone Press, 1967.

Turner, Christopher. "Conjugal Roles and Social Networks." *Human Relations,* 20 (1967), 121–130.

――――. *Family and Kinship in Modern Britain.* London: Routledge and Kegan Paul, 1969.

Udry, J. R., and Hall, M. "Marital Role Segregation and Social Networks in Middle-Class Middle-Aged Couples." *Journal of Marriage and the Family,* 27 (1965), 392–395.

Uhlenberg, Peter. "Changing Configurations of the Life Course." In *Transitions: The Family and Life Course in Historical Perspective.* Ed. Tamara K. Hareven. New York: Academic Press, 1978, pp. 65–98.

――――. "A Study of Cohort Life Cycles: Cohorts of Native Born Massachusetts Women, 1830–1920." *Population Studies,* 23 (November 1969), 407–420.

Vinovskis, Maris. "Angels' Heads and Weeping Willows: Death in Early America." In *Themes in the History of the Family.* Ed. Tamara K. Hareven. Worcester, Mass.: American Antiquarian Society, 1978, pp. 25–54.

Warshay, Diana W. "Sex Differences in Language Style." *Toward a Sociology of Women.* Ed. Constantina Safilios-Rothschild. Lexington, Mass.: Xerox Publishing, 1972, pp. 3–9.

Welter, Barbara. "The Cult of True Womanhood, 1820–1860." *American Quarterly,* 18 (1966), 151–174.

Wertz, Richard W. and Dorothy C. *Lying-In: A History of Childbirth in America.* New York: Schocken, 1979.

Wolford, Thorp L. "The Laws and Liberties of 1648." In *Essays in the History of Early American Law.* Ed. David Flaherty. Chapel Hill, N.C.: University of North Carolina Press, 1969, pp. 147–185.

Wood, Ann Douglas. "The Fashionable Diseases: Women's Complaints and Their Treatment in Nineteenth-Century America." In *Clio's Consciousness Raised: New Perspectives On the History of Women.* Ed. Mary S. Hartman and Lois Banner. New York: Harper and Row, 1974, pp. 1–22.

Young, James Harvey. *The Toadstool Millionaires: A Social History of Patent Medicines in America Before Federal Regulation.* Princeton, N.J.: Princeton University Press, 1961.

Young, Michael, and Peter Willmott. *Family and Kinship in East London.* Glencoe, Ill.: The Free Press, 1957.

Index

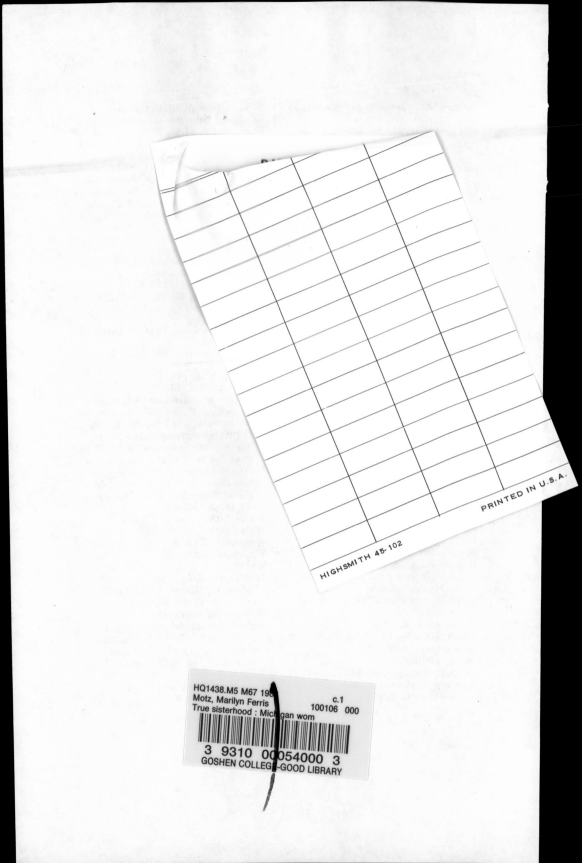

HIGHSMITH 45-102

PRINTED IN U.S.A.